Fathering at Risk

James R. Dudley, PhD, is a professor at the University of North Carolina at Charlotte. Previously he was on the faculty of the School of Social Administration at Temple University. He teaches in the areas of social work practice with families and groups, and research and program evaluation. He has conducted studies focusing on divorced fathers in the Philadelphia area and family-supportive policies of employers in Charlotte, North Carolina. He has published several articles and book chapters on fathering issues. His family-related professional work has included the Fathers Center in the Philadelphia area, divorce mediation specializing in shared-parenting agreements, and social work practice with families at the Philadelphia Society to Protect Children, the Philadelphia School System, and the Tressler Lutheran Services for Families in Harrisburg, PA. He is a Licensed Clinical Social Worker in North Carolina and is a consulting editor for *Family Relations, Journal of Baccalaureate Social Work; Professional Development;* and *Religion, Disabilities, and Health.* He has one son, Eric, whom he raised since the age of six in a successful joint residential custody arrangement. He is also the very proud grandfather of 2-year-old twin girls and a new baby boy.

Glenn Stone, PhD, is an assistant professor at Miami University in Oxford, Ohio. Previously he was on the faculty of the School of Social work at Indiana University. He teaches in the areas of social work practice, research methods, and the changing role of men in families. He has been involved in conducting research on nonresidential fathers and their children. He has also taken part in research on the effectiveness of divorce-education workshops. He recently completed an evaluation project focusing on the programs instituted under the Indiana Restoring Fatherhood Initiative. He has published articles on divorce and on nonresidential fathers. His professional work includes practicing for nearly 10 years as a marital and family therapist. He is a Licensed Clinical Social Worker in Ohio and is a consulting editor for *The Journal of Genetic Psychology* and *Genetic, Social, and General Psychology Monographs.* He is a member of the Practice Commission for the Council on Social Work Education. He is also the father of two daughters, Cara, 10, and Julia, 6, who have taught him much about parenting. They are very patient instructors.

Fathering at Risk

James R. Dudley & Glenn Stone

 **Prometheus Books**

59 John Glenn Drive
Amherst, New York 14228-2197

Published 2004 by Prometheus Books

Inquiries should be addressed to
Prometheus Books
59 John Glenn Drive
Amherst, New York 14228–2197
VOICE: 716–691–0133, ext. 207
FAX: 716–564–2711
WWW.PROMETHEUSBOOKS.COM

08 07 06 05 04   5 4 3 2 1

Library of Congress Cataloging-in-Publication Data

Dudley, James R.
    Fathering at risk / by James R. Dudley, Glenn Stone.
        p. cm.
    Originally published: Fathering at risk : helping nonresidential fathers. New York : Springer Pub Co., © 2001.
    Includes bibliographical references and index.
    ISBN 1–59102–129–4
    1. Absentee fathers—United States. 2. Father and child—United States. I. Stone, Glenn. II. Title.

HQ756.8 D83 2001
306.874'25—dc21

2001020647

Printed in the United States on acid-free paper

We dedicate our book to our children and grandchildren–
Cara, Julia, Eric, Michele, Elise, Hannah, and Ben.

Acknowledgments

Several people have helped us make this book possible by inspiring, assisting, and supporting us in special ways. They include Kay Pasley, Kathy Clark, John Franklin, Mary Lou Dickey, Patrick McKenry, and especially our wives, Joanna and Patty.

Other people are deeply appreciated for giving us considerable time from their busy schedules to read all or parts of our manuscript and for contributing helpful insights and suggestions to our evolving manuscript. They include Kathy Byers, Denise Schweitzer, Stan Meloy, and Becky Wilson.

We are also grateful to the assistance provided by our publisher, Springer Publishing Company, and its staff and consultants: Bill Tucker, Sheri Sussman, Jordan Kosberg, Jerilyn DePete, Elizabeth Keech, Sara Yoo, and Matt Fenton.

We also wish to thank countless unnamed fathers with whom we have spent time over the past 25 years in our research studies, professional practice, volunteer work, and friendships. Above all, they have taught us a great deal about fathering!

Contents

Innovative Programs

Foreword

In the last quarter century, fathers and fatherhood have attracted the attention of behavioral scientists, mental health professionals, policy makers, journalists, and the public at large. As a result, a veritable flood of scholarly articles and books have explored the varied faces and functions of fatherhood so thoroughly that fathers could no longer be described as "forgotten contributors to child development," as they were in 1975.

Indeed, fathers could hardly be forgotten as evidence accumulates documenting the extent to which they play important roles in the complex fabric of socializing influences that shape the course of human development. By offering or failing to offer financial support, by engaging constructively or destructively in partnerships with mothers, and by offering children stimulation, guidance and models, fathers clearly exert both direct and indirect influences on their children's development. More significantly, perhaps, their potential to affect the course of development for good or for ill is present, whether fathers live with their children in two-parent families or function from afar. The circumstances differ, of course, and these differences matter a great deal to the children and to their parents, but the potential and the mechanisms are similar, however and wherever the men and their children reside. Children who do not live with their fathers are at greater risk of relative psychological and economic abandonment, so it is important to pay special attention to the needs of circumstances of these increasingly significant groups of men and children.

The books and articles that have come to define our contemporary understanding of fatherhood fit into one of three major categories. Many, of course, are scholarly syntheses or monographs, designed to summarize portions of the professional literature for both specialized or broad audiences. Others are manuals designed to communicate strategies and skills to practitioners, and many of the remainder are polemics written to shape the social and political debate in the United States. Few are books like *Fathering at Risk: Helping Nonresidential Fathers* which addresses mental health professionals and trainees but builds upon the authors' clear familiarity both with the literature as well as their "in-the-trench" experiences.

Although these authors provide a broad review of the literature documenting the changing roles and perceptions of fathers in the United States, their concern is focused more narrowly on noncustodial fathers and their children. Dudley and Stone show that increasing numbers of children in the United States currently live apart from their fathers despite widespread emphasis in the popular and scholarly media on the formative importance of father-child relationships. Increasing proportions of these children, from all socioeconomic and ethnic backgrounds, have been born to unmarried mothers and either never or only briefly live with their biological fathers. Many others are separated from their fathers by their parents' divorce, while others are teen fathers, often psychologically, socially, and economically unprepared for parenthood. Although all three groups of fathers (divorced fathers, never married nonresidential fathers, and teen fathers) place their children at psychosocial risk, argue Dudley and Stone, they have both shared and differing concerns that merit the attention of mental health professionals. As a result, these authors strive to describe the particular circumstances of each group of fathers and then describe the types of intervention strategies most likely to help these men minimize the risks to themselves and to their children.

Both of the authors have taught for many years in schools of social work and their sensitive and sympathetic familiarity with the personal concerns of noncustodial fathers is apparent throughout the book. The sensitivity with which Dudley and Stone describe the emotions and dilemmas faced by noncustodial fathers and the mothers of their children, furthermore, is matched by impressively concrete and detailed suggestions for practitioners. The combination is important, because practical suggestions can easily become rigid solutions in the hands of less sensitive and experienced guides. Instead, because these authors provide carefully balanced and articulate rationales before offering suggestions for intervention, readers are well equipped to refashion the suggestions to suit individual circumstances.

Indeed, Dudley and Stone make clear that each noncustodial father is unique, even as a careful analysis of his situation, informed by familiarity with the literature on men like him, makes it possible to offer support and assistance that is both grounded in the literature and tailored to individual circumstances. Few books provide advice as clear and careful as that offered in *Fathering at Risk: Helping Nonresidential Fathers*. As a result, this book promises to be an invaluable asset to mental health professionals as well as to students seeking to acquire skills without too lengthy a period of personal "trial and error."

More effectively than any other text I can recall, these authors sprinkle the text with insightful and provocative questions designed to stimulate thoughtful introspection or discussion about important issues raised by the adjacent text. Most of the "Reflections" raise precisely the sort of question most likely to stimulate analysis that facilitates mastery of the content and its effective application to address the needs of individual fathers. In the hands of Dudley and Stone, therefore, "Reflections" become a remarkably effective pedagogical device.

Because an increasing number of children do not live with their fathers, despite increasing awareness that these circumstances place many children at risk, practitioners are being asked with accelerating urgency to address the needs of these fathers, for their own sakes as well as in the interests of their children. To practitioners working with such children, fathers, and partners, no other professionals offer as helpful and thought-providing a guide as do Dudley and Stone. *Fathering at Risk: Helping Nonresidential Fathers* offers invaluable guidance to mental health professionals, trainees, and students attempting to meet the needs of divorcing couples, nonresidential fathers and their children.

Michael E. Lamb
National Institute of Child Health
and Human Development

Preface

Preparing this book has been a rewarding and exhilarating journey for both of us (Jim and Glenn). The topic of fatherhood resonates well with us because we are both fathers, and one of us (Jim) is also a grandfather of three small children. While this is our first joint project, we have both brought to our work many prior years of involvement with fathering issues: our research projects; our professional practices with individuals, families, and groups; the assistance that we have given to many volunteer groups; our own personal experiences as members of men's and couple's groups; and not least importantly our experiences as fathers in our families.

While we are both happily married individuals and actively involved parents, we have a deep appreciation and empathy for nonresidential fathers, both those involved and uninvolved with their children. Jim's past joint custodial experience has enlightened him to the enormous complexities and demands of co-parenting apart, as well as the wonderful benefits that can accrue for the children. Likewise, both of us have encountered numerous disappointed, frustrated, and angry fathers and mothers over the years. While these experiences have often deeply saddened and frustrated us, they have also deepened our commitment to wanting to help reverse the troubling trend of increasing father absence.

Overall, the book provides both extensive knowledge about nonresidential fathers and recommendations for helping these fathers, particularly those "at risk." In both of these areas, we review the relevant current literature, including our own works. We use a "broad-brush" approach to cover considerable pertinent material on this topic and to organize and integrate it into a meaningful framework that can be useful for work with fathers and families.

In general, our book is distinguished from most others on the topic of fathering in at least three ways. First, we focus mostly on a subgroup of fathers, nonresidential dads, who are often a missing topic in the professional literature and course offerings in higher education. Second, a major emphasis is on a wide range of policies, programs, and other interventions that can help these fathers and their families. Third, the book is coauthored rather than edited which has helped us to synthesize and integrate it into a readable text for university students and professional practitioners.

At the most basic level, the book's intent is to promote what we believe is the children's best interest. We are interested in strategies that will actively involve both fathers and mothers in raising their children whenever this is possible. Our preference is that they work together as cooperatively as possible. When this cannot occur, we advocate for the best interest of the children, rather than blindly supporting fathers' or mothers' "involvement at all costs." We merely want to maximize the opportunities and minimize the barriers for men to be active and responsible parents.

We recognize and affirm that fathers vary widely in their racial identity and ethnic background, socioeconomic status, religious orientation, and family history. We particularly examine ethnic and racial diversity in fathering throughout the book by periodically giving attention to the special needs of African American, Latino, Asian, and White European cultural groups, as well as the influence of social class and poverty.

Nonresidential fathers are an increasingly diversified group in other ways as well. As we began writing this book, we discovered that our own work has focused more with divorced and teen dads and less with unmarried fathers. But we have discovered that the personal needs and circumstances of all three groups are more similar than different. One major difference is that unmarried fathers seem to have less parental rights and involvement, and very little public awareness or understanding. About one third of all births today, for example, are to unmarried women. In many of these cases, the fathers always have been nonresidential to their children, or they may not even exist in their children's eyes. Many are called "sperm fathers" because their sperm has been their sole contribution to their children; by design they are expected to disappear, never to bond or claim their offspring. Yet, a growing number of unmarried fathers' group are attempting to become more involved parents. And they are confronting major social and personal barriers, such as insensitive court policies and procedures, an absence of genuine services to help them in their parenting roles, and a general disregard for them beyond their paying child support.

The book is divided into four parts, in two major sections. The first part (chapters 1–3) examines the state of fathering and at-risk fathering in the United States. We document the reality of nonresidential fathers as a significantly growing segment of the population, particularly in comparison to 3 or 4 decades ago. Currently, for example, about one third of all children are estimated to be living apart from their biological father. One thing that is most troubling to us about this trend is that a large portion of these fathers have little or no meaningful contact with their children.

The first chapter highlights the trends of diminishing involvement and increasing absence of fathers. We also summarize the history of fathering in families over the past 2 centuries and the radically changing roles that fathering has undergone. Hopeful signs for fathers are also covered, including the recent social movements of Robert Bly, the Million Man March, the Promise Keepers, and others. The profound difficulties and challenges that males are likely to encounter are also highlighted, particularly the various external and internal barriers that interfere with their becoming effective parents. A grossly overlooked question is carefully examined: If fathers are significantly declining in such large numbers, why is more not being done to stop this dangerous trend?

Chapter 2 describes profiles of the three groups of nonresidential fathers who are the book's primary focus—divorced non-custodial fathers, unmarried fathers, and teen dads. The similarities and differences among these groups are identified and described. A case is made for claiming that the parental roles of most of these fathers are at risk. We sound a call for our society to do substantially more to help them in response to this claim.

What do we already know and what do we hope for about fathers? These are the main questions that are addressed in chapter 3. This chapter describes the evolving knowledge base on fathering. We review the studies that have focused on "father absence" and the known negative impacts on children. Further, we cite studies that document what "father presence" provides to children. We examine the unique contributions provided by fathers and highlight the importance of the father's role in child development. The tasks and challenges of fathering are described at the different stages of development—with infants, school-age children, teenagers, and adult children. We also briefly consider the importance of grandfathers. We close with reflections on what we hope for in the future.

Part II of the book introduces the focus for all of the remaining chapters—what we can do to help fathers. A central message is that we *can* do many things to reverse the dangerous trend of father absence. Chapter 4 offers a set of general strategies and principles for helping fathers. We emphasize the importance of enfranchising fathers in all that we do to help them. Other central principles include identifying and promoting the strengths of fathers, actively engaging fathers on the affective and spiritual levels, and being sensitive and responsive to their multicultural issues.

We take the position that children are usually better served if fathers and mothers are working together in cooperative ventures. Ideally, we believe, both parents have an inherent investment in their children, and both can do significantly more than one alone. We also believe that helping fathers needs to take into account the needs of mothers. We advocate several different ways of promoting active fathering, including promoting marriage, expanding the various joint custody models, and giving greater attention to the needs, rights, and responsibilities of teenage and unmarried fathers. We also recognize that cooperative parenting partnerships are not always possible or desired, and we discuss these important exceptions. We promote the idea that mother/father partnerships, particularly outside a nuclear family, need significantly greater institutional support from family courts, family agencies, schools, and other institutions.

Part III focuses on professional practice issues. Chapter 5 addresses the assessment phase of professional practice with nonresidential fathers. The special needs of most nonresidential fathers, and the topics to be considered in a holistic assessment are summarized. Also, several likely barriers to fathers receiving help are highlighted, including several gender biases that often exist in the assessment and intervention phases of help. Chapter 6 offers helpful suggestions for working with nonresidential fathers at various system levels. Practice issues are considered in work with individual fathers, fathers in family systems, and professional-led and self-help groups.

Part IV underscores the importance of policy and program initiatives in addressing the major risks confronted by nonresidential fathers. A selection of policy initiatives and program strategies that have been successful in helping many diverse groups of fathers and potential fathers is presented.

Chapter 7 offers a way for local communities to begin an exploration of the needs of fathers. A model is described for assessing the needs of fathers and their families and for determining the extent of at-risk fathering. A case study is presented as an illustration of how one county conducted such an assessment. Chapter 8 begins by describing policy initiatives directed toward nonresidential fathers over the past century and the residue arising from these historical initiatives. The major focus of this chapter is on recent policy initiatives that have the potential for promoting responsible fathering, including alternatives to welfare, initiatives to involve teenage fathers, and family-sensitive employment policies.

The next two chapters address the special needs of teen and unmarried fathers. Chapter 9 considers the help that teen fathers need. Stereotypes about teen fathers are debunked, and current trends in teen fathering are highlighted along with descriptions of various successful program models for helping teen fathers. Chapter 10 looks at the help that unmarried adult fathers need. Unmarried fathers make up the fastest growing of the three nonresidential fathers' groups. They are also the most diverse, ranging from the extremes of fathers in relationships often comparable to marriages to "sperm fathers" who are usually nonexistent to their children. Innovative intervention models are highlighted for helping unmarried nonresidential fathers.

Chapters 11 and 12 examine approaches and programs for involving fathers when they are faced with legal decisions related to divorce, custody, and child support. Chapter 11 focuses on post-divorce educational programs that help fathers and mothers understand the divorce process and the various options available to them. A bias is incorporated into these programs in favor of cooperation between the parents and avoidance of unnecessary adversarial encounters. Chapter 12 elaborates on additional ways to assist parents who separate from each other. Whenever fathers and mothers split up, we recommend that arrangements be made for helping them work out a cooperative plan to share parental responsibilities. The win/lose approach of adversarial legal proceedings poses problems and should only be used in certain circumstances or as a last resort. Mediation strategies are presented as a preferred alternative. Court mediation programs along with private mediation services are highlighted. We also examine helpful parenting agreements that address all of the post-divorce aspects of raising children.

In a brief afterword, we reflect on our visions and hopes for fathering in the future.

We have added some other special features to the book to assist the reader. Reflection and Perspective boxes are included throughout each chapter to engage the reader in further thought on the material that is being covered. Discussion questions are also added at the end of each chapter to assist the reader in summarizing and integrating key concepts. Descriptions of successful programs, referred to as "Innovative Programs," are highlighted throughout the book (and listed in the front on page viii), and a directory of fatherhood organizations and pertinent Web sites is included in the Appendix, to assist readers who want to begin implementing their own programs to help fathers.

I

Why Fathering Is at Risk

1

What Is the Problem?

Men have burdens as well as privileges in our society. So often, we emphasize the privileges and overlook the burdens. When we have such an unbalanced view, we fail to understand the needs and circumstances of a male, whether he is a child or grown man. Perhaps so many men have not succeeded in their marriages because the expectations of them have been so high and often contradictory. Married men are often expected to have such qualities as being the capable provider, aggressive competitor, wise father, sensitive and gentle lover, fearless protector, cool and controlled negotiator under pressure, and being emotionally expressive. (Goldberg, 1976, p. 151)

This chapter introduces many of the important topics and concepts of the book and examines the larger social context for fathering. The primary goal of the book is highlighted: helping nonresidential fathers become more actively involved in their children's lives. This chapter covers the following sections:

- The concept of fathering at risk
- Changing historical perspectives on fathers
- Differing views about the importance of fathers in families
- Problems faced by men
- Favorable and unfavorable views of fathers
- Focus on nonresidential fathers

It is important to begin by sharing some facts about the status of fathering in the United States (Horn, 1998):

- Approximately half of all marriages end in divorce.
- Approximately one third of all children under 18 years live apart from their biological father.
- In 1995 one third of all births were to unmarried women.
- More than 1 million children each year experience the divorce of their parents.
- A White child has one chance in two of living continuously with a biological father through the age of 18, while an African American child has one chance in four.
- Children who live apart from their biological fathers, on average, are more likely to be poor, to experience adjustment problems, be victims of child abuse, and engage in criminal behavior than children who live with both of their biological parents.

A frightening reality in all of these statistics is that countless fathers are absent from their children's lives. Furthermore, it appears that these numbers will remain high and possibly increase in the future if nothing more is done to reverse them.

The decline of the male role of fathering is one of the most serious social problems currently facing our society and we refer to this problem as fathering at risk. Being at risk is defined as exposure to loss or harm; a hazard; danger; or peril. We believe that the role of fathering in the United States is exposed to harm or endangered now more than ever. Individually, a man's fathering role is at risk whenever it is performed inadequately or is nonexistent. At a societal level, fathering is at risk if large numbers of men are either absent or are otherwise participating inadequately in their parental roles. An important reason to be concerned about fathering at risk is that children can become at risk as well, as described further in chapter 3.

Fathers have become absent from the family and child raising responsibilities at a dangerously rapid rate over the past several decades. The trend is particularly evident from 1960 to 1990, as documented by Table 1.1. While both fathers and mothers were present in almost 81% of family households in 1960, by 1990 both parents were present in only 58% of family households. Alternative family arrangements have not usually been favorable to involving the biological father, as the number of mother-only families has almost tripled and the number of stepfathers has almost doubled.

One particular trend may be the most alarming that adversely affects the future of fathering: About 30% of new families in 1990 were

TABLE 1.1   Percentage of U.S. Children in Various Family
Arrangements

Living With	1960	1970	1980	1990
Father and mother	80.6	75.1	62.3	57.7
Mother only	7.7	11.8	18.0	21.6
Father only	1.0	1.8	1.7	3.1
Father and stepmother	0.8	0.9	1.1	0.9
Mother and stepfather	5.9	6.5	8.4	10.4
Neither parent	3.9	4.1	5.8	4.3

Note: Hernandez (1993); U.S. Bureau of the Census (1981, 1991, 1992).

headed by unmarried parents, in contrast to 3% in 1960, and growing numbers of couples and single women living on their own are having children without marriage (U.S. Bureau of the Census, 1992). In the instances of single women who choose to raise their children without a father, fathers are becoming optional and are much less likely to stay in contact with their children and to provide financial and emotional support. If the current trends and attitudes continue, we suspect that the absence of fathers in families may become a cultural norm, particularly for some subgroups such as low-income families.

A more positive note suggests that the number of married-couple families with children may be stabilizing since 1990 (U.S. Census, 1997). The percentage of these families with children has dropped only 1% from 1990 to 1997. Also, the growth of single-parent families has slowed, increasing only 2% during the same period.

Reflection

Numerous family structures currently exist. The list includes households with two biological parents; single-parent households, extended-family households with additional family members such as grandparents; households with a biological parent and stepparent; shared custody two-household families; gay or lesbian families; and adoptive and foster families. In what kind of family structure were you raised? What was the structure of the family of origin of each of your parents? Is there a difference between how you were raised and how your parents were raised? If so, what were the advantages of each family structure?

HISTORICAL PERSPECTIVES

The role of fathers in families has changed dramatically over the past two centuries. These changes are closely linked to transformations in the economy and major societal changes such as war, mass immigration, depression, and social movements.

The Colonial Era

In the Colonial era of the United States, European American fathers were seen as primary and irreplaceable caregivers. Fathers were in charge of child-rearing even though they delegated many of these responsibilities to their wives. They were expected to teach their children moral and religious values and had control over most of the decisions. Because there was little separation between home and work, they were likely to have intense daily involvement with their family. Based on the economic demands of farming, their children were critical as laborers on the land; boys in particular worked alongside their fathers in the fields from dawn to dusk. Fathers were also viewed as the patriarchs in the family, a tradition that was passed down to them by the Protestant Reformation (Mintz, 1998). For example, they had a legal right to determine whom their daughters would date, and they gave approval of their children's marriages. Historical evidence suggests that many Colonial fathers sat in an armchair that symbolized their authority, while their wives and children sat on stools or benches. Letters of these early periods reveal that many fathers addressed their wives as "child," while their wives called them "mister."

Latino fathers from the Southwest were also viewed as patriarchs. One possible difference from their European American counterparts was that they gave special emphasis to patriarchy issues by emphasizing a "code of honor" in which their sons were to be manly and their daughters virgins until marriage. They also arranged their children's marriages.

Many African American fathers were slaves during the Colonial era. They wanted to be protectors and providers of their children, but they were often barred by their owners from acting in their children's best interest. They were often separated from their families when it served the needs of their owners; at times fathers were intentionally separated from their families if it suited the demands of the plantation. Many children and mothers were forcibly and cruelly separated from the fathers, often at the auction block (Billingsley, 1992). This had to be a low point in the lives of African American parents, as they were stripped of their very humanity and dignity.

American Indian fathers were experiencing very different circumstances 200 years ago as well, as they were increasingly losing their grip on their homeland and culture to European settlers. They had strong tribal identities and loyalty to their native tongue, their clan and extended family, and religious ceremonies. Strong patriarchal values were also evident in most tribes, with wives relegated to a lower status and submissive to their husbands. Unfortunately, the manhood of American Indians, like that of African Americans, was being stripped away as they were forced either to assimilate with the European victors or live on segregated reservations.

The Nineteenth Century

As our society became industrialized in the 19th and early 20th centuries, mothers began to replace fathers as the primary parent. With a shifting economy, young men found greater opportunities outside of agriculture (Fliegelman, 1982) and began taking jobs in industries, offices, or businesses some distance from their family homes. New jobs in factories and offices separated them physically and metaphorically from their families. This was a time in which the chasm between fathers and their families began to widen as home and work became two very distinct worlds. Greater numbers of fathers could no longer supervise and teach their children as they did when they worked together in the fields.

In 1839, the "tender years" doctrine, which was promulgated in British courts as a prototype for our laws, began to change radically the father's and mother's roles. According to this court doctrine, children younger than seven years of age had emotional needs that ostensibly only the mother was able to meet; hence mothers were automatically awarded custody upon divorce. Once the children reached the age of seven, custody of the children was given to the father and the mother was granted visitation rights.

A clear demarcation of parental roles emerged among the middle class in particular (Mintz, 1998). Women asserted their identities as nurturers and full-time mothers, while fathers were viewed as protectors and providers. The father's authority shifted to material and social resources outside the home—property, business connections, men's clubs, and other social networks.

The urban working class evolved differently. Unlike the middle class, these families were usually not able to survive on the father's income alone. Older children often were expected to go to work and contribute to the family's income; they also stayed with their families longer to help with economic survival. While this demand on the children imposed problems, one advantage was that many of them could work alongside their fathers in the factories. For economic reasons new households often were not established until a couple reached their 30s (Mintz & Kellogg, 1988). The employment conditions of working-class men were stressful and physically demanding. Sometimes work sites were far from the family home, which led to longer absences of the father. Immigrant and migrant fathers in particular often worked for extended periods away from their families who resided in another region of the United States or in another country (Griswold, 1993).

The Twentieth Century

Irresponsibility among fathers was more evident around the beginning of the 20th century. With industrialization, increased urbanization, and other social forces came increased desertions by fathers, wife-beatings, and physical abuse of children (Pleck, 1987). There was also more evidence of men avoiding their financial obligations to their children and ignoring them altogether. Alcoholism was more prevalent and was often linked to these negative deeds. Violence against wives was also more prevalent or at least more noticed.

Wars were another social force that negatively influenced fathering. The Civil War, the Spanish American War, the two world wars, Korea and Vietnam, and the Gulf War separated countless fathers (and, more recently, mothers) from their children. In some instances, such as during the draft for World War II, deferment was given to fathers before single males and husbands without children, but the demand for soldiers eventually drew tens of thousands of fathers into this war. Countless fathers died or came home to a family that was bound for divorce because of the impact of their absence and battle scars. Battle scars were particularly evident during the Vietnam era, partially because so many in our society disapproved of this war. When they returned to their families, fathers were often ill-prepared to be caring, nurturing parents because of the violence and trauma of war, drug and alcohol use, and the general disregard for humanity that they experienced.

The father's role as breadwinner was also strengthened in the early part of the 20th century because of gradual increases in wages, new child-labor and compulsory school attendance laws, expanded workers' compensation, and the New Deal measures of 1932. The domestic sphere of family life increasingly became the responsibility of the mother. In this transition, the mother's natural capacity to care for her children was allowed to become more visible and honored. The "tender years" doctrine of early child-rearing had become normative, and by the 1920s, laws strongly favored mothers as custodial parents. Many marriages were on more equal footing, and companionship became more possible.

After World War II, fathers were viewed as more personable family figures who could become psychologically close to their children (Pleck & Pleck, 1997), and many began to take on a more nurturing parental role. Most of these so-called new fathers emerged from the middle class, partly because their work environments offered more leisure time; yet this trend has affected fathers from all backgrounds to some extent. Fathers became more comfortable with showing affection towards their children, spending more time playing with them, and being identified less as the disciplinarian. These changes occurred over the span of only one generation. Recognizing that their own fathers were good providers and protectors but less skilled at nurturing, these men consciously decided to become the nurturers that their fathers were not.

However, while this new trend has been positive, these new fathers often were not taking on an equal share of parental responsibilities with their wives. Meal preparation, housekeeping, and the less desirable aspects of parenting like washing clothes and changing diapers remained the mother's responsibility. Popular 50s sitcoms such as "Father Knows Best" and "Ozzie and Harriet" reflected this new image, but these programs depicted and spoke primarily to White fathers (Pleck & Pleck, 1997): African Americans, Asians, and gay fathers were not yet allowed to fill these roles.

The 60s and 70s were a time of public scrutiny of African American fathers. The Moynihan Report, which was utilized for policy analysis during the Nixon Administration, was an indictment against these fathers (U.S. Department of Labor, 1965). The matriarchal family structure of the African American family was criticized because the fathers were absent, and the family structure was blamed for the disproportionately high number of African American families in poverty and of male teenagers committing crimes. While there may have been some truth to these claims, there were some flaws in the theory. African American families were quite diverse in socioeconomic class during this period, and the percentage of two-parent families was relatively high as late as the 1960 census. Two-parent African American families only began to decline around that time.

Finally, one of the most recent trends in fathering started in the 1970s. Many fathers began to participate in a more egalitarian relationship with their wives or partners, becoming highly involved in all child-rearing tasks (LaRossa, 1988; Pleck & Pleck, 1997). Large numbers became involved in the birth experience, joining their wives as partners in childbirth classes. Paternity leave from employment became a policy choice for many middle-class fathers, but the option was not usually exercised because of its likely adverse impact on their jobs. Fathers and mothers arranged their work schedules in concert with each other whenever possible so that at least one parent was with the children as much of the time as possible. Gender-neutral thinking was introduced, such as the notion of co-parenting and raising boys and girls without gender bias. With both parents working outside the home in the majority of cases, the father clearly was no longer the sole breadwinner. In relatively few instances, house-husbands emerged as an acceptable arrangement when the wife had greater earning power.

Yet co-parenting has by no means reached the masses. It is probably primarily a middle class, professional phenomenon, and it may be contradictory to other trends from the 70s such as the economic drive for prosperity and increased divorce. Ironically, divorce became a more acceptable option at a time when cooperation between men and women seemed to be at an all-time high level. Liberal no-fault divorce laws enabled parents more easily to disjoin without going through the complicated proceedings of proving fault.

While many fathers have been in the spotlight for becoming more involved in child-rearing, others have received increased attention for being irresponsible. Deadbeat dads have become a growing group in society that many feel needs to be reined in and forcefully required to pay child support. Unmarried-couple families also have significantly increased during recent times. In many ways, the 70s and 80s were a time of paradoxical trends with more emphasis placed on excessive individualism, but also a leaning toward making more sacrifices for children.

In 1970, the Uniform Marriage and Divorce Act enacted by most states promulgated a standard referred to as "the best interests of the children." For the first time, custody decisions were now made based on the children's needs and not the preferences of either parent (Kelly, 1994). Joint custody was first considered as an option in California in 1979, and by 1991 most of the states either allowed or gave preference to joint custody by statute (Folberg, 1991).

Since the 1970s, a backlash has been brewing among political conservatives partially suspected of being opposed to the women's movement (Coontz, 1992; Faludi, 1992). Opposition is evident in the intensified battle over abortion rights, the defeat of the Equal Rights Amendment, and other efforts to empower women. A conservative political alliance has called for a renewed commitment to "family values," greater support for marriage, school prayer, and other calls for a greater presence of religion, renewed antipornography battles, and a greater emphasis on morality in the schools. This loosely coupled movement has also sparked renewed attention for asserting custody rights among men. In actuality, the battles between the political left and right have revealed that both sides are advocating for a greater presence by fathers, albeit in different ways.

This historical summary reveals that the parental roles of men have changed significantly over the past two centuries. Their roles as caregivers and moral educators have lessened in importance and are much more likely to be shared or assumed by the mothers. Men are much less likely to be referred to as the head of their families beyond name or title. Even the father's role as the family breadwinner has been changing as women's economic status has improved. Nevertheless, many men have gained something new from these radically changing times. Currently, men have a new way of assuming their parenting role if they choose to do it. Many doors have opened to them so that they can invest themselves much more fully in their children's daily lives.

Reflection
As we reflect on the changing social landscape of fathering, we may be able to recognize such changes within our own families. Recall your own grandfather (or your great-grandfather if you remember him). Or try to identify an older male whom you know and admire who is 50 or more years older than you. What kind of father was this man when he was the parent of young children? What was his relationship with his wife? How did they share family responsibilities? How do you think that the socioeconomic conditions of his time shaped his parental role?

Men's Movements and Their Impact on Fathering

It can be said that some of the recent positive attention focused on fathering is linked with the issues and concerns raised by different men's movements (Messner, 1997) that emerged in the late 1960s. Although a majority of these movements did not directly deal with the issues of fathering, they did set the stage for genuine exploration of maleness that ultimately led to reanalyzing a man's role as father.

THE MYTHOPOETIC MEN'S MOVEMENT

Perhaps foremost among these movements was the mythopoetic men's movement brought to national prominence by Robert Bly in his 1990 bestseller *Iron John*. The basic belief of the mythopoets is that in many ways men have been damaged by negative socialization and trapped in harmful sex roles. According to Bly, one of the worst injuries that men have suffered is what he termed the father wound. As Bly stated: "Not seeing your father when you are small, never being with him, having a remote father, an absent father, a workaholic father, is an injury" (p. 31).

Bly's analysis of the deep confusion and alienation experienced by modern men goes back to the start of the Industrial Revolution. It was then, Bly says, as men moved off the land and into the factories, that fathers began separating physically and emotionally from their families. According to Bly, those most affected were young boys, who lost not only the emotional security of the father but the presence and participation of other, older men in their lives. Over time, men lost touch with what Bly calls the "male mode of feeling . . . something that gives the son a certain confidence, an awareness, a knowledge of what it is to be male." Clawson (1989) notes in particular how industrial capitalism has undermined much of the structural basis of men's emotional bonds with each other, as wage labor, market competition, and instrumental rationality replaced the more supportive male work relationships of the past (e.g., craft brotherhood, apprenticeships, and mentorships).

Bly maintains that men experience this mass exodus of the father (and older men) from their day-to-day lives as a great wounding. There is longing, grief, and anger at the loss, which gets buried deep within the psyche. The ramifications of this wounding lead men to distrust the older men in their lives and to depend too much on women. Men have been taught to cut themselves off from their emotions and to seek fulfillment through work and status.

Bly believes that one of the major problems in Western industrialized countries is that there is no ritualized movement from childhood into adulthood. He discusses how a woman can do a good job bringing up a baby boy through adolescence—and many single mothers are struggling to do just that—but she cannot initiate her boy into manhood without sacrificing her own femininity. This is a job only the older men can accomplish, and he feels that men in the Western world are reneging on this responsibility.

According to Bly, lacking the participation of the older men, boys are forced to turn to each other for initiation, increasing the allure of gangs, fraternity "animal houses," or other negative influences. As they may get older, they turn to the women in their lives, but Bly asserts that while most men learned about nurturing and vulnerability from women, those feelings never fully take until men see them exhibited in an older man. He maintains that this is what older males are uniquely qualified to do: to empathize with the younger boy and nurture him. The grown man can never fully do that for others, his wife, or his children, unless it has been modeled for him by a man.

It is Bly's contention that if men want to heal fully they must seek a definition of themselves from within and with other men. Men, Bly said, must learn to heal themselves and stop relying on women for all the answers to their problems and needs. Unfortunately, some interpreted this statement as antiwoman. Coupled with Bly's assertion that men need something "fierce" in their relationships with women, many feared that this movement was advocating a somewhat Neanderthal approach to women and the women's movement. Others suggest that what Bly was trying to say is that some of men's problems come from the growing societal message that there is something wrong with masculinity. Mythopoets would say that masculinity is acceptable, but they would be totally opposed to violence or oppression toward women and would not advocate these behaviors as a natural part of masculinity. The movement is very concerned with the poverty of men's relationships with their fathers and with other men in the workplace. It is Bly's insistence that they need a positive male role model to help them develop into healthy and well-adjusted men and fathers.

THE FATHERS' RIGHTS MOVEMENT

Other men's movements are more truly fathers' movements. They deal specifically with enhancing the role of fathers in the lives of children and often pursue social and political agendas to help bring this about. The first of these is called the Fathers' Rights Movement, which can be traced back to the early 1960s. These fathers are sometimes thought of as the "warriors" of the men's movements. They can be found on the front lines, advocating in such areas as child custody, child-support awards, divorce, and the rights of unmarried fathers. Members within this group are often politically conservative, although beliefs range across a wide political spectrum. A common theme voiced by members is their desire for a strong and active relationship with their children.

Parke and Brott (1999) note that these fathers emulated the women's movement by trying to make the personal political. Examples of this included lobbying local, state, and federal agencies to restructure the divorce and court system in order to provide more equitable treatment of fathers in the divorce process. However, many have noted that there is not just one fathers' rights group at this time but several hundred splinter groups offering varying degrees of support and capacity. Unfortunately, their social influence becomes questionable when claims that have little or no factual basis are made by their leaders. Parke and Brott (1999) cite the example of one who proposed that giving child custody to fathers in every divorce case would eradicate the need for Aid to Families with Dependent Children and save the government $50 billion a year. Such statements detract from the real issues that noncustodial fathers are trying to resolve. These types of comments also prove divisive and drive away potential supporters, both male and female. Fortunately there are segments within the movement that approach the issues with more inclusive pleas for supporting concerns that are vital to noncustodial parents. Women, particularly second wives, are active in many of these groups, and in some cases become informal leaders. They have a personal stake in this movement because the child-support issues and conflicts between their husbands and first wives can be detrimental to their own families and children.

THE GOOD FATHERHOOD MOVEMENT

Much of the impetus for this movement can be found in Blankenhorn's book, *Fatherless America*. The author promotes the idea that fatherhood is vitally important in our society and that the diminishing role of fathers in the family accounts for the dramatic rise in social problems over the past two decades, particularly among youth (Blankenhorn, 1995). Blankenhorn disagrees with those who simply call for more money to resolve the problems within single-parent families headed by mothers. Instead, he contends that money alone cannot replace the absent father. Followers of this movement are typically critical of deadbeat dads and other men who retreat from their parenting responsibilities. They have succeeded in getting media attention and have recruited high-profile celebrities like James Earl Jones to the mission. The movement permits females to be part of the cause and solicits advice from various well-known female writers (Barbara Dafoe Whitehead and Judith Wallerstein, among others).

Blankenhorn has drawn mixed reviews for his 12-point plan to combat the problem of fatherlessness. He calls for fathers to strive to become what he terms the good family man who sees himself as his wife's junior partner when it comes to parenting. He doesn't believe that fathers can be as fully involved with their children as the mother can and labels those men who aspire to become fully involved co-parents as the "new fathers." It is his contention that the new father is a mirage, and it is quite possible that Blankenhorn's good family man is actually a reincarnation of the one-dimensional breadwinner that many men have been trying to escape.

THE PROMISE KEEPERS

The Promise Keepers movement was founded in 1990 by Bill McCartney, a college football coach. This organization began with 72 men and by 1995 had attracted more than 600,000 men to its gatherings. Promise Keepers sponsor large gatherings usually in sports stadiums across the United States. The group raises about $3 million per event and the money is largely spent on organizing future rallies and developing a national network of men (Messner, 1997). It has successfully included large numbers of racial minorities in its membership and leadership, and it's most notable public gathering occurred when half a million Promise Keepers attended a rally in Washington, D.C.

Perhaps the heart of the Promise Keepers' appeal is that it offers solutions for men who feel that they have lost control over their lives. The content seems to appeal to men who are searching for ways to make up for their own perceived failures as husbands or fathers. Because it is a predominately religious movement one could speculate that it offers participants a chance to atone for past wrongs they have committed.

A recent qualitative study by Silverstein, Auerbach, and Grieco (1999) offers some additional information about why this movement has broad appeal. In their study, 22 men were interviewed in focus groups about their fathering experiences. Analysis found that they were experiencing gender-role strain as they tried to conform to traditional masculine role norms. The Promise Keepers movement provided them with an ideology and social support system that facilitated their becoming more involved fathers, while simultaneously reassuring them that they were the leaders of their families. Using these supports, the men were able to construct a more personally gratifying fatherhood identity.

Although many think that the motivation to improve as a husband and father is commendable, some observers are concerned with the specific means and ends that are seemingly encouraged by some in the movement. For example, Dr. Tony Evans (1994) wrote: "I'm not suggesting that you *ask* for your role back, I'm urging you to *take it back*. . . .There can be no compromise here. If you're going to lead, you must lead. Be sensitive. Listen. Treat the lady gently and lovingly. But *lead*!" (pp. 79–80). As can be expected, this sort of comment has led some to conclude that this movement is also about a return to patriarchy, and therefore has been met with considerable resistance from feminist authors. However, among many Christian women there is no apparent uproar over the Promise Keepers' desire to reinstate men as heads of the household. Stoltenberg (1995) reports observing hundreds of women taking part in the rallies across the country, and many expressed a desire to "meet and marry a man of Promise Keeper caliber some day" (p. 29). These comments imply the acceptance of a bargain where Christian women are willing to trade off elements of power within the marital relationship in exchange for a man's promise to be a responsible breadwinner, father, and husband. There's little outcome research yet to determine the full extent of the change that this movement has made in the members' lives in terms of improved relationships and improved self-image.

THE MILLION MAN MARCH

Nearly a million African American men converged on Washington, D.C., in October 1995 as another strong expression of support for responsible fatherhood. Though the march was led by Minister Louis Farrakhan and the Nation of Islam, African American men of many religious persuasions chose to join it while not claiming to endorse some of Farrakhan's controversial views. These men (and some women) voiced a collective proclamation to restore African American men's sense of moral responsibility and leadership in their families (Messner, 1997). The leaders of this march were responding at least in part to the major crises confronting many inner-city African American neighborhoods. As Anderson (1990) observed, most of the traditional African American adult male leaders had moved to the suburbs, men who had previously taught young males the value of hard work, family involvement, and contributing to the community. The vacuum they left behind has been filled by a new and troubling brand of male leaders including young street toughs, drug dealers, and gangs. The Million Man March was a call to respond to these social crises and to project a positive image of adult African American males by mentoring teens and by taking care of their families and communities (Messner, 1997). Countless volunteers surfaced after the march, seeking to be mentors with the NAACP, Big Brothers Association, and other groups.

THE MEN'S LIBERATION MOVEMENT

As the feminist movement emerged in the 1970s, a loose-knit men's liberation movement sprang up beside it. Male consciousness-raising, "male feminism," and concerns about gender inequities surfaced. Many male liberation groups strongly endorsed the messages of the feminist movement and began giving special attention to developing their feminine side (Messner, 1997). Special concerns were raised about how boys were socialized to be competitive, independent, and publically successful and how their socialization was stunting their capacity to express their full range of emotions and develop close relationships. A familiar expression associated with this movement was, "It's okay for boys to cry."

Reflection

List five messages about being a man that little boys in our culture are likely to hear. These messages can come from parents, peers, teachers, the media, and other sources (Rabinowitz & Cochran, 1994). List these messages on the chalkboard and discuss them in your class or group. What do these messages, particularly the most frequently mentioned ones, tell you about what little boys are exposed to?

Feminist thinking has helped to shape those in this movement as well as other men in the broader society. Silverstein (1996), a feminist writer, suggests that too much emphasis has been placed on the definition of fathering as being the provider in the public world and not enough attention paid to caretaking in the personal world of the family. This imbalance has been responsible for the inability of many men to be aware of and articulate their needs for intimacy and emotional connectedness. According to Silverstein, redefining fathering to reflect an emphasis on nurturing and caregiving as well as being a provider is the "next necessary phase in the continuing feminist transformation of our patriarchial culture"(p. 4). She adds that equitable sharing of the provider and caregiver roles will lead to greater marital satisfaction and improved psychological well-being for both partners.

In review, the men's movements of recent decades have inspired and fostered nothing less than a social transformation for men and their families. These movements have provided countless men with personal guidance and support, opportunities to bond with other men, and encouragement to claim the full extent of their maleness. These men's groups have also promoted many important themes pertinent to fathering. Male initiation into adulthood, fathers' rights, being a responsible father, mentoring young males, building both family and community, and developing the feminine side of fathering are examples. In general, the overall impact of these movements has been very positive for fathers' issues with a few noted exceptions.

WHY IS THE PROBLEM OF THE DISAPPEARING FATHER NOT TAKEN MORE SERIOUSLY?

When we consider the dramatic changes in the involvement of fathers in families over the past four decades or more, instinctively we want to ask why there is not more widespread concern. Some family scholars clearly see the growing trend of absentee fathers as the most critical problem confronting our society (Blankenhorn, 1995; Braver & O'Connell, 1998; Popenoe, 1996). These writers ask whether we would be so tolerant if it were women who were disappearing from families in such large numbers.

Yet other family scholars do not seem to view the absence of fathers with the same concern. Some may believe that this trend is an inevitable outcome of the diversity in our society and the more varied lifestyles that come with it. Others may see the effort to support fathers as a threat to the gains rightfully obtained by women. Their fear may be that absent men will return to their parental roles in families and reassert traditional roles and behaviors that could be oppressive, controlling, or violent.

Social forces of the past 40 years may help explain why a consensus has not been reached on reversing the decline of fatherhood, and the women's movement is one of these forces. This movement has made great strides in liberating women, particularly wives, from male dominance. Economically dependent on their husbands to a large extent until recent times, women are now realizing their own earning power in the workplace. This power has given them other options such as living alone or obtaining a divorce, when the alternative could be either spousal abuse or marital unhappiness.

Those in the women's movements may be concerned about efforts to reestablish marriage as the dominant family structure because of their fear of reversing women's economic and social gains. And many people are no longer convinced that the parenting roles of fathers and mothers are all that different, suggesting that fathers may not be indispensable as previously thought. Some recent authors, for example, suggest that children can be raised just as successfully by single mothers, extended families, and lesbian couples as they can by married couples (Silverstein & Auerbach, 1999).

Reflection

Delegates to the Southern Baptist Convention recently advised their wives to be "graciously submissive" to their husbands. How do you feel about this position? Do you believe it is unfair to wives? Do you think that such a position could be harmful to some wives?

Is it possible that the current state of male-female relationships is at a crossroads? Feminists might suggest that females are becoming liberated and men have not been as willing to adapt to these changes in women. Many men may still want to return to earlier arrangements in which gender roles were more distinct and mothers carried the bulk of the responsibility for child-care and housekeeping. Doherty (1997) asserts that the nature of male-female relations in parenting may be the crux of the problem. Thus, more attention must be given at all system levels to helping fathers and mothers work together to raise their children, whether within or outside marriage.

Another social force likely related to the decline of fatherhood was the sexual revolution of the 1970s. Coupled with more effective birth control technology, it significantly loosened the link between sexual activity and pregnancy. *Roe v. Wade* (1974) also provided the option of legal abortion, which became for many another form of birth control and eliminated the worry about unwanted pregnancy. Sexual activity became a pleasurable act, not just one of procreation, and as it became more prevalent between men and women outside of marriage, marriage in turn became less of a necessity for sexual intimacy.

The incidence of family violence has also increased significantly during the past 30 to 40 years, or it may be that family violence is reported more fully because it has become less acceptable in our society. Because of the women's movement, more women have assumed greater political influence and demanded that these problems that usually victimize women be stopped (Faludi, 1992). Family violence, substance abuse, and other harmful behaviors previously considered the private matters of families are now considered public issues that need to be addressed.

The women's movement, the sexual revolution, and the public attention paid to family violence have been linked to the phenomenon of the disappearing father in some important ways. As divorce has increased, more women than men typically have been the initiators. Men, viewed in the past as the head of the family and in some cases as the perpetrators of family violence, have become linked more consciously with women's oppression and victimization. Women are leaving men in larger numbers for other reasons as well, such as boredom with marriage and disappointment with their husband's capacity to be intimate (Braver & O'Connell, 1998).

Yet the link between these and other social forces and fatherhood issues has not been that simple or clear. Husbands as well as wives have been seeking marital separation and divorce in growing numbers, and a father is no longer considered essential to procreation, owing to the available technologies. Increasingly, unmarried couples are choosing to have babies, and many single women are giving birth to children on their own. Marriage may be becoming much less essential for some people in meeting such basic needs as sexual pleasure and raising children. Perhaps even more men than women perceive this new age as preferable to the past, because they have become the beneficiaries of greater sexual freedom and independence and a less structured concept of parenting.

Another explanation for society's tolerating the problem of the disappearing father is the trend toward greater consumerism, with its emphasis on a comfortable, materialistic lifestyle, particularly among the middle and upper classes. As our economy continues to expand, more attention is paid and expectations increase for the good life filled with material comforts, leisure, and pleasures. Although greater wealth can be beneficial to children and their parents, consumerism can become an end in itself and lead to neglecting our children. It can also attack some of our traditional societal values such as helping others and contributing to the improvement of the larger community.

Yet consumerism and a materialistic lifestyle are not likely to be relevant explanations for absent fathers in all groups in society. Many minority families, and poor people generally, are likely faced with racial and class discrimination as well as employment barriers even during times of economic prosperity. Economic opportunities available to the dominant culture are often denied to them, thwarting their attempts to provide materially for their families and to successfully parent (Allen & Connor, 1997).

In brief, we are concerned about our dominant culture's apparent complacency with the phenomenon of absent fathers. Our dominant culture is changing, and the ethical fibers that have held families together in the past seem to be weakening or at least are in question. We wonder if we would be so complacent about these patterns if the situation were reversed and women were disappearing from families. We suspect that more likely we would be alarmed and urgently calling for new ways of helping women return to their roles as mothers.

Why then has the trend of disappearing fatherhood been tolerated and perhaps even accepted by so many in our society? Doherty (1997) reminds us that these are contradictory times for fathers, the best of times and the worst of times. On the one side are those who speak of the traditional virtues of good fathering, the mounting evidence of the fathers' importance to child development, and nurturing as a new aspect of good fathering. On the other side emphasis is placed on the negative indicators, that fathers are becoming less involved as parents, are not assuming their financial and relational responsibilities, and are no longer essential to families beyond economic reasons. Some cite statistical indicators documenting how children in fatherless families are worse off in practically every indicator of social and psychological well-being, (see chapter 3 for details) while others call for an economic solution: "If only absent fathers would meet their financial obligations, all would be well for single-mother families." As Doherty explains, we seem at risk of either elevating fathers to the status of saviors of children or of trivializing their importance in the family.

Reflection

Do you think that fathers are essential to families and child-raising? If you think that they are not, do they provide an important or even unique role in the raising of children? What do they offer to children? If fathers are absent from families, what do you think is lost for the children?

PROBLEMS CONFRONTING MEN

Why are so many males not assuming an active parental role? Let us begin our exploration of some of the problems confronting males in our society and how we can bring them back into their families. Men in United States society are likely to face any or possibly all of the following problems:

Societal Barriers and Mixed Messages About Effective Fathering

Many barriers—obvious and subtle, interpersonal and institutional—confront males as they contemplate their child-raising responsibilities. Societal values and biases are among the most formidable barriers. Boys and men receive numerous conflicting messages about who they are supposed to be. For example, are they to be independent or interdependent, emotional or in control of their emotions, active in child-raising or successful in their outside careers? These conflicting messages are even more prevalent in the new millennium as equality between the sexes becomes an increasing reality. Men need help in understanding how these conflicting societal messages are woven into their lives. They also need help in affirming what they have to offer as fathers.

The Hazards of Being Male: Surviving the Myth of Masculine Privilege reminds us that

> men have burdens as well as privileges in our society. So often we emphasize the privileges and overlook the burdens. When we have such an

unbalanced view, we fail to understand the needs and circumstances of a male, whether he is a child or grown man. Perhaps so many men have not succeeded in their marriages because the expectations of them have been so high and often contradictory. Married men are often expected to be the capable provider, aggressive competitor, wise father, sensitive and gentle lover, fearless protector, cool and controlled negotiator under pressure, and emotionally expressive. (Goldberg, 1976, p. 151)

Having all of these qualities is unrealistic for most men and in many ways communicates confusion and contradiction. Goldberg goes on to identify several binds that are imposed on many males as they grow up:

1. Gender: He is raised mostly by his mother and other females such as a grandmother and female teachers. However, he is expected to throw off this female identity by the age of 5 or 6 and replace it with a male identity.
2. Feeling: He is discouraged from expressing feelings like crying and desiring hugs and other forms of physical affection from his mother by a certain age. Yet he is later criticized for not revealing his more vulnerable feelings and needs as an adult.
3. Breadwinner: He is expected to be a reliable, productive economic provider for his family. Yet if he takes this role too seriously, he may be accused of neglecting his children or of not being around them enough at home.
4. Autonomy: He is expected to be strong and independent and not to depend upon others for help. Unfortunately, this can lead to a denial of his need for others.
5. Health: He is taught to minimize his complaints about physical pain if he is to be a real man. Further, he is taught not to give in to his bodily ills and injuries. Yet if he follows such advice, he may be laying the foundation for chronic illness and early death.

These and other societal binds should not be misused to overlook the rightful responsibilities of men as parents and employees. Nevertheless, they are real binds or challenges that can deeply and painfully interfere in men's lives. We may, in some cases, be helping men by exploring these binds or dilemmas that confront and confuse them. We can also address these binds by initiating changes in policies and service provisions. For example, we can help institute stronger family-supportive employment policies that not only permit but encourage fathers to take paternity leaves when they have new children.

Negative Stereotypes of Men

With a relative lack of understanding in our society about why so many men are uninvolved fathers, stereotypes and misconceptions are allowed to continue to flourish. Without question, these stereotypes are evident in the behaviors of many males in society. But we also need to remember that they are stereotypes and reflect negatively on fathers in general. Furthermore, these stereotypes serve negatively as models for teenagers and young men who want to become active in their children's lives and are searching for ways to do so. When few positive images of men are readily evident, such stereotypes can influence the developing self-image of males, diminishing the likelihood that they will pursue an active, nurturing role with their children. As our society promotes these negative stereotypes of men, we create a self-fulfilling prophecy: boys become men with limited capacity and interest in raising and nurturing their children. The following are examples of such stereotypes:

- Teen fathers and other unmarried fathers can be overlooked or presumed to be uninterested in having a parenting role.
- Men who do not pay child support are labeled deadbeat dads, meaning that they want to avoid assuming the financial responsibilities of parenting and don't care about their offspring.
- Divorcing men who seek a sole or shared custodial role of their children are suspected of foul play, of avenging their former wife or using custody as a divorce proceeding tactic to get the upper hand.
- So-called traditional fathers in families have little to offer their children beyond discipline and protection. In these cases, the nurturing role must be assumed by the mother by default.
- The bumbling father is a favorite media image of the father who is incompetent in his efforts to parent. He usually doesn't know how to cook, wash clothes, houseclean, or prepare the children for school.

Perspective: The Elian Gonzales Case

Elian Gonzales, a young Cuban boy, was rescued at high sea in the Straits of Florida while escaping Cuba with his mother in late 1999. He was the lone survivor. His relatives in Miami were quickly given temporary custody while this case began to unfold. Juan Miguel Gonzales, Elian's father, lived in Cuba and shared custody of Elian with his mother. He had seen Elian regularly, almost daily, before the escape occurred. Yet Juan Miguel Gonzales was largely dismissed by many U.S. citizens as insignificant to the child's welfare even though he was the sole surviving biological parent. Many people had already decided that Elian had to be "saved" from returning to Communist Cuba. Several months later, Juan had to travel to the U.S. to retrieve his son, and even then he was faced with many legal obstacles. What if Juan Miguel Gonzales had died escaping Cuba and Elian's mother waited for Elian's return to Cuba? Do you think that the concern about returning Elian to Cuba would have been a serious consideration or would he have been returned immediately?

Public Policies That Discourage or Deter Active Fathering

Many public policies, like negative stereotypes, tend to undermine an active fathering role:

- Aid to Families with Dependent Children, the former public assistance program for families with financial needs, usually required the exclusion of fathers for families to be eligible.
- The sole emphasis of the Child Support Enforcement Agency is to expect that nonresidential fathers pay financial support, which reinforces a narrow view of what men have to offer their families—money. Only recently have the family visitation rights of fathers begun to be recognized as legitimate public goals.
- Most welfare reform initiatives almost exclusively focus on the males' employment preparation and overlook their need for counseling and support services related to being successful parents.
- The emphasis in teen-parenting programs focuses almost exclusively on helping teen mothers and ignores the importance of teen fathers. Similarly, teen-pregnancy-prevention programs

focus largely on the responsibilities of the young female and virtually ignore the responsibilities of young males.

- Many family service agencies and school counseling programs assume that the mother is the primary provider, design their services for mothers, and communicate low expectations for the fathers' participation.

Deficit Perspectives of Men as Fathers

Have you noticed that in many ways fathers are not viewed very highly in society? Have you noticed how the media—ads, movies, and magazines—portray men as self-centered and self-absorbed, highly competitive, bungling as fathers, sexually promiscuous, preoccupied with their own needs, and prone to violence? Relatively little of the media emphasizes fathers as caring for their children and partner, being socially concerned, and cooperative. In general, a deficit perspective on fathering seems commonplace, with the focus being on their problems or limitations.

A deficit model of men seems to prevail in much of the professional literature, especially in the social science literature. Family texts, for example, give far more attention to mens' problems than to their strengths (for example, their problems with substance abuse or domestic violence). While these problems are essential to cover, too little content seems to focus on men as valuable family members. In short, men can be subtly depicted as the problem family member who needs to be singled out with social control interventions. Less evident is content on the assets and potentials of men to their families, their capacity to be nurturing parents, role models for their daughters and sons, and an important source of guidance about future careers and citizenship.

More than mothering, fathering seems to be a culturally driven family role. What our culture encourages or supports has a major impact on the definition of the father's role. And as mentioned in the historical analysis earlier in this book, our culture has had widely varied expectations of fathers over time, from moral educator and primary caregiver to nonessential care-giver.

Blankenhorn (1995) presents an example of a deficit perspective. He claims that society has a responsibility to devise and enforce an acceptable role for fathers. Blankenhorn goes on to say that men do not volunteer for fatherhood; they must be conscripted into it authoritatively by the culture. He adds that men are not ideally suited to responsible fathering and are "inclined to sexual promiscuity and paternal waywardness" (p. 4). He views the current state of male identity in our society as bound to fail because our society has failed to create or sustain a set of norms for acceptable fatherhood. As Blankenhorn warns:

> [Our current society's story of fatherhood] reveals . . . both a failure of collective memory and a collapse of moral imagination. It undermines families, neglects children, causes or aggravates our worst social problems, and makes individual adult happiness—both males and females—harder to achieve. (p. 4)

According to Blankenhorn, men in American society are no longer instilled with responsibility to family and community. Instead a cultural void has led to a decline in children's well-being and a rise in violence, particularly against women. Blankenhorn clearly views the cause of the disappearing father to be inherent in the male species. Only the culture of society can harness men into responsible parenthood.

Hawkins and Dollahite (1997) espouse an alternative to the deficit perspective that they refer to as generative fathering. They point out that a deficit model of men and fathers is particularly evident in much of the professional literature. They cite labels used in family scholarship as one source of this evidence, including references to men and fathers as uninvolved, uninterested, fearful of intimacy, distant, unskilled, abusive, and oppressive. According to this model, men choose to be uninvolved with their children and they are unmotivated to change their ways. While Hawkins and Dollahite recognize that this deficit model is manifested in many fathers, by no means do they see it in all. Most important, they believe that a deficit model is not the place to begin to understand and help fathers who have gone astray. Unlike Blankenhorn, they do not lay the responsibility for this deficit model on the biological and social makeup of males.

The problem with a deficit model is that it masks what men believe in and can do. We believe that the vast majority of men love their children and want to be good fathers. Also, every man has strengths, some more than others, that can enhance their effectiveness as parents. According to Hawkins and Dollahite (1997) the deficit model is itself an obstacle for men. This model does not give adequate attention to the potential in males for further maturation and development. Every human being has the potential to grow and develop further, and this should be the expectation of anyone seeking help. The deficit model can also obscure what most men feel, believe, and want. While men may often have differing sides to their feelings, beliefs, and desires, this model consistently emphasizes the negative side—men as incapable, uncaring, and uninterested, rather than their opposites.

Inadequate Preparation for the Multifaceted Responsibilities of Parenting

Young men are usually introduced to the work world—to vocations, work skills, a trade, careers in corporate life—within their schools and families. But what about their family responsibilities? Where do they learn to develop empathy for others, supportive and collaborative skills, mentoring roles, a capacity to listen, and other qualities inherent in effective parenting?

Although neither sons nor daughters can be perfectly prepared for family life these days, females typically are given more attention because of the traditional view that they will raise their children. Preparation for parenthood mostly comes from one's own parents, and girls usually have better modeling from their mothers than boys have from their fathers. Many women report having had a close relationship with their mothers and some firsthand experience assisting their mothers in parenting; men are less likely to make such a claim. While fathering roles are gradually changing, most boys still have a father who is not well prepared to nurture, who is usually absorbed in his work or is absent altogether. The apparent lack of interest in a parenting role that many young men manifest may be an unconscious imitation of their own father, an intergenerational pattern widely evident in society, or a product of societal images promoted by the media and other sources.

FAVORABLE VIEWS OF FATHERS

Dollahite, Hawkins, and Brotherson (1997) construct an alternative to a deficit paradigm called generative fathering. Erikson (1950) referred to generativity as a psychosocial task of human development that refers to actively caring for the next generation. Generativity refers to expanding one's concerns beyond self to one's children and others of the next generation. Fathering is ultimately about generativity, loving and caring for one's children. According to Dollahite and associates, generative fathering is "fathering that meets the needs of children by working to create and maintain a developing ethical relationship with them" (p. 18). This perspective emphasizes what is possible and desirable rather than what reality may describe. What can and ought to be done by fathers, mothers, families, and communities is the key issue. This perspective offers an ethic of fathering calling for both an obligation by fathers to become committed to their responsibility and an effort by all of us to enhance their abilities to be good parents.

African American men, in particular, too often have been viewed from a negative perspective. Researchers have focused mostly on the problems of African American males and families, with an emphasis on abnormality and dysfunctional issues (Allen & Connor, 1997). For example, most studies have focused on economically deficient, socially vulnerable families and then attempted to make inferences to African American families in general (McAdoo, 1981). Such studies have inevitably produced many harmful stereotypes, such as highlighting the matriarchal family structure and its absent father. A generative perspective leads us to seek to discover the strengths of African American fathers and families. Their capacity for adaptation, family unity, and stability sustained over these past four centuries of extreme hardship are indeed strengths worthy of further exploration (Mirande, 1991). Afrocentric standards need attention as well, such as the value placed on collectivity over individualism and family and kinship group obligation over being an autonomous father (Asante, 1989; Oliver, 1989).

Reflection
What are your views about men in general? Fathers in particular? What images come to mind when you think about fathering? Are these images positive or negative? Where do you think these images come from?

A central theme running through the book is an emphasis on a strengths perspective. To succeed in helping fathers, we *must* emphasize the positive qualities of men that are often overlooked. All males have assets to affirm and build upon, and any assistance to men should begin there. This does not suggest that we should overlook the personal problems of fathers. Only that we should explore these problems and the eventual solutions with a respect, openness, and hopefulness for these men and their potential for change.

We believe that all men have special strengths that are to be identified and recognized. In some cases it may take more time and effort than others to discover their personal strengths, but discover them we must. Men are often unaware of their special strengths or gifts, or they may lack the self-confidence needed to identify them. When this is the case, we must begin by helping them affirm this part of who they are.

Our perspective includes a belief that virtually all males have an inherent psychological need to parent their children. We operate from a perspective similar to Dollahite, Hawkins, and Brotherson (1997) that men want to be good fathers and that they have the inherent ability and the potential to do so. We must begin with the belief that men love their children deeply even though many may not be aware of the depths of this love. Sometimes they need help in discovering the love that is deep inside them as well as their inherent qualities that are waiting to be developed. Men want to participate in raising their children, just as women do. Men want to contribute to their family's well-being and bond with them.

Reflection

How much did your father or father surrogate invest in his parental responsibilities? Did you have enough direct contact with him? Do you recall other ways in which he was involved in your life that were important to you? How important is direct interaction between a father and his children?

We recognize that some men have problems and many have serious problems, such as substance abuse, that can block or divert their parental instincts. We approach the help that they need with the full realization of these problems, large and small. Adult or teenage males may lack the immediate motivation to activate their parental desires. They may also lack specific knowledge and skills that are needed for effective parenting. Nevertheless, we discourage the application of a deficit model mind-set that accentuates their part in creating their problems and overlooks their strengths. Such a perspective will inevitably lead to a self-fulfilling prophecy wherein we suspect that they cannot be responsible parents, and then discover this to be true.

Questions for Discussion

1. Is fatherhood as important to the family today as it was 100 or 200 years ago? Why or why not?

2. Blankenhorn (1995) states: "Being male is one thing. Being a good father is another. The latter no longer seems to be the pathway to proving the former." What is your reaction to his point? Have masculinity and fatherhood become disconnected as suggested by Blankenhorn?

3. How have the radical changes in the family over the past 200 years changed the role of fathering for the better? for the worse?

GLOSSARY

A glossary is included to help us to consider alternative terminology when traditional terms can be harmful to fathers. For example, in a single-mother household the father could be residing somewhere else and spending significant, intimate time with his children. By referring to this family as a single-parent family we are overlooking or ignoring the father's role. Other preferred terms are listed below followed by traditional terms that could be problematic to fathers.

Glossary of Preferred and Problematic Terms

Preferred Term	Traditional Term
Single-parent household	*Single-parent family* often overlooks family members outside the household.
Nonpaying father	*Deadbeat father* implies that all fathers who do not pay child support are capable and unwilling.
Co-parents	Use of *custodial* and *visiting* parents suggests that one parent assumes all of the responsibilities.
Primary residence	Use of *custody* can overlook an important role played by the other parent.
Primary and secondary residential parents	*Custodial* and *noncustodial*. parents can suggest that one parent is clearly superior to the other.
Living with or spending time with the other parent	*Visitation* suggests that parents visit their children.

2

Profiles of Three Groups of Nonresidential Fathers

There are many reasons why 'nonresidential fathers,' as you have put it, withdraw or remain removed. Maybe many would like to take responsibility, but feel that they would be leaving themselves wide open for a life filled with difficulties and feel it is just easier to walk away from their responsibility. Maybe they don't feel like they could take the stress or fear of never knowing what's going to happen next. To get into this situation, somewhere along the line they have made mistakes and just fear making more [mistakes] and messing up their children's or their own lives even more. Maybe some fathers don't have a conscience or don't let it bother them. Maybe some don't care as much about family ties or what a genetic bond means, as I do. Whatever the reason, I think you will find that the majority of fathers who have decided not to take responsibility really feel the burden of their choice . . . more than they would ever admit. (Unmarried father's comments to one of the authors)

In this chapter, we describe three primary groups of nonresidential fathers: divorced fathers, teen fathers, and older unmarried fathers. These three groups will be a continuing major focus throughout the book. This chapter highlights several topics describing the circumstances of these three groups, including

- Their common problems and challenges
- Custodial issues for divorced fathers
- The concerns of remarried fathers
- What we know about unmarried fathers
- The challenges of teen fathers

Virtually any group of fathers in our society could be at risk of not adequately fulfilling its parental role. They may be married, unmarried, or divorced; young or old; from any socioeconomic level, and from any racial, ethnic, or religious group. Although we have chosen to focus on three specific groups of nonresidential fathers, we wish to stress that many other groups of fathers could have been the focus as well. For example, fathering could easily be at risk in any of the following circumstances:

- A married father who is excessively absorbed in his job and neglects his wife and children is likely to be placing his fathering at risk. His psychological and physical absence from the family easily can be harmful to both his wife and children.
- Dual career couples could be putting their parenting at risk if either or both of their careers result in neglecting their children's basic needs.
- A single custodial father could be unprepared for many of the tasks involved in sole parenting because he has not had earlier training or practice in such parental tasks as nurturing, establishing and respecting personal boundaries, or preparing nutritional meals.
- A military father away at war could be placing his family in jeopardy by his absence and possibly by dragging the violence that he has internalized from his war experience into his family's life after returning home.
- Fathers in prison are a special group whose parental role is at risk. Such fathers are likely to bring harm to their families by their absence and by the negatively perceived meaning that their absence could have for their family.
- Abusive fathers, whether residential or nonresidential, are a particular group of men needing special attention. These fathers are placing their families at risk because of the dangers and harm inflicted by their violence.

The focus of the book is on nonresidential fathers, a large, diverse group of fathers who are among the most vulnerable to being at risk in the United States today. These nonresidential fathers include divorced fathers, teen fathers, and unmarried fathers.

This chapter identifies some of the important ways that these three nonresidential groups are similar to one another and thus face common challenges to their parenting. It also highlights some of the ways that they are different, particularly in their personal and social circumstances, and describes the diversity within each of these groups. In addition, we note that these groups are not always mutually exclusive. For example, teen fathers could also be members of one of the other groups, divorced or unmarried, as well. However, we consider teen fathers as a distinct group because of their relatively young age and stage of personal development.

COMMON PROBLEMS AND CHALLENGES

We characterize these three groups of nonresidential fathers as at risk in their parenting roles because they are highly prone to following a pattern of diminishing their contact with their children.

Doherty (1998) offers a conceptual model that identifies many considerations that can influence how well a father functions. It includes factors about fathers, mothers, their relationship, their children, and the larger contextual issues, all of which can influence the parenting role of nonresidential fathers. Factors in interaction with each other can have even more impact. We give special attention to many of those factors that pertain to fathers, mothers, and their relationship as well as the larger contextual factors. Factors pertinent to the children, while important, are not a major focus of this book. Figure 2.1 illustrates the factors of Doherty's model.

Two key pivotal challenges are likely to influence a father's role. First, challenges can exist when a father lives physically apart from his children. A separate living arrangement can make it very difficult both psychologically and physically for a nonresidential father to stay involved with his children (or a mother with hers). Efforts to adjust to a separate living arrangement sometimes can be quite troublesome and bewildering. Nonetheless, fathers will need to make this adjustment and accept the reality of a separate residential arrangement if they are to succeed in their parenting. Doherty's model can be useful here in identifying factors that may be important in helping a father adjust to living apart. Factors about fathers are all relevant. A co-parental factor that is particularly important is the custodial arrangement (joint or noncustodial). Having joint custody can provide fathers with more rights and responsibilities as parents and more confidence in their parenting role. Contextual factors can also be important, such as expectations of their culture and their social supports.

Second, fathers could have difficulty arranging quality time with their children because they must depend upon a cooperative relationship with the biological mother. The possibility is obvious of conflicts arising after the uncoupling of the parents' intimate relationship. Anger,

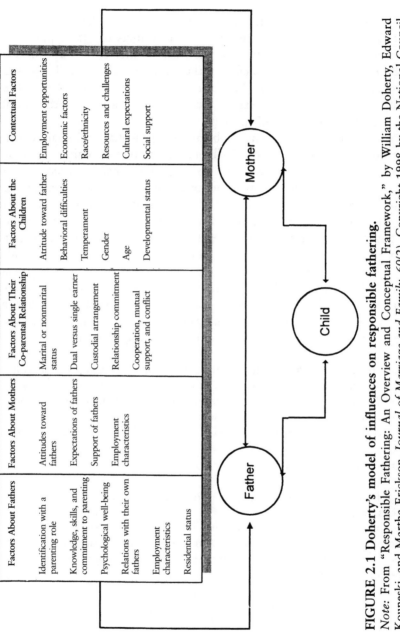

Factors About Fathers	Factors About Mothers	Factors About Their Co-parental Relationship	Factors About the Children	Contextual Factors
Identification with a parenting role	Attitudes toward fathers	Marital or nonmarital status	Attitude toward father	Employment opportunities
Knowledge, skills, and commitment to parenting	Expectations of fathers	Dual versus single earner	Behavioral difficulties	Economic factors
Psychological well-being	Support of fathers	Custodial arrangement	Temperament	Race/ethnicity
Relations with their own fathers	Employment characteristics	Relationship commitment	Gender	Resources and challenges
Employment characteristics		Cooperation, mutual support, and conflict	Age	Cultural expectations
Residential status			Developmental status	Social support

FIGURE 2.1 Doherty's model of influences on responsible fathering.

Note: From "Responsible Fathering: An Overview and Conceptual Framework," by William Doherty, Edward Kouneski, and Martha Erickson, *Journal of Marriage and Family, 60(2).* Copyright 1998 by the National Council on Family Relations, 3839 Central Ave. NE, Suite 550, Minneapolis, MN 55421. Reprinted by permission.

disappointment, resentment, indifference, a sense of failure, jealousy, or a desire for vengeance are all possible feelings of either parent. If not managed well, such feelings could easily interfere with efforts to arrange quality time between a father and his children. Factors in Doherty's model that may be important in facilitating cooperation include many of the co-parental factors, factors about mothers, and contextual factors for both parents.

These two pivotal challenges—being nonresidential and being dependent upon collaboration with the biological mother—combine to create numerous hurdles for these fathers to overcome. There is a tendency at this time in the family life cycle for such fathers to be perceived as relatively unimportant to the survival of their children, regardless of their prior importance. As many nonresidential fathers have stated, this secondary parental status offers little in legal rights and minimal sympathy and support from most judges and attorneys in times of trouble. Judges take a strong stand in enforcing child support issues, which assist custodial parents, but often feel less comfortable addressing visitation or access issues (Emery, 1994). As a result, fathers often feel punished by the legal system while their former wives are perceived to be treated more positively (Arendell, 1995). One father gives an example of this:

> One thing that really irritates me about the court system here is that you can be married for 10 years, and you can be a loving, wonderful father for 10 years. And . . . in my instance, [my wife] met the other guy and decided to run off with him, and the minute that she left, I was no longer a worthy father. I got visitation! (Umberson & Williams, 1993, p. 389)

Another had this to say:

> I believe that the system (judges, attorneys, etc.) have [sic] little or no consideration for the father. At some point the system creates an environment where the father loses any natural desire to see his children because it becomes so difficult, both financially and emotionally. At that point, he convinces himself that the best thing to do is to wait until they are older. (Pasley & Minton, 1997, p. 124)

Demographic Trends

Information selected from the U.S. Census and relevant research studies sketches a general profile of families and fathers as they have changed over time.

MORE CHILDREN ARE WITHOUT THEIR BIOLOGICAL FATHERS

The percentage of all fathers living with their biological children has declined considerably from 1960 to 1990. In 1960, 17.5% of all biological fathers lived separately from their children, increasing to 22.4% in 1970. In 1980, this figure was 32.2%, and by 1990 the number had reached 36.3%. Unfortunately, data is not available after 1990 to determine if these trends continue or are stabilizing.

DECLINE OF MARRIED PARENT HOUSEHOLDS WITH CHILDREN CONTINUES THROUGH 1995

Other census data attempts to capture the changes in family composition since 1990. As Table 2.1 suggests, married couples with children continued to decline as late as 1995. An interesting footnote is that single-father families have increased more than single-mother families, and made up about one out of every five single-headed families in 1995. Table 2.1 can be somewhat misleading, however, as families headed by "women with no husband present" or "men with no wife present" could be either single parents or unmarried partners. "Unmarried cohabiting parents" was not considered a category in these census data.

TABLE 2.1 Changes in Family Composition 1970 to 1995

	1970	1995
Married couples with children	40% of all households	25% of all households
Families headed by women with no husband present	5.6 million	12.2 million
Families headed by men with no wife present	1.2 million	3.2 million

Note: U.S. Bureau of the Census (1995).

THE NUMBER OF CHILDREN LIVING IN UNMARRIED FAMILIES IS INCREASING MORE THAN IN DIVORCED FAMILIES

It is also important to explore trends related to the children in divorced, unmarried, and widowed families. Table 2.2 is an expansion of Table 1.1 (Percentage of U.S. Children in Various Family Arrangements in chapter

TABLE 2.2 Percentage of U.S. Children in Single or Blended Families
1960 to 1990

Living With	1960	1970	1980	1990
Mother only	7.7	11.8	18.0	21.6
- never married	3.9	9.3	15.5	31.5
- divorced	24.7	29.7	41.6	36.9
- separated	46.8	39.8	31.6	24.6
- widowed	24.7	21.2	11.3	7.0
Father only	1.0	1.8	1.7	3.1

Note: Hernandez (1993); U.S. Bureau of the Census (1981, 1991, 1992).

1) and provides such data. This table examines the percentage of children living in divorced, separated, unmarried, and widowed families, with married families and remarried stepfamilies being excluded. As the table indicates, the percentage of children in all single-mother families increased from 7.7% to 21.6% from 1960 to 1990. At the same time the percentage of children in single-father families tripled from 1.0% to 3.1%. Among all single-mother families, the percentage of children living with divorced mothers has remained fairly stable since 1960. Combining divorced and separated single-women families, their overall total actually decreased by 10%. In contrast, the percentage of children with never-married mothers has soared since 1960, growing from 3.9% to 31.5% of all single-mother families. These figures strongly suggest that the major increases in nonresidential fathers over the three decades have been among unmarried families.

Reflection

Since the largest increases in nonresidential fathers have been among the unmarried, it's important to consider their special needs and challenges. What kinds of help would they possibly need in strengthening their parental roles?

RACIAL AND ETHNIC TRENDS

Racial and ethnic differences are evident across all three fathers' groups. It might surprise some readers that most children from all ethnic groups were raised in husband-wife marriages in 1960. Before the 1960s, for example, African American families with both parents present were as high as 75% (Billingsley, 1968; National Research Council, 1989). In 1991, babies born out-of-wedlock had increased to 22% for Whites, 38% for Latinos, and 68% for African Americans (National Center for Health Statistics, 1993).

Furstenberg (1995) draws attention dramatically to this pattern by stating that parenting apart has become "standard practice" in recent years for most African Americans, Puerto Ricans, and low-income whites in the inner cities. This translates into enormous numbers of children growing up without their fathers in their homes, particularly in racial minority and poor families. Yet Manning and Landale (1996) claim that for most White and Puerto Rican women, unmarried co-habitation appears to be a transition to marriage while this does not seem to be the case for African American women.

DIVORCED FATHERS

Currently, almost half of all new first marriages will end in divorce, and some forecast that in the future, divorce will occur in two thirds of recent marriages (Castro-Martin & Bumpass, 1989). In 1998, 19.4 million adults obtained divorces, representing 9.8% of all adults (U.S. Census, 1998).

Divorced dads are typically distinguished from one another by their custodial status: sole, joint residential, joint legal, and noncustodial. Fathers with sole custody have increased considerably over the past 30 to 40 years, but still remain a small percentage of all divorced dads. They were approximately 1% of all families with children in 1960 and increased to about 3% by 1990.

Fathers with joint residential custody have the next highest level of custodial responsibility. They share residential care of their children with the biological mother on a more or less equal basis. This group of fathers is also a relatively small percentage of all families. While an accurate count is difficult to come by, they are estimated to be less than 5% of all divorced families (Nord & Zill, 1996).

Joint legal custody fathers have the next highest level of custodial rights, sharing responsibility for major decisions about their children with their former wives. However, these fathers are not likely to share equally in the residential care of their children unless they also have joint residential custody. About 17% of all custodial arrangements are comprised of joint legal custody (Nord & Zill, 1996).

By far, the largest group of divorced fathers is classified as noncustodial. These fathers live separately from their children, have few rights as parents, and vary widely in their parental involvement, from seeing their children regularly, such as every other weekend, to having no contact at all.

Noncustodial fathers appear to be the custodial group at greatest risk when it comes to fulfilling parental responsibilities. Fathers with joint legal custody have some legal rights and responsibilities and are thought to be less at risk (Braver & O'Connell, 1998). In contrast, sole custodial fathers and joint residential custody fathers have substantially more parental rights and residential responsibilities. Fathers who are sole custodial parents have their children living with them most, if not all, of the time and assume major decision-making responsibility. Joint residential custodial fathers, by definition, share residential responsibilities of their children with their former spouse. While fathers in this group are likely to have widely divergent living arrangements with their children, on average they live with their children approximately half of the time. They carry significant custodial rights, which they share with their former spouse. For these reasons, joint residential custody could be viewed as the preferred arrangement for fathering after divorce when it is feasible, can be voluntarily arranged, and benefits the children.

A Closer Look at Noncustodial Fathers

While little was known about noncustodial fathers in the past, this diverse group has gained increasing attention from family scholars in the past 10 to 15 years (Depner & Bray, 1993; Fox, 1985; Lund, 1987). A major contribution to this relatively new stream of research are the firsthand views and experiences of these fathers. Without such studies in the past, incomplete and often erroneous explanations have been offered about noncustodial fathers, resulting in harmful stereotypes and misconceptions.

Before this new research emerged, information about noncustodial fathers was derived largely from interview studies of the custodial mother. In this regard, it is important to note that noncustodial fathers are likely to have perceptions that are different than their former spouse, the custodial mother. Braver and O'Connell (1998) point out how common it is for divorced spouses to give very different versions of the same event or situation. Neither spouse is usually consciously aware that there could possibly be another version than their own. What they may be doing is bending or distorting events to back up their own position or perception of reality, and it is important to note that each typically identifies him- or herself as the hero and the spouse as the villain. Furthermore, such parents are more likely to focus anger and blame on the other parent than on themselves.

In studies that have compared the responses of previously married spouses, divorced fathers tended to give more credit to the value and extent of their involvement with their children than did their former spouse (Ahrons, 1983; Goldsmith, 1980). The conflicting nature of these responses suggests that studies of custodial mothers have not provided a totally accurate understanding of post-divorce families. When combined with studies of mothers the recent surge of studies of noncustodial fathers offers a more complete understanding of these post-divorce families.

How can we explain these differing and sometimes conflicting views about the attitudes and practices of divorced, noncustodial fathers? One way is to adopt the view of Furstenburg (1988) and others who claim that there are "good" and "bad" dads no matter where you look. The conflicting messages are likely to come from the "bad" dads, and the reasoning could go something like this: Some will strive to be good parents and will succeed at it, while others will show little drive or determination to make a go of it and will likely fade away. The ones who fade away will more likely blame the mother than admit to their own failings as parents.

Another, possibly more palatable explanation for the ambiguity of information is that reports about divorced fathers are likely to take sides with either the father or mother, as conflict and adversity are unavoidable to some extent when parents separate. Inevitably, we should expect that some stories about nonresidential fathers will be more favorable and others will be less so, depending on who is describing them.

Reflection
Collecting research data from some men can be a challenge for the researcher. At times, fathers' views are left out of studies due to this issue. Why do you think it can be so difficult to collect research information from some men? What steps would you take to improve this situation?

Favorable Profiles of Noncustodial Dads[1]

Favorable and unfavorable views about noncustodial fathers can be found in the literature. One favorable profile of divorced non-custodial fathers comes from a summary of the qualitative findings of five

---

[1]This section excerpted from "Noncustodial Fathers Speak About Their Parental Role," by James Dudley, *Family Court Review, 34*(3), pp. 410–426. Copyright 1996 by Sage Publications, Inc. Reprinted by permission of Sage Publications, Inc.

available studies from various sections of the United States (Dudley, 1996). Overall, the similarities in the general findings of these five studies are striking (Arditti & Allen, 1993; Arendell, 1992; Dudley, 1991c; Kruk, 1992; Umberson & Williams, 1993).

Perceived Loss Was Considerable

Most of the fathers in these studies reported experiencing considerable emotional distress from their divorce experience, and the loss of their children from their daily lives was of great importance to them. Their pain was related to seeing their children only intermittently and according to a prescribed schedule and feeling a sense of loss of control over their children's daily lives and events.

Concern About Focusing Only on Finances

The noncustodial fathers in these five studies had other common experiences. They were dissatisfied because they perceived that others (the biological mother, attorneys, courts, etc.) were only interested in their financial obligations to their children and not in their child-raising obligations as well. They wanted to be more to their children than a source of money. An illustration comes from the comments of one father: "Most divorced fathers do not feel that they shouldn't pay child support—it's that we think that we are more to the children than the man who sends the check" (Arditti & Allen, 1993, p. 471).

Desire for More Time With Children

Related to the deep sense of loss, many of the fathers in these five studies claimed to want sole or joint custodial responsibilities and more time with their children. Some also felt that sole custody for the mother was not in their children's best interest. One father explained it this way:

> One thing that very few people are really able to appreciate is that whoever it is who does not have custody, whoever it is who moves out of the house—that you are out there, you are in your flat or your room or whatever—you are away from your children, and your wife, and they are in a family home, in their familiar surroundings, your wife has the

children there (be they crutches, or be they a great joy), but they are people who care about each other, they are a threesome, and you are an isolated one—that can be absolute desolation, and you really can't . . . ever start to perceive how isolated one feels in the absence of your family. And that I think is perhaps the greatest tragedy of all. One may say verbally "That's really difficult," but if you face that for 3 or 4 years, it's really a hard cross to bear. (Kruk, 1992)

CONFLICTS WITH FORMER SPOUSE

Another frequent theme in all of the findings of these studies was the difficulty that these fathers had in getting along with their former spouses, difficulties that often had an adverse effect on their personal adjustment. Many of these conflicts resulted from the divorce itself.

Perceived interference with the fathers' visitation arrangement, for example, was a major source of conflict. Sometimes, former spouses interfered directly, by changing the children's schedule to conflict with the visitation. Other times the reported interference was indirect, such as saying negative things to the children about their father that affected the children's attitudes towards visits. For example, one father said:

If the mother is manipulative and is still attempting to get back at you, the mother can make the children feel guilty for wanting to see you. And this happened with my children. My children would come over crying. And the reason why they were crying was because their mother brought them over crying, saying, "I don't want to make you see your dad, but the judge made me do it, and I can't do anything about it, and you're just going to have to do this. . . . And so sometimes you ask yourself . . . would the children be better off without me, just to avoid the stress, and would I be better off? (Umberson & Willliams, 1993, p. 391)

DISSATISFACTION WITH COURT DECISIONS

Many of these fathers complained about the divorce proceedings and consistently voiced the opinion that the divorce courts were unfair. One father's observation was this:

I feel the justice system as we know it now is a joke. It makes all parties bitter toward each other, especially if you have a former spouse that uses the system for revenge and gets away with it. The judges are extremely

one-sided, and most lawyers don't care or represent you properly. They
are only in it for the money. I don't care for a system where judges can
sit in their ivory towers and lawyers can play "let's make a deal" with
your life. (Arditti & Allen, 1993)

Dissatisfaction with the court decisions about custody in particular was
a point of contention for these fathers, and most were dissatisfied with
their visitation and child support arrangements. One father's disillusion-
ment about the court's position on these issues was expressed as follows:

I sense that the legal system's prevailing attitude is that for the most part,
fathers don't really desire or care to have custody. This couldn't be
further from the truth. Fathers as a group are no more or less capable of
being single parents than mothers. (Arditti & Allen, 1993, p. 469)

In short, the noncustodial fathers of these five studies portrayed
themselves quite differently than the common stereotypes of fathers as
disinterested or lacking a sense of responsibility for their children.
These findings suggest a vastly different profile of a noncustodial father—one who loves his children and suffers when he cannot see them
frequently enough and one who wants to be more actively involved
and carry significantly more family responsibilities.

Unfavorable Profiles of Divorced Fathers

Contrasting views about noncustodial fathers are also evident and
need to be considered. Numerous noncustodial fathers belong to
fathers' rights groups that offer support and advocacy to redress
what they perceive as unfair legal advantages for mothers in the
divorce courts. Some of these fathers may reflect a profile different
than the ones presented above. Bertoia and Drakich (1995) conducted a study of 28 fathers and four mothers in four fathers'
rights groups. (The mothers were likely second wives to these men.)
They found contradictions between the public rhetoric of these
groups and their private views, which the researchers characterized
as "self-interest posturing." The public position voiced by some in
these groups, was that fathers of the 1980s and 1990s were making
positive changes such as becoming more involved in all family activities
and favoring affirmative action for women in the workplace; privately,
however, these fathers admitted to wanting to "delegate to the mother
all or most of the child-care responsibilities."

According to Bertoia and Drakich, members of these fathers' rights groups claimed that there is reverse discrimination against men in the courts. While they publically claimed to want fathers to be more seriously considered for sole custody and joint custody, many of these fathers admitted privately that their position in supporting custodial fathers is a strategy not for equality in parenting, but for a return to the more traditional roles of parenting in which fathers are breadwinners and mothers are child-care providers.

Another portrayal of noncustodial fathers seems unduly severe but is included here in an effort to provide a diversity of views. Blankenhorn (1995, p. 151) suggests that nonresidential fathers are destined to fade away from their parental responsibility. Pessimistically, he calls "visiting father" a contradiction in terms, saying that combining "visiting" and "fathering" leads to a collapse of parenting. His dramatic portrayal of a divorced nonresidential father is as follows:

For most divorcing couples, the marriage ends in bitterness, guilt, and pain. A small civilization has died. The children stay with the mother. The father moves out and tries to move on. When he does so, he may suffer enormously. He may have the best intentions about not divorcing his children. But despite these feelings, most of these men lose the essence of their fatherhood. They drift away from their children almost as surely as they move away from their former homes and drift away from their former wives. This is sad. But it is the pattern.

We do not concur with Blankenhorn's depiction because it does not fit the reality of most men's experiences that we know. The major challenge is not the father. In our view, most noncustodial fathers seem to want continued contact with their children. The major challenge is in arranging continued contact in a way that both serves the children's needs and fosters cooperation between the parents.

Reflections

Which of the descriptions of divorced noncustodial fathers do you see most prevalent in your experiences: the hurt but persistent dad who works hard to stay involved, the manipulative dad who misrepresents his motives about wanting involvement with his children, or the dad who cannot seem to adjust to a visiting role and gradually gives up and withdraws?

Remarried Fathers: A Special Subgroup of Divorced Fathers

Divorced fathers who later remarry are a special subgroup of divorced fathers. They have two families who expect their involvement: their biological children and their newly constituted family. Fathers who remarry are usually living with stepchildren, not their own children. In 1990, 10.4% of all children in the U.S. were living with their mother and a stepfather, while fewer than 1% were living with their father and a stepmother. These percentages have not changed much over time: 5.9% of all children had been living with their mother and stepfather in 1960, and less than 1% had been living with their father and a stepmother.

Divorced fathers who remarry are likely to have special circumstances that are different from other divorced fathers. Not only do they have the added demand on their time of two families, but they are also faced with divided loyalties. Pasley and Minton (1997) suggest that remarried fathers face greater parental-role ambiguity because they are caught between two competing families and conflicting loyalties. Remarried fathers are likely to form firm boundaries with their new spouse and children, resulting in reduced contact with the children in their first marriage (Buehler & Ryan, 1994; Seltzer, 1991). Also, in comparison to married fathers, remarried fathers tend to have relationships with their biological children from their first marriage that are more detached, conflictual, and problematic (Hetherington & Clingempeel, 1992). In addition, remarriage by either spouse can create stress in the original co-parent relationship (Wallerstein & Blakeslee, 1989).

Remarriage occurs rather quickly for many fathers and mothers. About 50% of men and 33% of women remarry within 1 year of divorce (DeWitt, 1994; U.S. Bureau of the Census, 1990). A father's adjustment to divorce and remarriage involves redefining his role both with children and stepchildren. Confusion in their role with stepchildren is likely and can undermine the development of cooperation with the mother of their biological children. A decline in the father's contact with his biological children is a likely result (Maccoby & Mnooken, 1992). The least contact often occurs when only one parent remarries; this may be the result of a need of the new stepfamily to build stronger bonds (Hetherington, Arnett, & Hollier, 1988; Maccoby & Mnooken, 1992). One study found that fathers were more likely to diminish their contact with their children when their former wife remarried, possibly because of difficulties adjusting to the presence of the new stepfather and greater stressful contact between the former spouses (Buehler & Ryan, 1994).

When fathers remarry they take on additional financial and child-raising responsibilities for their new stepchildren, which can result in a decline in financial support as well (Buehler & Ryan, 1994: Seltzer, 1991). They are also faced with many new challenges. They must establish an essentially new family household for the occasions when their children visit, with new rules, routines, expectations, and new relationships with their children (Blankenhorn, 1995); at the same time they must establish a new family household with their new wife and stepchildren.

One child, Ari, age 14, expressed her worries about being replaced by her dad's new family after he had remarried:

[I feel] left out a lot of the times. And one thing I really worry about is that I think they want to have a baby, and I know that if they do, it will be just like a replacement for me. That's because I only see my dad on weekends, and since he would see the baby more than he'd see me, he'd probably grow to like it more than he likes me. (Blankenhorn, 1995, p. 151)

UNMARRIED FATHERS

Unmarried families have only recently attracted the interest of researchers and the U.S. Census because of their dramatic increases. Generally, reliable statistics and information on unmarried couples and unmarried single mothers and fathers are difficult to find. Prior to 1990, the census only had indirect methods of identifying unmarried cohabitation. In 1990, "unmarried partner" was added as a response category to the question about the relationship of others in the household to the primary householder. However, this additional category does not identify a group about whom we have special concern: nonresidential unmarried fathers.

Accurate and reliable information on unmarried families may be difficult to obtain because such family configurations tend to change more frequently than other families. For example, how many unmarried single mothers began as single parents and how many began as unmarried couples living together? Also it would be interesting to know how committed unmarried couples are to each other when they begin to live together. Widely varying levels of commitment are suspected, with some couples eventually choosing marriage and others dissolving soon after they are constituted.

Our primary interest is with nonresidential unmarried fathers who are even more difficult to identify because they are not living with their children. Unfortunately, the U.S. Census does not attempt to consider the fathering role of these men; the children of these fathers most likely reside with single mothers who are unmarried. We address this problem by examining unmarried fathers whether they are residential or nonresidential because many residential fathers are likely to become nonresidential. And if unmarried residential fathers are assisted, they may be able to strengthen their bonds with their children over the long term.

Diversity Among Unmarried Fathers

Unmarried couples living together consist of an exceedingly diverse group of people, particularly with regard to the level of the father's commitment to his family. Some unmarried relationships appear a lot like marriages, while others bear little or no resemblance to marriage (Cohen, 1999).

An unmarried father could be deeply committed to his partner, and the couple may consider themselves married without the formal sanctions. Such a couple may plan ahead, often with the utmost care, to have offspring, and both may become actively involved in parenting their child. In time they may decide to get married. As an example, John describes his relationship to Debbie:

> Debbie and I have been together and committed to each other for over 4 years, 2 years before Shandra [their daughter] was even conceived. Both of us have been married before and both of our marriages ended in disasters. My ex-wife was constantly complaining that I wasn't making enough money. Otherwise, she just ignored me. I couldn't wait to dump her. Debbie and I have so much more going for us. And we decided not to taint our relationship with another marriage vow. Presently, we are committed to each other more than ever . . . and we both want the best for Shandra.

In contrast, unmarried relationships can be short-lived and uncommitted. Some unmarried fathers have no intention of becoming involved as a parent. They are a casual acquaintance of the biological mother, or they may not even know her. Blankenhorn devotes an entire chapter of his book, *Fatherless America,* to the men he calls sperm fathers. These fathers may be doing a favor for a female friend who wants to get pregnant or may be selling or donating their sperm to a sperm bank. He makes no secret of his contempt for this type of father, using terms like minimalist father, a one-act dad, no more purposive than a drop of sperm, or a father of cash nexus and short-term exchanges (Blankenhorn, 1995, p. 171). To him, these men are the least responsible of all fathers and pose a serious threat to the future of fatherhood. Sperm fathers may represent as many as 30% of all fathers of small children. Up to 10% of all births resulting from artificial insemination by donors are to unmarried mothers.

Derrick is an example of a sperm dad who later tried to change his status to that of an active parent. At the age of 18, Derrick had casual sex with several different women before enlisting in the army. To his surprise, two of those sexual encounters resulted in the birth of a daughter to one woman and of a son to another. Five years later, Derrick returned from the army considerably matured and began to realize how important his children were to him. Over the next year he maintained fairly regular phone contact and occasionally visited his son, Jed, because the boy's mother encouraged him. But the mother of his daughter, Jean, who lived within 15 miles of Derrick's apartment, wouldn't allow him near her. He has tried to make contact with his daughter but has only been able to secretly observe her on occasion when she was leaving school. At this point Derrick reports heightened frustration, as he desperately wants more time with both of his children before they are fully grown.

Reflection
What are your personal reactions to the men that Blankenhorn refers to as sperm fathers? Do you think that *sperm father* is a reasonable term to use in describing them? What suggestions do you have for attempting to involve these fathers with their children if they have such interest? What difficulties do you anticipate these fathers having with their children once their children find out how they were conceived?

Numerous other types of unmarried fathers fall between these ex-tremes of a deeply committed father and a sperm father. Some of these men may be in a serious relationship with a woman, with no intention of having a baby, and find themselves accidently pregnant. Or they may have a casual dating relationship or even a one-night stand that results in an unplanned pregnancy. These could be relationships of convenience where little if any thought has gone into being together; it just seemed to happen. A strong physical attraction may have led to a sexual encounter, and sex may be the only glue that currently holds them together. Or perhaps two teens have been emotionally bonded to each other for some time when an unexpected pregnancy occurs. The teen father pulls back because he becomes frightened by the responsibilities of becoming a parent. Unfortunately, many of these unmarried relationships share common characteristics—little stability, vulnerability to conflicts, and being prone to breaking up.

Unmarried parents are faced with very complicated and challenging initial circumstances when they have not planned for a baby. Many questions are likely to confront them: Should they have the baby or get an abortion? What if they disagree about what should be done? Would one parent want to go it alone if the other chose to walk away? Can they stay together long enough to provide a stable family or is their relationship too tenuous or temporary? Can their relationship withstand the demands that a new baby will bring? Will all that they value in their relationship be compromised if they have a baby? Are other things in their lives a higher priority? Can they afford a baby?

Available Statistics

According to U.S. Census statistics, the percentage of divorced parents has remained fairly stable since 1960 while the percentage of unmarried parents has soared (see Table 2.2 for details). Less than 4% of all single-mother households were unmarried in 1960, in contrast to just over 30% by 1990. In 1998, about 28% of all children under 18 years of age (19.8 million children) lived with just one parent (U.S. Bureau of Census, 1998). The vast majority of these children (84%) lived with their mother, and about 4 in 10 lived with a single mother who had never married. Clearly, these figures indicate that single parents and unmarried couples are family groups that must be given greater attention. These figures may even suggest that marriage and parenthood are becoming largely separate, unrelated institutions for some groups.

McLanahan and Sandefur (1994), however, caution that the distinctions between children born in and out of marriage have become blurred. They found that about one third of all children born outside of marriage are born to formerly married mothers. Another one fourth of such children are born to unmarried couples who are cohabiting, and two thirds of them will eventually get married to each other.

We know the least about unmarried fathers in these families, as indicated by the sparseness of this topic in the professional literature. Also, unmarried fathers are often difficult to identify, particularly if their legal status is not connected to their child and if their initial commitment to their child is low or nonexistent. Paternity establishment rates for children born out of marriage tend to be relatively low and vary widely across states. Arizona, for example, has a rate of 5.5% in contrast to Georgia with a rate of 67% (U.S. House of Representatives, Committee on Ways and Means, 1993).

A disproportionately high percentage of unmarried fathers are young and are in many cases teenagers (McKenry, McKelvey, Leigh, & Wark, 1996). However, government sources suggest that these trends are changing. The majority of nonmarital births have been to adult women in recent years and they are increasing (National Center for Health Statistics, 1995). While 51% of all unwed births in 1970 were to women 20 years or older, unwed births to such women increased to 71% in 1992.

Del Carmen and Virgo (1993) point out that economic circumstances are closely linked to ethnicity and unmarried status. They claim that among these groups the primary determinant of family formation and marital separation without a divorce is financial well-being. Family configurations have to be determined based on the best strategies available for accessing resources to raise children. An extended family structure is often a viable strategy among some ethnic minority parents; in these cases, however, mating patterns with males become secondary. Likewise, unmarried status for men is linked to economics. Men who are faced with low-paying, unstable jobs, barriers to better jobs resulting from racial discrimination, and low levels of education may be discouraged from marriage and family responsibilities because of their limited capacity as breadwinners (National Research Council, 1989). In contrast, higher income mothers, mostly White, more often choose remarriage as a strategy for accessing resources for children.

Clearly, the economic circumstances of many lower income men have discouraged them from making a marital commitment to a wife and children. Furthermore, their subcultures have not considered marriage as important as other socioeconomic groups do. Chris is an example. Chris is a 20-year-old father who broke up with the mother of his two children and is currently committed to another girlfriend. He explains, "I want to stick with her [his girlfriend]. I wouldn't mind marrying her, but until I get settled down, like I said, until I get settled . . . we just got to get settled, you know, job, j-o-b, with benefits. That's what I'm going to shoot for" (Johnson, Levine, & Doolittle, 1998, p. 38).

Yet unmarried fathers are not all from low-income backgrounds. In the past, unmarried fathers were thought to be mostly poor, but these trends are changing as well. More recently, larger numbers of unmarried fathers are emerging in the middle class. In 1980, 18.4% of all births occurred to unwed mothers, and the number increased to 29.5% in 1991, with increases in all socioeconomic groups.

The relationship between Beth and Benny is an example. Benny explains that he was once married to another woman. He claims that he was a successful salesman with a large company bringing in a six-figure salary. He worked day and night and seldom saw his wife. By all accounts, he had made it—both he and his wife had all the material comforts that they could ever want—but one thing was missing. He was profoundly unhappy and depressed, and Benny eventually bottomed out. He began drinking and soon left his family and moved to another region of the country. Benny blames his problems mostly on his marriage and states adamantly that he will never make the mistake of getting married again. Beth and Benny are now talking about having a baby together.

Racial differences have been evident in marital status over time. White unwed births have increased from 11% of total White births in 1980 to 22% in 1991. African American unwed births have increased from 55% of all African American births in 1980 to 68% in 1991, while Latino unwed births increased from 24% to 38% (National Center for Health Statistics, 1993; National Center for Health Statistics, 1982). White women are thought more likely to divorce their husbands than African American women (87% versus 62%). In contrast, African American women are more likely than Whites to separate but not divorce (33% versus 8%). Thus a higher percentage of African American than White women are likely to be experiencing a series of cohabitating partners without marriage.

Mexican American families, more so than Puerto Ricans and Cubans, tend to remain married, two-parent families across the life span (Frisbie, 1986). Asian American families, in contrast to most other minority groups, have the lowest proportion of households headed by women and the lowest divorce rate (Momeni, 1984). The largest Asian American groups in the U.S. are Chinese, Filipino, and Japanese. The migration of family members to this country is an important factor of influence, particularly among immigrant populations such as Mexicans, Asians, and Puerto Ricans. Migration can increase the risk of divorce for couples of many ethnic groups (Del Carmen & Virgo, 1993).

Parenting Role of Unmarried, Nonresidential Fathers

Among unmarried nonresidential fathers, levels of contact with children have been reported to be lower than that of divorced fathers. In one study, 40% of unmarried fathers had no contact with their children in the past year compared to 18% of previously married fathers (Seltzer, 1991). However, one segment of unmarried fathers is very active in parenting: The proportion of unmarried fathers and previously married fathers who had contact with their children at least once a week were similar (20% versus 25%). The financial participation of unmarried and divorced fathers differs considerably, however, with 29% of unmarried fathers and 64% of divorced fathers reported to be paying child support.

A study by McKenry and colleagues (1996) also investigated the parental roles of fathers of various marital statuses. Unmarried nonresidential fathers were found to visit their children less frequently than divorced and separated fathers, and they felt that they exercised less influence in decisions regarding their children. On the other hand, those who were active were involved in a wide range of activities with their children like the other fathers, including leisure, religious, school, and highly interactive activities. Also, these unmarried fathers were as satisfied as other fathers with their custody arrangements and with the quality of their relationships with their child's mother. These findings suggests that many unmarried nonresidential fathers are actively involved with their children and are an important part of their lives.

TEEN FATHERS

Large-scale studies that provide accurate information about teenage dads are still somewhat scarce (Marsiglio, 1995). Thus, what is known about them is drawn mostly from small studies with convenience samples along with feedback from teen fathers in parenting and other teenage clinical programs.

A startling statistic is that a large percentage of teen fathers are probably not teenagers at all. For example, Danziger and Radin (1990) found that teen mothers in an AFDC (Aid to Families with Dependent Children) sample in Wisconsin ranged in age from 16 to 23 years, and the fathers of their children ranged from 16 to 38 years. Another study involving a Baltimore sample found that fathers of infants born to White teenage mothers were four years older than the mothers, and fathers of African American teen births were 2 to 3 years older (Hardy, Duggan, Masnyk, & Pearson, 1989). These statistics remind us that teen fathers by no means account for all of the births to teen mothers. We need to consider young adults as well.

Perspective

A national profile of unwed teenage fathers suggests:

- Most teen unwed fathers do not later marry their child's mother.
- Generally, they are less well educated than non-parental teens.
- They started sexual activity at earlier ages.
- They were more likely to be raised in a low income family.
- Many spend time with their child, but this mostly occurs soon after their child's birth.
- About one third pay child support but at low levels.
- Unwed fathering is most widespread among young African American men.
- Interventions have been successful in deterring teens from becoming unwed fathers.

(Lerman & Ooms, 1992).

About Teen Mothers

BIRTHS TO UNMARRIED TEEN MOTHERS

Ample statistical data are available on teenage mothers, their pregnancies, and birth experiences. The percentage of births to unmarried teen mothers has increased over the past several decades (U.S. General Accounting Office, 1998). In 1995, 78% of teen births were to unmarried mothers in contrast to 14% in 1957. Older unmarried teens between 18 and 19 years old are responsible for most unmarried teen births. Considering race and ethnicity, African American teen mothers were predominately unmarried (95%), while 68% of Latino teen mothers and 68% of White teen mothers were unmarried when their babies were born. By region, teens in the South and Southwest had the highest unwed teen birth rates.

UNPLANNED PREGNANCIES

Teen births reportedly are usually unplanned (Alan Guttmacher Institute, 1994). Seventy-three percent of all births to teenagers and about 86% of all births to unmarried teens are not planned. These teen mothers explain that they would rather be pregnant later or not at all. By race, 75% of African American teen births were unintended, compared to 67% of White births and 46% of Latino births.

Reflection
How would you help a teen father who is involved in casual sex to consider the possible negative consequences of his sexual behavior on the baby? on the biological mother? on himself? How could you help him grasp what would be expected of him if he wanted to be a responsible father?

INVOLUNTARY SEX

The potential for violence is important to assess in relationships between males and females. In this regard, many teen mothers are reported to be the victims of rape and molestation (Alan Guttmacher Institute, 1994). In one study, 60% of teenage mothers who began to have sex before the age of 15 reported having involuntary or forced sex. Forty-three percent reported having *only* forced sex.

INFLUENCE OF FAMILY STRUCTURE AND INCOME

Factors correlated with teenage pregnancy include the family structure of the teen mother's parents and their income. If the parents of African American teen mothers were single, the teen was more likely to become a teen mother as well; however, this was not the case for White teens (Wu, 1996). Living in a two-parent family was associated with less risk of giving birth by White and Latino teens but not African American teens. The income of the teen mothers' parents had differing effects by race. Lower socioeconomic status was related to increased risk of pregnancy among Latino teens but surprisingly a lower risk for African American teens. Socioeconomic status had no effect on White teen pregnancies (Manlove, 1998).

SOCIOECONOMIC FACTORS

Predictors of teenage parenting are influenced by socioeconomic factors. Teens from low-income families are 9 times more likely than higher income teens to have a child (Alan Guttmacher Institute, 1994). Teens from lower income families also begin having sex earlier than higher income teens and are less likely to use birth-control methods and to seek abortions. School factors can also be important. One study found that among teens in lower income families, those who were doing poorly in school or were not planning to complete their education had childbearing rates 5 to 7 times higher than other teens in the same ethnic groups in their schools (Abrahamse, Morrison, & Waite, 1988). Other studies found that once teens became unwed mothers, they were placed at higher risk for lower educational attainment, lower wages, and higher risks of poverty (Hardy & Zabin, 1991). These negative effects were particularly evident among African American women (Bronars & Grogger, 1994).

Teen Father Involvement

Findings of smaller studies of teen fathers have been beneficial in challenging many potentially harmful stereotypes about teen fathers (Rhoden & Robinson, 1997). Although teen fathers are considered uncaring and uninvolved, new data suggests that some are just the opposite, that fathering is a central part of their lives. Many teen fathers want to become active parents despite stereotypes to the contrary. Hardy and colleagues (1989), for example, reported that approximately 90% of the teen fathers in their study spent some time with their children during the first 15 months of life. However, the frequency of this contact declined markedly over time.

George conceived a child when he was a teenager. Now, 5 years later he struggles to make a commitment to raising his daughter, Joy, but he is confronted with intense conflicts with Joy's mother because she doesn't want him involved. George, an unmarried nonresidential father, shares part of his story:

> I had a brief relationship with Althea, my daughter's mother, during a semester break from college while visiting my parents. I was 19 years old at the time and Althea was 17 and attending high school. When Joy was born, Althea named another man as Joy's father and then married him. Two months later, she told him that he wasn't Joy's father but would not say who the biological father was. Five years later, I found out about this story and realized that Joy was born 9 months after my short sexual encounter with Althea. After some sleepless nights, I decided against Althea's will to take a blood test to find out if I was the father. The results were 99.9% positive so I decided to commit myself to raising Joy as a nonresidential father. I did this despite the enormous problems and conflicts that I anticipated that I would face in the future. I knew that by this time, after 5 years had passed, that I was "off the hook." But what was more compelling was my determination to have my daughter know her father.

EDUCATIONAL AND EMPLOYMENT ISSUES

Studies indicate that teen fathers tend to be disadvantaged both educationally and in employment. Danziger and Radin (1990) report from their study that teen fathers usually did not complete high school by the time of their child's birth. Only about half of them were employed either part- or full-time. Another study found that being a White teenage father is associated with low self-esteem, a perceived lack of control over one's life, and conservative sex role attitudes, while African American teen fathers were not characterized this way (Pirog-Good, 1995). Generally, fathers of teen births are less well-educated, have lower academic abilities, commit more crimes, and are more likely to have economically disadvantaged parents compared to other comparable young men. Also, these differences are much larger for White unwed fathers than for African Americans when compared to their peers (Marsiglio, 1995, p. 325).

LOW INCOME, INNER CITY TEEN FATHERS

Other studies of teen fathers reveal somewhat different profiles. Furstenberg (1995) conducted lengthy interviews with 20 low-income, inner-city teen fathers in Philadelphia, all African American. As in any group, he found both "good" and "bad" fathers, but more examples of the latter. Most of these teen fathers lived separate from the biological mother. All but a few grew up without their own father present. One recurring theme was broken promises to their children and the mother, such as failing to provide financial help and not being around consistently.

One teen father, Lionnel, indicated at the birth of his son that he loved him a lot and planned to be with him to avoid putting his son through the experience that he had with his absent father (Furstenberg, 1995, p. 126). But 7 years later he wasn't paying child support and was resigned to losing contact with his son even though this "weighs on him." Lionnel is also unemployed and recovering from an illness. By contrast, Ricky was a good dad who still has regular contact with his 4-year-old daughter. Ricky is reportedly the only steady male figure in her life and seems to have a reputation for looking out for his daughter, her mother, and her mother's other children.

Furstenberg (1995) reported that these teen fathers embarked on parenthood without preparation or planning; they and their girlfriends wanted to have sex but seemed unprepared for the consequences. Having a baby was the option they usually chose over having an abortion. And in many cases these young men and women looked forward with pride and joy to having their own offspring once pregnancy occurred. In most instances, these teen fathers acknowledged that the baby was theirs, particularly if the baby resembled them; some, on the other hand, denied being responsible for the pregnancy. *Negotiated parenthood* was a typical means of assuming responsibility. Such an arrangement involved "a short period of bargaining with the expectant mother following pregnancy, ending in a resolution to make a go of it" (p. 131). Making a go of it, however, was regarded conditionally by these fathers and warily by the biological mothers. Family and friends also had their influence on whether or not the couple would both stay involved. Three of the teen mothers explained why some fathers eventually opted out:

- "That's how most of them are. I mean they get scared."
- "I guess failing, maybe failing the child or not standing up to the mother's standards or something. It takes too much for them."
- "He wasn't scared. He's just spoiled and he always had everything his way." (p. 134)

Most of these fathers were unable to provide regular child support because they were unemployed or had a haphazard work situation, and most were unreliable as child-care providers, showing up sporadically when they wanted. The biological mothers wanted these fathers to spend more time with their children, while the fathers needed to withdraw, feeling that they could not meet these expectations.

In brief, most teen fathers seem to want to become involved with their children, but they also must face many of their own unmet developmental needs. Rather than being denigrated for their shortcomings and blamed for some of the stereotypes mentioned earlier, they need help to meet their own developmental needs and to delay parenthood (or having additional children) until they become ready. Responsible sexual behavior and respect for women are important aspects of the preparation that they need. Chapter 9 offers more understanding of teen fathers and introduces program interventions for assisting them in their parenting.

Questions for Discussion

1. How are the needs of nonresidential fathers from various backgrounds similar? How are they different based on whether they are divorced, unmarried, or teenagers? How are they similar and different based on their race and socioeconomic status?

2. What views do you hold about divorced, unmarried, and teenage fathers that may be based on stereotypes? What do you think are the origins of these stereotypes?

3. Jot down some ideas that you have about helping these nonresidential fathers. As you read on, compare your ideas to the ideas that are proposed in later chapters.

3

What We Know and What We Hope For

[I]t is clear that the absence of the biological father reduces children's access to important economic, parental, and community resources. The loss of these resources affects cognitive development and future opportunities. Thus, the evidence strongly suggests that family disruption plays a causal role in lowering children's well-being. (Sara McLanahan, 1998, p. 91)

This chapter explores the existing research concerning the role and importance of fathers in child development. Information will be presented about fathers with their infants and preschool-children, their school age children, their teens, and parenting issues with adult children. A special effort will be made to focus on *father presence* versus *father absence* research. Consideration will also be given to the role that grandfathers can play in the lives of their grandchildren. Readers of this chapter should have an increased understanding of the following areas:

- How fathers influence child development
- Fathering as a developmental process
- Research supporting the importance of *father presence*
- Issues fathers face across the developmental life span

We assume that the needs of children in families are paramount and that their needs should always be taken into account as we investigate ways of helping both fathers and mothers. This chapter will highlight the importance of the father's role in child development. The tasks and challenges of fathering will be described at different life stages (prefathering, new fathers, fathers in later stages, grandfathers, etc.).

One of the first questions to consider when exploring the case for fathering is to examine just what we mean by father involvement with their children. Lamb (1986) developed a typology of a father's involvement with his children that includes three major types:

* Interactions with the child
* Accessibility, psychology and physically, to the child
* Responsibilities for the care or welfare of the child

Lamb's expansive typology opens our awareness to a wide array of activities that could be considered an aspect of father involvement. Although we believe that some of the father's involvement should include quality interactions with the children, many other types of activities falling under the categories of accessibility and responsibilities should also be recognized as important, valued aspects of parenting. This broad definition of involvement encourages men to plug into their children's lives particularly where they have the greatest strengths. This typology supports a culturally varied explanation of involvement. Mirande (1991) reports that ethnic minority fathers, for example, have a different sense of being with their children than do European American fathers. Puerto Rican fathers may place more emphasis on disciplining their child and less to child care (Sanchez-Ayendez, 1988), and Asian American fathers may give the greatest emphasis to being breadwinners (Suzuki, 1985).

Using Lamb's typology researchers have been able to explore the impact of father involvement upon child development. Often the importance of father involvement has been implied by research delineating the outcomes for children who do not have fathers in their lives, while a growing number of research projects have attempted to measure the impact of father presence. In an interesting book that explores issues of father involvement (*Father Facts*), Wade Horn presents findings from numerous studies suggesting that father absence is hazardous to the physical, educational, and psychological health of children (Horn, 1998). Here is a sampling of some of the findings that Horn recounts:

* In a recent study (Sedlak & Broadhurst, 1996) found that compared to their peers living with both parents, children in single parent homes
  —had a 77% greater risk of being physically abused
  —had an 87% greater risk of being harmed by physical neglect
  —had a 74% greater risk of suffering from emotional neglect

- In a national study by Cooksey and Fondell (1996) of 1,250 fathers of school-aged children, it was found that children who lived with both biological parents did better in school than children in all other family types. Children living with single biological fathers and children living with stepfathers did significantly worse academically than children living with both biological parents.
- Heiss (1996) reported that both Black and White students from single-parent homes were more likely to have discipline problems than students who lived with both biological parents. This study used a nationally representative sample of over 2,300 youths.
- In a longitudinal study of 1,197 fourth-grade students, Vaden-Kiernan, Ialongo, Pearson, and Kellam (1995) observed "greater levels of aggression in boys from mother-only households than from boys in mother-father households."
- A study (Angel & Angel, 1996) using a nationally representative sample of 6,287 children aged 4 to 11 indicated that children in single-parent homes are more likely to experience emotional problems and use mental health services than children who live with both biological parents.
- Beman (1995) found that the absence of the father from the home affects significantly the behavior of adolescents and results in greater use of alcohol and marijuana.

Many would contend that these findings support the need for the ongoing presence of a father in a child's life. In essence, many claim that if fathers are not in the home, children are placed at risk for various problems in the areas of health, psychological well-being, schooling, and even criminal activities. Others would suggest that perhaps the findings are not as clear-cut as Horn presents them. First, it is noted that many studies fail to account for the socioeconomic differences that exist between single-parent homes and dual-parent homes. Critics suggest that in actuality these studies are measuring the impact of poverty on children. Second, other critics suggest that these studies are based on correlational data and therefore it is not possible to draw cause-and-effect inferences from these types of studies.[1] Third, and perhaps most important, critics assert that these types of studies tell

---

[1]McLanahan and Sandefur (1994) present interesting data from their national study that suggests that not all findings about the importance of father involvement are correlational. Their research found strong statistical evidence that several outcome measures for children were directly connected to father involvement levels in a cause-and-effect relationship.

little about the impact of father presence. They recommend completion of studies that focus on what fathers offer while in the home versus what seems to happen when they are not present.

Reflection
Why is it so important to distinguish between father-absence research and father-presence research? Why can't we assume that they are measuring the same things?

It becomes painfully obvious that questions about the role and importance of fathers in child development are not simply left to the realm of child-development experts. When one asks the question, How important are fathers in the lives of their children? one enters the sociopolitical arena as well. This question is the crux of numerous battles raging within our society. It is one of the foundations of the men's rights movements. Advocates for welfare reform often cite the impact of the old welfare system on the involvement of married and unmarried nonresidential fathers with their children. These welfare-reform proponents claimed that the old system encouraged women to leave the fathers of their children and that it provided the financial support to do so. Other writers have talked about "father hunger" that exists in children who grow up in fatherless homes. Gallagher (1998) describes this as "an ache in the heart . . . a longing for a man, not just a woman, who will care for you, protect you, and show you how to survive in the world" (p. 165). Fatherlessness has also been identified as the reason for higher rates of criminal activity, depression, and school problems among children from single-mother families. Fathers and their importance to children have become a flashpoint in the social and behavioral sciences.

The downside of all this conflict is that it becomes difficult to advocate for the importance of fathers in families without appearing to be attacking or criticizing other family forms. As soon as one states that fathers are important to the healthy development of their children, it may be interpreted that single-mother families are inferior and unhealthy. It is this type of dichotomy that can lead to misunderstanding of the issue and lack of progress in the area of father research, family policy, and program development. It is hoped that this chapter can present the facts about the role of fathers with their children in a way that supports healthy fathering without attacking other family forms.

It is also our intention to strike a balance in addressing the conflict that exists about the importance of fathers to their children. A developmental perspective will be presented that attempts to highlight research on the effects of father presence as well as father absence.

FATHERING ACROSS THE LIFE SPAN: RESEARCH, TASKS, AND CHALLENGES

Much of the writing and research that exists about the importance of fathers to children and child development has focused on father absence. The research question seems to boil down to this: What negative things happen in families in which there is no father? While this line of research has given us some information about the potential adverse impact that the loss of a father can have on children, it does not focus on a strength or generative approach to fathering that we have advocated within this book. Focusing on the impact of fatherlessness can also further heighten the dichotomy between the family where a father is present and any other family form in which there is no father. In this chapter we will attempt to provide information relevant to father presence when at all possible. However, since this a fairly new way of exploring fatherhood we will need to present information from the father absence research area as well.

Prefathering Stage

Men can begin to view themselves as fathers even before the child is born. This change in self-identity can have a profound effect on the level of connection the father may begin to feel with the unborn child. Unfortunately, research in this area has been lacking. There has been some preliminary research indicating that fathers who attend prenatal classes report more satisfying experiences with the newborn child. In an early study of father-child attachment, Peterson, Mehl, and Leiderman (1979) found that the participation of the father in the birth, and his attitude toward it, were the most significant variables in predicting the father's attachment to the infant. The results suggest that it is very important to provide prenatal education and to structure the birth environment in order to obtain maximum participation and involvement of fathers. However, most of the remaining research in this area has focused on the psychological changes that mothers experience as a result of preg-

nancy; very little information is available regarding the psychological changes that fathers undergo (Dragonas & Christodoulou, 1998).

In a study of adolescent fathers, it was found that males who had
maintained long pre-pregnancy relationships with their mates tended
to be more supportive of them prenatally and to perceive themselves as
maintaining closer relationships with both the mothers and infants
after delivery (Westney, Cole, & Munford, 1986).

The prefathering stage also seems to initiate a father's sense of
attachment toward his unborn child. Fathers may become keenly aware
of their new responsibility to care for and protect the family; it's a
common response for new fathers. There is limited formal research in
this area but an abundance of anecdotal information. One father began to wear his seat belt in the car after he learned that he was going
to become a father because, as he said, "I no longer had any right to
die." Another father recounted his experiences after taking part in the
delivery of his child. Exhausted, he returned home and noticed that
the stairs to his house were in need of repair. In his words,

> I had never given any thought to those steps before, and neither had any
> of the hundreds of people who had made their way up and down with-
> out injury. But the thought occurred to me that a new mother carrying
> a new baby would soon be climbing those rickety stairs. So, exhausted
> as I was, I got out the power saw, some wood, a handful of nails, a
> square, and a hammer. For the next 3 hours, I built steps. (National
> Center for Fathering, 2000)

Fathers in the stage of attachment may develop a keen sense that
their lives have a higher purpose and that their actions have very real
and powerful consequences. The father may see that rickety steps can
have dire consequences for his child and family.

Reflection

Fathers often learn certain expectations of their role as father from
their culture, friends, colleagues at work, and the child's mother.
One of the most important expectations will come from their own
view of fathering which is often based on how they were fathered.
Interview an expectant father about the ways his father influenced
his ideals about fathering, and about his views on what the child's
mother expects from him as a father. Consider how these questions
raise issues related to your own ideas about fathering.

New Fathers With Infants and Preschool Children

We have grown in our understanding of the reciprocal nature of the socialization process between father and child. Fathers influence the development of their children and in turn are changed and socialized by their children (Fogel, 1997). Unfortunately, we have very little research data that details either the specific impact that father involvement has on children or the psychological changes in the father that children elicit. Once again, much of our understanding has been focused on the mother-child relationship. Even when efforts have been made to increase our understanding of the role that fathers play in child development, the information has tended to be based on maternal reports of father involvement and importance. Very little firsthand data collected directly from fathers or children exist (Fitzgerald, Mann, & Barratt, 1999).

The lack of information on new fathers is particularly disturbing given the growing numbers of fathers who are involved in the primary care of their preschool children. According to a report by the Population Reference Bureau, about 20 percent of preschool children in 1991 were cared for by their fathers (both married and unmarried) while their mothers worked. This number was up from 15 percent in 1988 (O'Connell, 1993). What are the special needs and challenges for these new fathers involved in the primary care of their young children and infants? A recent study by Soliday, McCluskey-Fawcett, and O'Brien-Mof (1999) suggests that new fathers may be experiencing unexpected adjustment problems of their own. Their study looked at the postpartum affective experiences of couples. Mothers and fathers completed questionnaires on coping, marital satisfaction, stress, positive and negative affect, and depression 1 month before the birth and then 1 month postpartum. More than one fourth of both mothers and fathers reported elevated depressive symptoms. How would these elevated levels of depression affect a new father's ability to provide primary care to his child? What do we know about ways to help the new father overcome such feelings of depression? It is obvious that more work is needed in this area.

Research on the impact of father presence in the lives of young children is becoming more available. Biller (1993) found that children with an involved father were exposed to more varied social experiences and were more intellectually advanced. Biller also asserted that infants with two involved parents can cope better with being alone with strangers and also seem to attend more effectively to novel and complex stimuli. Krampe and Fairweather (1993) found that a positive father-child interaction can promote a child's physical well-being, perceptual abilities, and competency for relating with others, even at a young age.

These documented differences in children where the father is present are interesting, but they really don't tell us all that is important. They inform us that there is a difference, but not what might be causing the difference. Surely it is more than simply having a man around the house. The question becomes, What is it that fathers bring to parenting that might help explain these outcomes?

One area in which a father's parenting style is most obvious and very important with young children is play (Parke & Brott, 1999). Research has consistently found that mothers and fathers engage in different play styles with their children. Mothers tend to engage in more visual games with their infants and are more verbal with them. Men, on the other hand, are far more physical in their play with children. Yogman and Brazelton (1986) report clear differences in the ways mothers and fathers played with a group of infants 2 weeks to 24 weeks. Mothers tended to speak softly, repeating words and phrases frequently and imitating infants' sounds followed by periods of silence. Their communication was characterized as a burst/pause pattern, a rapidly spoken series of words and sounds followed by a short period of silence. Fathers were less verbal but much more tactile. They touched their infants with a rhythmic tapping more often than mothers. Father-infant play shifted rapidly from peaks of high infant attention and excitement to valleys of minimal attention. The authors observed the following:

> Most fathers seem to present a more playful, jazzing up approach. As one watches this interaction, it seems that a father is expecting more heightened, playful response from the baby. And he gets it! Amazingly enough, an infant by two or three weeks displays an entirely different attitude (more wide-eyed, playful, and bright-faced) toward his father than to his mother. (p. 33)

You might be saying to yourself, This is "just play." How important can it really be? Yet it seems that this type of interaction can have what could be termed remedial effects on even at-risk infants. Yogman, Kindlon, and Earls (1995) assessed the effect of father involvement on intellectual and behavioral outcomes of 985 low-birth-weight preterm infants. These researchers followed the children longitudinally from birth to 3 years. They reported that most fathers played a meaningful role as play partner with their high-risk infants. Approximately 75% of fathers were reported to play with the baby every day at 12 , 24, and 36 months. The average IQ score for the high-involvement subgroup was 6 points higher than for the low-involvement group. This held true even after adjusting for family income, neonatal health, and paternal age. It seems evident that the importance of play activity should not be overlooked as an important contribution of fathers to their young children.

Reflection
Does the type of play by fathers described in the research fit your memory of play with your own father? How was it different than what was noted? What impact did your father's play have on you?

Other researchers have suggested that differences exist between mothers' and fathers' interactions with their children in areas other than just play. Some suggest they may use very different, but complementary communication styles. In a study of 42 families of young children, mothers were found to be more likely to use indirect forms of communication, including questions, directives, and suggestions, while fathers tended to use direct forms of communications such as imperatives. Mothers in the study were found to be less direct and tried to bring about compliance and cooperation from their children. Fathers in the study offered a model of directiveness and self-assertion. In measures of compliance or obedience toward their mothers and fathers, although girls did not differ in their rates of compliance with mothers and fathers, boys showed higher levels of compliance to their fathers than with their mothers (Power, McGrath, Hughes, & Manire, 1994).

It becomes apparent, therefore, that the new father can play an integral role in the social, intellectual, and psychological development of his child. The challenge is perhaps how to avoid a societal tendency to evaluate parenting skills strictly based on mothering. Rather than seeing this as an either/or situation, we would contend that while mothering is extremely important to the developing child, fathering has its own special place in the process.

Fathers and School-Age Children

Children are faced with many challenges as they begin attending school. They are required to be more autonomous and self-confident, while at the same time following rules not based on relational standards. Not "I do things because I love the person making the rules"—but rather adhering to impersonal rules—that is, "I do things because those are the rules, regardless of the lack of a relationship with the person making them." This can be a difficult transition for many children (and for parents, too!). Children growing up with the opportunity to experience a wide range of communication styles may have an easier time adapting to these changes. A recent survey of more than 20,000 parents (National Center for Education Statistics, 1997) found that when fathers are involved in their children's education, including attending school meetings and volunteering at school, children were more likely to get As, to enjoy school, and to participate in extracurricular activities and less likely to repeat a grade.

School also becomes one of the first real tests for children in terms of social skills. Those who are able to express empathy and other prosocial skills are more likely to make friends and ultimately to be more successful within the school setting. As practicing clinical social workers, the authors can attest to the number of cases that are referred for help based on a child's inability simply to get along with his or her peers. What role can fathers play in helping with the intellectual and social growth of the school-age child?

Several researchers have explored the role of fathers in the development of empathy in children. In a 26-year longitudinal study on 379 individuals (Koestner, Franz, & Weinberger, 1990), researchers found that the single most important childhood factor for developing empathy is paternal involvement. Fathers who spent time alone with their kids performing routine child care at least twice a week raised children who grew up to become compassionate adults. In another study of 47 first-grade boys and their married parents it was found that fathers who participated more in child care had sons who were more empathetic than sons whose fathers did not participate often in child care (Bernadett-Shapiro, Ehrensaft, & Shapiro, 1996).

In terms of prosocial behaviors, research has consistently demonstrated that father presence can have significant positive effects, particularly for boys. In literature on father absence, there seems to be a tendency of children for whom there is no father to engage in a wide range of unacceptable, unwanted behaviors (Coney & Mackey, 1998). In addition, studies reveal that even in high-crime, inner-city neighborhoods, well over 90% of children from safe, stable, two-parent homes do not become delinquents (Richters & Martinez, 1993). In a longitudinal study of fourth-grade students, researchers observed higher levels of aggression in boys from mother-only households than from boys in mother-father households (Vaden-Kiernan et al., 1995).

Perspective: Cross-Cultural Research

It is important to note that evidence exists cross-culturally of the important role that fathers can play in the development of their children. In a recent study by Williams, Radin, and Coggins (1996), an attempt was made to determine the relationship between the quantity and quality of father involvement in child-rearing and the academic and social school performance of children (ages 3 to 11) among *Ojibwa Indian* families. The researchers obtained questionnaire and interview data from 17 Ojibwa families of the Bay Mills Indian Community in Michigan. Results indicated that the fathers' spending a greater amount of time as primary caregivers was associated with higher academic achievement and better social development, almost exclusively for boys. Factors that were associated with more paternal involvement included greater participation by the father's father in his upbringing.

The impact of father absence on adolescent and adult lifestyles was examined based on interviews with 999 adults from father-absent and father-present families in *Hungary* (Bereczkei & Csanaky, 1996). It was found that father-absent boys were more likely to participate in rule-breaking behavior. Both boys and girls from widowed families evidenced a higher degree of various forms of noncompliant behavior.

In a study by Booth (1995) among *Swazi* migrant workers, the effects were explored of prolonged father absence on their young children's preparedness for a formal school setting in traditional African society. Test data from 80 children (ages 5 to 8) identified skills acquired before formal schooling that contributed to the ability to read, write, and compute. Results indicated that children of absent migrant fathers were less prepared than children whose fathers were present.

In summary, it is quite apparent that the role that fathers play with their school-age children can have a significant impact on a child's social, emotional, psychological and cognitive well-being. Children raised with a positive father influence seem to benefit from this contact and are often better able to meet the multiple challenges presented by schools, peers, and other adult authority figures.

Perspective: Parent Absence or Poverty—Which Matters More?

A heated debate exists over the relative importance of poverty versus father absence with regard to child development. What do you think? Which do you think has a more powerful influence over child development? McLanahan and Sandefur (1994) used five different, nationally representative samples of young adults. They report finding that children from one-parent homes are about twice as likely to drop out of high school as children who live with both biological parents. Students who experienced family disruption have dropout rates that are higher than students who did not experience family disruption. The differences were:

- 17 percentage points among Whites
- 13 percentage points among Blacks
- 24 percentage points among Hispanics

McLanahan completed another national survey in 1997. Based on her review she suggested that family structure may be more important than poverty in determining behavioral and psychological problems, while poverty may be more closely associated with issues related to educational attainment.

Fathers and Teens

It has been noted that the study of fathers and their relationships with their teens is still very much in the beginning stages (Hosley & Montemayor, 1997). Several critical issues that need further exploration in this area include such issues as (a) to what extent are there differences between fathers' and mothers' relationships with their teens?; (b) do father-teen relationships differ from father-child relationships?; and (c) what is the impact of the father-adolescent relationship on teens?

Hosley and Montemayor (1997) reviewed the literature on how fathers and mothers differ in their relationships with their teens. It should be noted that the information is this area is rather scant. Only about 1% of the studies on teens from 1984–1991 dealt exclusively with fathers versus 48% dealing with mothers. Hosley and Montemayor report that a number of these studies found that fathers were described as more distant and less intimate than mothers. Daughters often described their fathers as "uninvolved." In contrast, teens were more likely to describe their relationships with their mother as close, affectionate, and filled with self-disclosure. Unfortunately, these descriptions play into the deficit model described earlier. It is possible that teens were being asked to evaluate the father-teen relationship based on female standards of communication. Hosley and Montemayor (1997) suggest that new ways of measuring and assessing parenting need to be developed. They point out that "scales assessing intimacy define intimacy from a traditionally feminine point of view (i.e., sharing feelings) rather than being sensitive to the ways in which fathers feel they are intimate" (p. 176).

So what does this mean? It is possible that fathers are more likely to show intimacy through sharing an activity or helping out in some way (for example, watching a movie with a son or daughter, or fixing the broken door to the bathroom) versus verbal expressions of love and intimacy.

More recent research has focused on the special issues that challenge adolescents and the positive role that fathers can play. During adolescence there is an ongoing redefinition of parent-adolescent relationships (Smollar & Youniss, 1989). One key task of the adolescent period is identity formation and consolidation. During the senior year of high school, individuals must begin to make commitments to specific goals and pathways. With decisions to be made about future work and educational plans, adolescents frequently turn to their parents for advice. In two-parent families, the level of discussion with parents about academic and vocational plans is substantial (Hunter, 1985).

However, noncustodial fathers are less likely than married fathers to be the primary source of discussions about school, careers, or feelings (Smollar & Youniss, 1985). It is still not clear whether decreased opportunities for discussion are related to adjustment problems for youths during late adolescence. There is also need for further research to determine whether male or female adolescents are affected by these differences in contact.

Other researchers have been concerned with the role that fathers play in the development of a healthy sense of masculinity in adolescent males. Beaty (1995) explored the extent to which adolescent males experience different peer adjustment and masculine self-image as a function of father deprivation. A sample of 40 middle-school boys (20 father-present and 20 father-absent) rated each other on scales measuring these factors. Results indicate that father-absent boys showed a poorer sense of masculinity as well as poorer interpersonal relationships than did father-present boys.

Fathers and Adult Children

A common misunderstanding is that parenting ends once the child reaches adulthood. It's as if there is a parental on-off switch that gets moved to the off position once the predetermined age of adulthood is reached. Of course as most parents and young adults can attest, parental concern, love, and attempts to guide the young adult do not stop magically once the child reaches that age. Very little research exists in the area of fathering and adult children. An exception to this can be found in a study by Amato (1994). In this study an attempt was made to determine the importance of the father-child relationship for young adult offspring (mothers were also studied). Amato collected information from a national sample of 471 young adults and found that the closer children were to their fathers, the happier, more satisfied, and less distressed they reported being. These results are consistent with those of Barnett, Marshall, and Pleck (1992). However, whereas Barnett and colleagues could only find evidence on the influence of fathers over sons, Amato's study found that both sons and daughters experienced gains as a result of having a close relationship with their fathers. This is an important finding as some child developmental researchers suggest that fathers are more important in the development of sons than of daughters (Lamb, 1987; Radin & Russell, 1983). The Amato study found no evidence to support this view among young adult offspring. The only statistically significant interaction involving the sex of the child indicated that closeness to mothers was more strongly related to psychological distress among sons than daughters. Overall, father-child relationships appear to be as closely bound up with the well-being of adult daughters as with adult sons.

   Another interesting finding in Amato's study was that the elapsed time since last contact between young adults and their parents had little impact on the degree of importance they placed on the relationship. As you may imagine, it is quite possible that some adult children may not feel close to their parents but still continue to have frequent contact with them out of a sense of obligation or because the parents initiate contact. Other children may have little contact with their parents yet still feel a strong emotional bond. It is quite possible that it is the emotional bond rather than the level of contact that is bound up with adult sons and daughters' sense of well-being.

Reflection
Consider the ways that your father continues to be a parent to you now that you are an adult. How do you respond to these parenting efforts? How has your father adjusted to his role as the parent of an adult child? How have you adjusted to his new role?

ADDITIONAL RESEARCH

Various studies have noted that there seems to be little difference between mothers and fathers regarding the degree of affection that they feel toward their adult children. Aldous (1987) found that when mothers and fathers were interviewed separately they did not differ in their descriptions of the affective quality of their relationship with their children. Other studies have noted that older African American and Hispanic American fathers are even more likely to describe their relationships with their adult children as close, warm, and affectionate (Bengston, Rosenthal, & Burton, 1990; Taylor, 1988).

Unfortunately, these studies and much of the subsequent research in this area have done little to help us understand *how* fathers (and mothers) actually contribute to their children's well-being. What are the helpful behaviors that fathers lend to their adult children? Are fathers more important at some times in adult children's lives than in others? Under what social contexts do fathers influence children? These questions might be best answered through use of qualitative research in which fathers are interviewed directly. One such study that attempted to gain a more in-depth understanding of fathers of adult children was conducted by Nydegger and Mitteness (1991). In this study, men aged 45 to 80 were interviewed about the history and quality of their relationships with their children. (The researchers also interviewed one of the adult children of the fathers.) These interviews provided valuable information about how men enact the fathering role with their adult children. Several key gender differences were noted, for example, fathers reported that they found it easier to understand their sons than their daughters, and that they were more demanding and critical of their sons than their daughters. Fathers also reported that they were concerned about socializing their daughters into the male work world and wanted to help ease their entry into a career and monitor how well their daughters were doing in their careers.

Often researchers neglect the reciprocal nature of father-child relationships. This holds true for understanding the give-and-take aspects of a father's relationship to his adult child. It seems that fathers can benefit emotionally and psychologically from healthy relationships with their adult children just as the adult children can benefit from a good relationship with their fathers. Very little research has examined the value that fathering has for fathers of adult children. In an indirect measure of this phenomena, Lewis (1990) found that fathers experienced pleasure in their ability to provide help to their adult children. In another study by Harvey, Curry, and Bray (1991) it was found among rural Canadian parents, that the fathers' happiness was strongly associated with the degree to which fathers believed their adult children could count on them. Fathers reported less satisfaction if they felt that they had to count on their children for assistance. It would seem that many of the caretaking roles developed by fathers with their young children are carried over into their perception of what constitutes a happy and satisfying relationship with their adult children.

Grandfathering

It's estimated that well over 90% of older adults with children are grandparents (Roberto, 1990). Numerous researchers have suggested that grandparents can serve as a vital source of emotional and instrumental support for children (Cherlin & Furstenburg, 1986; Denham & Smith, 1989). We are also living in a very special time in which grandparents are still alive well into the adulthood of their grandchildren (Mills, 1999). Basically this means that the grandparents of today have a unique opportunity to influence their grandchildren for many years, not just through childhood but well into the grandchild's young adulthood. Despite these demographic shifts, the media and professional literature provide only limited specific information of older men's relationships with adult children and with grandchildren (Thomas, 1994). Most scholarly work in the area of grandparenting continues to focus on the relationship between grandmothers and their grandchildren.

Reflection

Consider your relationship with your grandfather. In what ways does your grandfather provide support? How is grandfathering different from fathering?

The few studies that do provide a degree of focus on grandfathering present some interesting results. Mills (1999) examined the connection between the adolescent-to-adult role transition by individuals and their perceptions of intergenerational solidarity with their grandparents. The findings from this study indicated that adult role transitions were more closely related to grandchildrens' solidarity with grandfathers than with grandmothers. In a recent qualitative study (Waldrop, 1999) efforts were made to explore the mentoring capacity of grandfathers. The findings from this study revealed the importance of life lessons that men teach their grandchildren. The respondents expressed strong desires for transferring values to their grandchildren's lives and indicated a desire for teaching interpersonal relationships. Through this involvement, they educate through life experiences and serve as mentors for their grandchildren. This mentoring role makes a positive contribution to the lives of grandchildren and to the identity of grandfathers.

There is some evidence that the degree of importance placed on grandfathers in the lives of their children differs somewhat based on race and ethnicity. Kivett (1991) explored racial differences in the centrality of the grandfather role and in the factors related to its importance among older Black and White males. Interviews were conducted with 48 Black and 51 White males aged 65 and older living in a rural area. Results suggested that the grandfather role is more vital for older Black men than for White men. These differences in centrality of the role were mainly a result of race and not economic or structural factors. Higher centrality of the role among Blacks was observed in the following areas: (a) household structure; (b) association with grandchildren; (c) grand-filial expectations; (d) help given to grandchildren; (e) feelings of closeness; and (f) perceptions of getting along with grandchildren. There were some areas in which both Black and White men reported similar views on grandfathers. Grandfathers were seen as more affectionate than functional among both older Black and White men. In addition, there were racial similarities in terms of the ranked importance of the grandfather role, in the amount of help received from grandchildren, and in grandfather-grandchild harmony. This study lends support to the view that grandfathering has a strong cultural component.

Much more extensive work is needed in order to increase our understanding of how grandfathers effect the lives of their adult children and their grandchildren. Additional research is needed to increase our understanding of the racial/ethnic differences that exist in the importance placed on grandfathers.

SUMMARY AND WHAT WE HOPE FOR

Information has been presented within this chapter that addresses "What We Know." We would now like to make some suggestions relevant to the second part of the chapter title "What We Hope For." Based on the various findings from the research discussed within this chapter we would hope for the following:

1. We need to conduct additional research on the issue of father presence. While there is a growing consensus that father absence is potentially detrimental to child development, we do not have clarity on what specific fathering behaviors make a difference when the father is present. Is it the difference in play? Is it the differing socialization efforts of fathers, or is it simply the economic resources that fathers bring to the child? These are a few of the numerous questions that need further exploration.

2. We would hope that fathers begin to appreciate their own strengths and what they might bring to child development. It seems that far too many fathers are uncertain about the contributions that they can make to the well-being of their own children, beyond that of being the breadwinner. It would also be helpful if others could appreciate the strengths that fathers bring to child-rearing as well (mothers, grandparents, family workers, the court, etc.).

3. We would hope to continue to expand our knowledge of the role that fathers play with their adult children and the role that grandfathers play with their grandchildren. We are in a unique period in which fathers can live to see their children grow old and live to see their great grandchildren born. Additional research could improve our understanding of how this phenomena is affecting men and how they are responding to the opportunity to parent across the life span.

4. Because we are in a period of extreme social change (divorce, increased life expectancy and parenting across the life span, etc.) we would also hope that more support and educational services will be offered to men attempting to adapt to their changing roles. What does it mean to be a nonresidential parent or a grandfather in a divorce situation? How does one enact those roles? In some ways, we are living in unprecedented times; it should not come as a surprise that many men (and women) are having difficulty knowing how to be a "good" father or grandfather. To some degree, these roles are socially determined, and therefore we may need to help those who are struggling with the changing social landscape.

5. It is also our hope that society will explore further ways to prevent the occurrence of nonresidential fathering. Given the inherent difficulties in the role of nonresidential father, we hope that efforts can be made to explore the reasons for failed relationships (both marital and nonmarital), unwanted pregnancies, and teen pregnancies.

There is significant research indicating that fathers can have a positive and meaningful effect on the development of their children throughout the life span. While it is true that some fathers may not always contribute in the ways mentioned in this chapter, it is important to note that for a growing number of men, the role of father has a high degree of saliency for them from the point of their child's conception to their own death. Many men are expanding their roles as caregivers and nurturers to their grandchildren through their mentoring and affectionate behavior as grandfathers. Additional research is needed in each of these developmental areas to better understand the specific processes involved in effective fathering, as well as research into ways to provide programming to assist fathers with their developmental transitions as fathers.

Questions for Discussion

1. In what ways does the behavior of the father who talked about his desire to fix the steps resemble what is commonly called female nesting behavior?

2. Why is play such an important activity for children? Why is it important to consider the different play activities of mothers and fathers?

3. Amato (1994) discusses the role of fathers with their adult children. Are there other ways that you see fathers playing a significant role with their adult children? What are some examples?

II

What We Can Do

4
Principles and Strategies for Promoting Effective Fathering

John was a father who returned to a group counseling session after having dropped out for several months. When John showed up at the session, Brian Hawkins, the group leader, ran to the door to greet and embrace him and to welcome him back to the group. Brian later explained that he would never choose to be judgmental, casual, or indifferent toward fathers like John. According to Hawkins, there is no room for pretentiousness or game playing; being genuinely compassionate is what helping these men is all about. (Hawkins, personal communication, March, 1999)

In this chapter we amplify our perspective for helping fathers and describe principles and strategies that can be utilized in helping fathers.

OUR PERSPECTIVE

Our perspective informs how we help fathers and their families. It suggests that those of us who intend to help fathers and their families must prepare for the work ahead. The following principles are the ones that the authors value the most:

• We embrace a strengths perspective rather than one that emphasizes fathers' deficits.
• We must be prepared to help fathers and their families at all system levels of intervention rather than limiting our attention to only one level such as individual counseling or legislative action. Sometimes several levels of intervention must be considered simultaneously.

81

• Fathers must be fully engaged in this process of help, particularly on the affective and spiritual levels, if true change is to occur.

• We must pay serious attention to the differences as well as the similarities manifested among nonresidential fathers. A multicultural perspective is employed in which we are sensitive to differences in race and ethnicity, socioeconomic status, age, sexual orientation, religion, and numerous other aspects of diversity and take them into account.

• Our values lead us to select approaches that help fathers cooperate with other family members rather than work against them. This is particularly important with regard to the biological mother of their children. We use several proven collaborative and conciliatory philosophies and practices that promote this effort.

Strengths Perspective

Helping nonresidential fathers requires taking into account their special circumstances. Many of them feel superfluous and unimportant as fathers and can sense keenly that no one really cares about them as parents. Many also may be unprepared for the emotional demands of parenting their children. Stereotypes like deadbeat dad and absent father are likely embedded in their consciousness as reminders of what society may think of them.

In light of these and other difficulties, a strengths perspective needs to be the vanguard of any help that is provided (Saleebey, 1997). Every father has assets that are worthy of recognition but that may be overlooked. As an ally of fathers, we can help create a climate in which they can rediscover these assets and hope for and seek something of value for themselves and their family.

We can begin helping fathers by asking them to identify their assets. Sometimes an asset is revealed in a man's facial expression or his demeanor—a smile, a sense of humor, or a discerning look. Strengths are evident in his loyalties, insights, patience, cultural heritage, pride, and survival skills. We can detect his strengths in his stories about his family and himself and in parent-child concerns that are raised. If a father talks about his children, that is likely a strength; undoubtedly, they are on his mind. What he shares may be positive—bragging about them or sharing their achievements, but negative comments have strengths embedded in them as well. For example, expressing anger can be a strength as the depth of his anger may reflect the depth of his love for his children. If his story is about being shut out of their lives or sensing that he is unimportant to them, he may be revealing both vulnerabilities and potential desires. Certainly, his stories need to be heard by someone who cares about him as a father, someone who can tell him that he is important to his children and encourage his attempts to become more active in their lives. It may never be too late for this, even in John's case:

> I have been addicted for over 20 years—all of my son's life. Most of that time I could hardly take care of myself. Now that I am slowly getting my life together, I don't know how to reenter my son's life and I am afraid of rejection. (Dudley, 1991c, p. 281–282)

Reflection

Do you think that it is too late for John to attempt to reenter his son's life when his son is already 20 years old? If you think it's not too late, how would you attempt to help him? How could you build upon some of his strengths? If you think it is too late, why do you think this?

Strengths can be easily identified, or camouflaged, concealed, and difficult to discover. Some nonresidential fathers may have a number of strengths that readily present themselves, like Ahab, a teen nonresidential father who told the story about how he attempted to protect his daughter from her stepfather's abuse:

> I have learned that not everyone in the world is born with human decency. I have learned that if you want your rights and the rights of others, particularly minors, to be attained, you had better stand up and fight like hell for them! I have learned to never give up on what you truly believe is right. That your self-respect is the most valuable thing you can possess. I have also learned that the bond of a biological father and child cannot be destroyed.

Ahab had few rights as a parent, but he was determined not to stand by while his daughter's safety was in jeopardy. His love for his daughter is deeply felt even though he has never lived with her for more than one night at a time. His moral indignation for the abuse that was being inflicted upon her was steadfast and revealed his instinctual desire to protect her. He could have easily turned and walked away, but he didn't.

All System Levels

Helping nonresidential fathers and their families calls for a prepared-ness to intervene at multiple levels. They may need *individual help*—intensive counseling, useful information, or just someone to listen. They may need help finding and utilizing community resources. This help may include affirmation of their right to seek such services, nego-tiating a bureaucratic maze, or simply support and encouragement.

Fathers can be helped effectively by groups of all kinds. Men may benefit the most from groups of other fathers, and self-help groups, in particular, can be invaluable. These groups offer men what most wom-en seem to be able to obtain without joining a group: intimate conver-sations with others of the same sex about their personal needs and problems. Counseling or therapy groups can also be useful whether mixed or all-male. These groups are particularly beneficial to fathers who have significant difficulty communicating their feelings or per-sonal problems.

Couple's and family-focused interventions are also important for promoting cooperative relationships between a father and other family members. Even though two parents have decided to uncouple, they can still benefit from couple's counseling that helps them to under-stand each other in their parental roles. Family therapy involving all family members can also be relevant because the family system still exists, though in different form. The concept of a nuclear family can be replaced by a binuclear family, in which two family households coexist, supporting each other as one larger social unit. This binuclear family concept is readily achievable for families with joint residential and joint legal custody arrangements; bi-nuclear families can also be relevant when one family member carries sole custody.

Numerous types of program interventions can be introduced to address a wide range of needs of fathers and their families. Chapter 11 describes a particular type of program that educates fathers and moth-ers about the divorce process, various options in obtaining a divorce, and the advantages of cooperative negotiations. Programs are described in other chapters including employment training for unemployed or underemployed dads; father-child play groups; parent training work-shops; spiritually oriented programs for fathers; and fathers' advocacy groups.

The workplace should not be overlooked if we are to succeed in getting fathers involved. It is the place where men spend most of their waking hours; it is also the family's primary rival for a father's time. Most employers tend to overlook their responsibilities for supporting fatherhood; in contrast, some are at the forefront in establishing creative family-supportive policies. For example, employers can help fathers by offering paid paternity leave when a new baby arrives. Flexible work schedules offer fathers free time during the day or week when their children may need them. Family-oriented workshops can be offered on the job, along with individual and family counseling. And financial benefits are needed that support families, including a flexible sick-leave policy that can be used to care for sick children, subsidies for day care services, tax-free health care and child-care spending accounts, and comprehensive family medical insurance coverage. Chapter 8 addresses some of the innovative ways that the workplace can be changed to be more father-friendly.

Social movements are also an effective way of bringing broad social changes for fathers and families. Men should be informed about these movements and be encouraged to get involved to the extent they can. One such movement has been led by the poet Robert Bly. He has offered countless retreats on "the masculine father," which has captured the hearts of tens of thousands of men. Bly has been particularly valuable in helping men get in touch more deeply with their masculine instincts for parenting. Other national movements such as the Promise Keepers, a national Christian-based group, and the Million Man March, an African American men's march, have drawn hundreds of thousands of fathers to a renewed commitment to their family responsibilities. Other movements supporting fatherhood have been evident on the local level, such as the initiative in Davidson County, North Carolina, which is presented in chapter 7.

The media often have a negative influence on good fathering. Images of the Marlboro Man; the bungling, incompetent dad; Don Juan; the gun-slinging cowboy; the tough cop; and the mass slayer all convey men that have little, if any, concern for parenting children. Ads, sitcoms, documentaries, movies, news programs, and other media outlets could do much more to promote positive images of men. Images of a responsible father, in particular, are needed—one who is kind and compassionate, who communicates intimately with his children and guides them along a responsible life-path, and who teaches them courage, morality, and social ethics.

Finally, policy changes that promote fatherhood are needed. Policy changes are needed in all kinds of organizations, including private corporations, schools, human services and health care agencies, religious organizations, and, of course, government. Policies are usually made more often by men than women, and White men in particular have had a major influence over policy-making. Yet ironically, men have too often created policies that are self-defeating to fathers and families, or they have overlooked new policy initiatives that could support dads.

New policy initiatives need to be mandated, including welfare reform initiatives that promote genuine self-sufficiency, school policies that involve fathers in their children's education, family agency policies that give more attention to assisting fathers, and government policies of all kinds that recognize and promote responsible fatherhood. While punitive policies such as the Child Support Enforcement Agency are sometimes necessary as a last resort, policies that voluntarily promote responsible parenting need to be given priority. Chapter 8 focuses on policy initiatives that can make a positive difference in men's lives.

Reflection
Had you thought about the various system levels of importance in the life of a nonresidential father? Which levels of practice appeal to you? How could you incorporate multilevel interventions in your practice efforts?

Affective and Spiritual Levels of Involvement

As mentioned in chapter 1, males experience many binds or contradictions in our society. The feeling bind is one example. By the age of 5 or 6 a boy is typically discouraged from expressing feelings like crying and desiring hugs and other forms of physical affection. Then as an adult he is criticized for *not* revealing his needs and vulnerable feelings. Another bind is evident in the realm of autonomy. Men are expected to be strong and not to depend upon others for help; yet these behaviors lead to denial of their needs to be cared for and nurtured. Many men end up being wounded and defeated from these binds. They may have chronic difficulties in expressing their feelings and revealing their vulnerabilities, particularly to other men. An internal tape keeps telling them that they can solve their problems on their own.

We are learning that most fathers experience considerable emotional distress from a divorce or uncoupling experience (McLanahan & Sandefur, 1994). Many reveal that the absence of their children from their daily lives is a major trauma. The pain related to seeing their children only intermittently and according to a prescribed schedule can be humiliating. Yet this may be difficult for men to admit to. On the surface, it appears easier to deny that anything is wrong and to walk away. Anger and outrage are likely to be healthier responses, such as complaining that their child's mother has disappointed them or that the court system has treated them unfairly. Helping these men necessitates our hearing their anger-filled stories. Many men can only get in touch with their vulnerable feelings and feelings of loss by first expressing their anger. We must begin where fathers are, often emotionally wounded and entangled in their family crisis, to succeed in leading them through to a satisfactory solution.

Fathers are likely to be spiritually wounded as well. Robert Bly (1990) suggests that men need to feel the pain of grief. This grief stems from the losses that a man has experienced all along his life journey, such as a loss of his father, a marriage, a child, or a job. Bly claims that men must descend into the deep places of their soul and find their accumulative grief to discover what manhood is all about. Boys who grow up with an addicted, abusive, or absent father can find themselves with a hole in the soul where anger, mistrust of males, and wounded self-esteem end up paralyzing them.

Engaging men spiritually requires preparation. We must be sensitive to their particular religious and spiritual affiliations and disciplines. If they believe in God, healing their wounds may involve helping them open up to his healing power. Several male spirituality books offer ways to help with this healing (e.g., Culbertson, 1992; Osherson, 1992; Pable, 1996). Spiritual work can involve reevaluating life goals and priorities, recognizing one's limited power and energy, appreciating anew one's children and the time that can be spent with them, rediscovering life instincts, and considering new generative paths to follow for the remaining years of our lives.

Our spirituality is often overlooked as a source of power for expressing our commitments to fatherhood. Dollahite, Hawkins, and Brotherson (1997) remind us that fathers are called by the next generation—our children's generation—to meet their basic needs and to prepare them to parent the next generation. This is an ethical obligation that fathers must make if we are to continue to succeed as a society, and a father's inner spiritual being may be the most important place to explore his motivation to assume this obligation. Similarly, the religious affiliations and involvements of fathers may offer some of the most valuable social supports for bringing about this ethical obligation.

Reflection
How could your spiritual beliefs serve as a strength to you in your practice? How would you work to ensure that your own spiritual beliefs do not dominate those of your clients?

Diversity Perspective

Diversity is an extremely important aspect of fathering and family life. We can easily err by assuming that the experiences of others are likely to be similar to ours. Although we have much in common that needs to be claimed—for example, a parental instinct to love and guide our biological offspring—diversity abounds in the human experience.

GENDER

Diversity by gender is most evident in the functions of families. If male and female differences are not apparent when two people are joined together, they are inevitably apparent when they separate. Though male and female roles in families are increasingly becoming blurred, gender differences based on our biological makeup and socialization cannot be ignored. Women, for example, have been traditionally treated as subordinate to men in almost all aspects of life— in employment, government, and politics. The family may be the only place in society where they enjoy a semblance of equality with men, and perhaps in some instances preferential status because traditionally they have been the primary parent responsible for raising the children.

RACE AND ETHNICITY

Differences based on race and ethnicity are also important to consider. Throughout this book, we point out how African Americans, Latinos (Cubans, Puerto Ricans, Mexicans, and others), Native Americans (numerous tribes), and Asian Americans (Chinese, Japanese, Korean,

Vietnamese, Filipino) are different from the majority White European American population. It is important to remember that there is tremendous diversity within each ethnic group as well. For example, African American fathers are not all alike, just as White fathers are not.

SOCIAL CLASS

Income and social class levels also differentiate the attitudes and behaviors of fathers and their families. Socioeconomic status can even have as significant an influence on families as race and ethnicity, as evidenced by the numerous similarities that we find in diverse groups of families within each income level. An inadequate income, for example, can have drastic negative consequences for families. Fathers who are unemployed are often considered unnecessary or even detrimental to their family's livelihood if they remain present. The obvious influence on the family of a man's low income and insufficient earning power suggests how critically important it is to promote employment policies that lead to decent jobs for fathers (and mothers). The breadwinners in every family must be assured an adequately paid, stable job if the family is to survive.

SEXUAL ORIENTATION

Gay fathers are confronted with an additional layer of problems beyond the usual ones besetting most men. They are likely to be suspected of being unprepared for parenting because of societal ignorance about their sexual orientation (Patterson, 1995; Patterson & Chan, 1997). Gay men and lesbians are often faced with discrimination in the courts, for example, on decisions about custody and visitation.

OTHER DIFFERENCES

Differences are evident in countless other ways based on religion, age, the region of the country, and whether one is from an urban, suburban, or rural area.

Conciliatory and Collaborative Perspectives

Children significantly benefit when fathers and mothers are cooperating. Several studies have revealed that the two most detrimental family circumstances for children following divorce are an absent parent and severe and continuous conflicts between a father and mother (Johnston, Kline, & Tschann, 1989; Wallerstein & Kelly, 1980). Conciliatory and collaborative approaches to problem-solving are needed to promote cooperative relationships. Adversarial and other competitive approaches should be avoided or used only later because of a likely exacerbating influence.

Divorce and other court proceedings are a pivotal event for encouraging or impeding cooperation and collaboration between two uncoupling parents. The choice of strategies for divorce proceedings is likely to have a long term influence on the quality of the family's relationships. As will be discussed in more depth in chapter 12, cooperative strategies should be employed whenever possible to help parents work out the necessary decisions of divorce and plans for ongoing parenting. Divorce mediation strategies are usually the preferred approach for negotiating plans for cooperative parenting. In contrast, the win/lose approach of adversarial legal proceedings has often been found to be problematic for negotiating a divorce and working out successful parenting arrangements.

Family mediation services are also beneficial at other times. For example, men may need help in learning how to communicate effectively with their former spouses, their children, a step-parent, or other significant parties. Once a divorce agreement or a parenting agreement has been completed, mediation services can also be enlisted to implement the agreement or to resolve problems that may arise.

The philosophy and principles of conciliatory and collaborative strategies are central to providing help to nonresidential fathers (Fisher & Brown, 1988). The following principles are among the most important:

- being unconditionally constructive in the relationship
- keeping the relationship open by communication
- understanding each other's interests
- discovering common interests
- creating a balance between reason and emotions in communications
- being honest and reliable
- using persuasion rather than coercion
- valuing and respecting each other

Reflection

In a study by Stone and McKenry (1998), it was found that while many nonresidential fathers continued to report angry feelings toward their former spouses after the divorce, they were still able to identify objectively positive mothering qualities. What is the significance of this finding for workers attempting to enact conciliatory and collaborative strategies with parents after separation or divorce?

PRINCIPLES AND STRATEGIES FOR PROMOTING EFFECTIVE FATHERING

Professionals who work with nonresidential fathers and their families propose several action principles and strategies that we support. Some derive from rather complex theoretical models while others are stand-alone strategies that seem to work.

1. Embrace a Broad Definition of Father Involvement

We view fathering to include a broad range of activities. As well as spending time with the child, fathering can entail such things as arranging a visit to the pediatrician, attending a parent-teacher conference, telephone calls with children, washing the child's laundry, shopping for their food or clothes, paying bills that affect the child's welfare, praying for a child, and contemplating the choice of a new school for a child to attend.

We subscribe to Lamb's typology of a father's involvement (1986) to include three major categories:

• Interactions with the child
• Psychological and physical accessibility to the child
• Responsibility for the care or welfare of the child

Interactions can include almost anything done with the child, such as bottle feeding, playing games, talking, reading a book together, playing ball, hugging, and changing diapers. *Accessibility* can refer to any activity in which the father is available even though he is not in direct interaction with his children. Examples are preparing a meal or washing the laundry while the child watches television, reading a book in a room nearby where the child is playing, or working outside while the child plays inside. *Responsibility for the care or welfare of the child* refers to many different types of activities on behalf of the child that do not involve direct interaction, such as planning after-school activities or arranging a neighborhood car pool for an event on the weekend. It could also include nonbehavioral things like reflecting on the child's immediate or future needs or considering the details of the child's birthday party.

We recommend promoting a father's involvement all along this broad continuum of activities on behalf of children. This view encourages men to participate in their children's lives in numerous ways. We do recommend that every father spend some regular, quality time in direct interaction with his child. Beyond some quality contact, however, a father can often choose areas of involvement in which he has strengths. And fathers of different cultural backgrounds can vary their involvement in response to cultural factors.

2. Enfranchise Fathers as Parents

Braver and O'Connell (1998) investigated 31 possible reasons why divorced fathers in their study could have disengaged from their children and found one reason clearly superior to all of the others: feeling parentally disenfranchised. Whether because of a judge who decided against them for custody or a former spouse who opposed their continued involvement, they felt they had no real rights of parenthood anymore. These disenfranchised fathers who felt that they were being rejected as a father were the ones that most likely discontinued contact with and support for their children. They still had concern for their children and were not deadbeat dads initially, but something happened that motivated them to withdraw because they felt they were not valued as a father.

Fathers often complain that they are overlooked or demeaned as parents. These complaints are most likely heard during court proceedings for divorce and custody. Custody rulings are more likely to be made against them than for them. Also, public policies more often seem one-sided in favor of enforcing their child support obligations and downplaying their visitation agreement. As one father put it, "That's all I am to my children—a monthly check" (Braver & O'Connell, 1998, p. 196).

3. Promote Support for a Father's Parenting Identity

Ihinger-Tallman, Pasley, and Buehler (1995) state that a key element in determining a father's involvement with his children after divorce is his identification with being a parent. His identity with his fathering role is based on several factors, including

- the commitment to his various parenting roles after divorce (e.g., provider, disciplinarian, nurturer)
- the salience of these parental roles in relation to his other roles (worker, new husband, stepfather)
- the degree to which his view of himself as a father corresponds with the views of his significant others (former spouse, children, new lover, new spouse, coworkers)

Ihinger-Tallman and colleagues (1995) go on to say that the people in a father's social network can positively influence his identity as a parent. For example, it is important that his former spouse value him as a parent and value his parenting ability and that his co-parental relationship with his former spouse be cooperative. He is also more likely to be active if he receives positive encouragement for his parenting behavior from other people in his life such as a lover or new wife, his friends, coworkers, and employers. Also, if he has a negative perception of his former spouse's parenting skills, he may be inclined to become more actively involved to protect his children. Ihinger-Tallman and associates (1995) also identify personal factors that positively affect his involvement, including good emotional health, a higher level of economic well-being, and a stable employment history.

Reflection

How can we measure a father's parenting identity? McPhee, Benson, and Bullock (1986) created the *Self-Perceptions of the Parental Role Scale* as one means of measuring parenting identity. Although their instrument was originally designed to measure a mother's parenting role identity, it was used successfully by researchers (e.g., Stone & McKenry, 1998) to evaluate a father's parenting role identity. The *Self-Perceptions of the Parental Role Scale* measures: parental role satisfaction, perceived competence in parenting, the level of investment the parent has in his role, and the salience of the role for the individual—how important the parenting role is compared to other roles in his life. How might such a scale be of use in your efforts to evaluate intervention effectiveness?

4. Implement Culturally Sensitive Interventions

It is always important to incorporate a multicultural approach in the helping process. As we indicated before, men are very different in many ways across racial and ethnic identities. One way to ensure that race and ethnic issues are considered is to ask ourselves the following questions (Allen & Connor, 1997):

- Are my interactions and interventions informed by traditional paradigms *or* am I using paradigms that encompass the realities of the particular cultural group?
- Are my interactions and interventions based on pathology and deviance or inferiority *or* am I using a perspective of strengths and positive attributes of the person?
- What aspects of my interactions facilitate or block opportunities for empowerment, including ethnic pride and racial self-identification?
- Do I help these men identify opportunities to learn from each other about survival and thriving in their culture?

Other general suggestions for developing a cross-cultural approach with fathers and their families are

- Explore cultural issues that may have an influence on parental roles, such as the importance of extended family and ancestry, specific gender roles, and views about child raising.
- Consider asking the family to explain pertinent aspects of their culture when you lack understanding.
- If the family's race or culture is different from the worker's, be sensitive to the possibility of the need to pay particular attention to building trust.
- Affirm the value and importance of the family's cultural identity.
- Explore and be prepared to address issues of racial or ethnic discrimination if they are evident.
- Explore important religious or spiritual beliefs that are mentioned or inferred.
- Consider particular cultural rules in the family regarding communication, such as who communicates with whom?

- Be sensitive to the family's views about space, such as where the first contact should take place (home, office, somewhere else?)
- Consider how the family uses space in the larger community. Are some areas used and others avoided for employment, recreation, leisure, schools, etc.?
- Don't overlook the importance of social supports from churches and other spiritual groups, social clubs, friends, extended family, and others.

5. Utilize a Holistic, Multiservice Approach

People are multidimensional and need help that potentially addresses all of their dimensions. Fathers, for example, may need help not only with parenting but also with employment, and individual counseling. Teen dads may also need educational support. Two exemplary programs that are holistic and multidimensional in nature are highlighted here as illustrations. Both programs are primarily directed to teen dads.

FATHERS IN TRAINING (INNOVATIVE PROGRAM)

Brian Hawkins is the founder of Fathers in Training (FIT), a program located in Virginia Beach, Virginia. This program is directed to young fathers who are not actively involved in their children's lives and are not usually living with the child's mother. Hawkins targets family members who receive services from the Department of Social Services (DSS) in Virginia Beach, and his program is funded by DSS. Fathers voluntarily join this program, and those with a history of sexual misconduct with children are excluded. This multiservice program comprises several components, including group counseling and parent training, employment assistance, educational assistance, community outreach, and case management. His training workshops focus on personal development, life skills, building relationships, and health and wellness along with the responsibilities of fatherhood. These components recognize the teen dads' multidimensional lives and their needs as both young men and fathers.

Hawkins's program is based on several basic principles. First of all, it attempts to prevent childbirth until a teen is ready for this responsibility. This primary prevention effort is achieved by offering training and education to these young men as early as possible. Hawkins's program also prepares teenage males for the responsibilities of fathering, including a committed relationship and marriage, financial self-sufficiency, and emotional readiness to care for a family.

When unmarried teen fathers have children, Hawkins encourages them to establish paternity at birth. Health care agencies are involved in this critical process of establishing paternity and recognizing and involving the father at the beginning of the child's life. The earlier these fathers get involved or are enfranchised as parents, the more likely they will remain in their children's lives.

Many of the services of FIT involve the fathers in relationship-building with others, including their children. Emotional bonding work is important in the group counseling sessions, as the participants are encouraged to talk with other fathers about the real issues in their lives. The program leaders continually stress the teens' strengths, encouraging them to hold up and claim their gifts within the groups. Importantly, relationships between the program's leaders and the participants model this bonding. Hawkins and other leaders go out of their way to communicate their concern, respect, and love for the participants. As an example, one participant returned to a group counseling session after having dropped out for several months. Rather than being judgmental, casual, or indifferent toward this participant, Hawkins ran to the door to greet and embrace him and to welcome him back to the group. According to Hawkins, there is no room for pretentiousness or game playing; being genuinely compassionate is what helping these men is all about. He indicated that the men he recruits for helping roles must be willing to do their own personal work related to male and fathering issues.

THE FATHERHOOD PROJECT (INNOVATIVE PROGRAM)

James Levine is the founder and director of another exemplary program, the Fatherhood Project of the Families and Work Institute in New York City. Levine is a nationally known leader of fatherhood efforts (Levine & Pitt, 1995). The Fatherhood Project emphasizes the need to provide help to fathers and fathers-to-be without taking issue with their marital status. While this program recognizes marriage as a preferred option for most child-raising, it also recognizes that marriage may not be feasible for all families and that it may be counterproductive to impose it on many fathers. Working with fathers and their families *where they are* is a critical basic strategy.

Like Hawkins's Fathers in Training program, Levine's program is multiservice-oriented. It offers individual counseling and group services, heath care efforts to establish paternity and father involvement at birth, employment assistance, parent training, and collaborative work with social agencies that serve families with children. This project has overall strategies similar to those of Hawkins's program (Levine & Pitt, 1995, p. 6):

- Preventing men from having babies before they are ready emotionally and financially
- Preparing men for the emotional, legal, and financial responsibilities of parenting
- Establishing paternity at childbirth as an important legal connection
- Involving fathers in developing a connection with their children
- Actively supporting them in their various parenting roles

Levine's group has learned some important lessons in more than 20 years of work. First, they state that the power of expectations cannot be overestimated (Levine & Pitt, 1995, p. 8). Low expectations of fathers from the agencies established to serve them will lead to a self-fulfilling prophecy, while high expectations are a catalyst for making things much more likely to happen. Second, social supports for fathers have a critical impact on their relationships with their children. The father's own father or another person who is a mentor can be a catalyst in promoting an active relationship with their child. Third, women play a critical role in promoting the father's parental relationship. The mother of his children, in particular, can have a major impact by how much she encourages and supports his parenting, and his wife or partner also has a potentially strong influence. In addition, the many female staff members representing relevant agencies that can serve the father have an important role to play.

Reachable moments are noted in their strategies. Besides childbirth as the most opportune time to reach and involve the father, entry of the child into preschool is another important time. This is probably the second major social institution after the hospital to enlist the involvement of fathers. Passage into adolescence is another reachable moment, as the child is making the transition to manhood and needs nurture and guidance from a father figure.

6. Additional Strategies That Are Essential

Finally, we offer several specific strategies that should be considered when intervening to help fathers and their families.

A. Encourage a cooperative parental relationship with the mother of the children. Fathers fare much better in their relationships with their children when there is cooperation between the parents. If the former wife is the custodial parent, her perception of the father and his parenting are usually critical to his continued involvement (Ihinger-Tallman et al., 1995). The mother is the gatekeeper to his children and if she encourages his involvement, he is more likely to remain active. Why? Because he feels enfranchised as a parent!

B. Emphasize cooperative strategies in the family court. A shift in court-sponsored programs is needed that promotes greater cooperation between the two parents. Custody and divorce proceedings too often are adversarial in nature and counterproductive to the possibility of successful co-parenting after divorce. Cooperative strategies need to be given greater preference, including different types of nonadversarial proceedings, parent education about the impact of divorce on children, and mediation services to formulate parenting agreements and resolve family conflicts.

C. Give greater consideration to the father's parental rights and responsibilities in court matters. A father often feels that he has been stripped of his parental role when his former wife is awarded sole custody, particularly when he seeks custodial rights. And if she makes it difficult for him to see his children during prescribed visitation periods, which is often reported to happen, he feels even less control as a parent. Joint legal and joint residential custody provide men with parental rights in partnership with their former spouses. Joint legal custody in particular sends a message to a father that he still is his child's parent. Braver and O'Connell (1998) found from their study that fathers with joint legal custody had significantly more frequent contact with their children and were more likely to pay child support than fathers with no custodial rights. Joint legal custody requires that parents make major decisions together, such as where a child will attend school, receive religious education, or obtain medical care. Fathers who receive joint custody become parentally enfranchised and are likely to go to greater lengths to assume their responsibilities to their children than those without any custodial rights.

Perspective: The Children's Act of 1989

In England, the Children's Act of 1989 has been lauded as landmark legislation that shifted the focus in the British child-welfare court system from protecting children to preserving families (Pine & Warsh, 1996). Attempts were made to create child-centered laws that were more flexible and easier to understand. One of the highlights of this legislation was the re-organization of the divorce court system to emphasize conciliation between divorcing parents on behalf of the children; in essence the court system became a family court. Emphasis was placed on using social workers to work with families to reach agreements that were in the best interests of the children. When the British court becomes involved in making judgements that affect children they must consider such issues as (a) the discernable wishes and feelings of the child; (b) the child's physical, emotional, and educational needs; (c) the likely effect of any change in the child's circumstances; (d) any harm that the child has suffered or is at risk of suffering; and (e) how capable each of the child's parents is in meeting the child's needs. The shift in focus has helped to create a court atmosphere that is less adversarial and more cooperative between divorcing parents. A greater allowance has been made for shared parenting and shared residence. How would you compare the U.S. divorce court system with the one evolving in Great Britain? What changes would you like to see in our current system?

D. Establish legal paternity as early as possible if the father is not married. Teen and other unmarried fathers particularly need incentives and support to verify their identity voluntarily. Pathways to enfranchisement are evident in efforts to involve teen fathers early in the life of their child. Establishing a teen father's paternity is an example. By certifying his paternity, we are validating him as an important person in his child's life. Furthermore, establishing paternity must be coupled with other services that encourage him to participate in child-raising and to contribute financial assistance.

E. *Involve fathers in assuming child-raising responsibilities in a timely way.* Strategies for involving dads must be timely. Fathers and mothers going through a marital separation should be encouraged to work out a cooperative parenting plan immediately that actively involves both parents. Temporary custodial and visitation arrangements established during the marital separation period are often the preferred permanent choice of judges if they have been successful. Similarly, meaningful involvement of teen and older unmarried fathers should be encouraged before the time of a child's birth. If the mother consents, an unmarried father can be involved in a variety of ways, including supporting the mother in a healthy pregnancy, attending birthing classes, assisting in the birth process, and caring for the child soon after the mother and child are released from the hospital.

F. *Help fathers become effective economic providers.* The economic capacity of a father is paramount, as virtually all nonresidential fathers are expected to assume some financial responsibilities for their children. If a father can be a successful breadwinner, he will be encouraged to become involved in other parental roles such as child-raising and decision-making. In this regard, enfranchising a father includes maximizing his likelihood of success as an employee. Unemployed and underemployed teen and older fathers may need substantial help with employment if they are to fulfill their financial obligations. Job training and preparation and educational assistance are essential ingredients of this strategy.

G. *Encourage marriage and its legal commitments as the preferred option for promoting the children's long-term well-being.* Marriage is the most effective way to ensure parental stability in the children's lives. Marriage encourages a stronger, more enduring commitment of the parents to their children and to each other than do alternative arrangements. Marriage can be promoted in numerous creative ways without being imposed; for example, through various public policies, human service interventions, and by emphasizing cultural values. This strategy is not relevant when marriage is not feasible.

SUMMARY

Principles and strategies that are important to our approach include choosing a broad definition of what constitutes parenting activities, supporting a strong parental identity for fathers, and choosing interventions that will enfranchise fathers. Other characteristics of our approach include assisting fathers at many system levels of intervention, utilizing a holistic approach, intervening in a timely way, asserting the legal rights and responsibilities of fathers, and encouraging marriage when it seems feasible and can benefit the children. Our approach also gives special attention to identifying a father's strengths, being sensitive to multicultural issues, engaging fathers on the affective and spiritual levels, and emphasizing cooperation among family members.

Questions for Discussion

1. Interview a father and encourage him to identify his strengths as a person and a parent. How easy was it for him to identify his strengths? Did this approach seem to energize or empower him in any way?

2. Ask a father to identify the activities that he participates in as a parent. Next, ask him to rank these activities, with the most important ones listed first and the least important ones last. How do his activities fit with Lamb's typology mentioned earlier in the chapter?

III

Professional Practice Considerations in Work With Fathers at Risk

5
Assessment Issues for Practice With Nonresidential Fathers

After 10 years Tom and Mary decided they could no longer stay married. They reached a dissolution agreement after meeting with a trained mediator, and they agreed to joint legal custody of their three children; however, sole physical custody was given to Mary.

Not long after the separation, Tom began to miss everyday contact with his children. He began to feel depressed, anxious, and overwhelmed and also found it difficult to sleep and to focus on his work. He felt powerless over these feelings because he had never experienced them before.

Tom also found it hard to adjust to his solitary lifestyle. Although he had shared many of the household tasks with Mary before the divorce, there were many skills in maintaining a household that he had never learned.

Tom had been taught that real men were supposed to be able to handle hard times and that they never asked for help or talked about their painful emotions. As the depressed feelings increased, Tom began to feel more and more that he was a failure for letting something like this get to him.

Unfortunately, Tom began to use an old style of dealing with painful emotions: He began to drink. Drinking seemed to provide an escape for him from the pain; it numbed the feelings of depression, anxiety, failure.

Asking for professional help seemed out of the question. What can be done to make it easier for Tom, and other fathers like him, to seek support and guidance in dealing with the painful emotions experienced as part of nonresidential parenting?

This chapter will help the reader gain a clearer understanding of the special needs of nonresidential fathers. The chapter provides information on what issues should be covered by practitioners who wish to conduct a holistic assessment with nonresidential fathers. The purpose of this chapter is to help the reader to

- Describe the special needs of nonresidential fathers
- Identify the various barriers that exist to fathers receiving help
- Identify the areas that should be included in a holistic assessment of nonresidential fathers
- Identify the various gender biases that exist in assessment and intervention

It has been well researched and documented that children often experience significant adjustment problems when their parents separate or divorce (Amato, 1994; Guidubaldi & Cleminshaw, 1985; Hetherington, Cox, & Cox, 1978). Our society is very concerned about how children make it through this very difficult time. As a result many wonderful programs have been developed to help children cope when their parents separate. There are even programs to help children deal with their feelings about absent fathers or mothers in situations in which the absent parent never lived in the home. These types of programs are necessary and help millions of children adjust better to the losses they have experienced.

Other studies have focused on the pain and anguish that mothers experience as a result of divorce or separation. We know that women often go through a wide range of negative reactions as a result of a breakup, including depression, anxiety, hopelessness, and feeling overwhelmed by the situation (cf. Kitson & Roach, 1989; Lorenz et al., 1997). Because of these findings, special outreach efforts and intervention programs have been established in order to provide single mothers with extra emotional and financial support and guidance to get them through these difficult times. Once again, these types of programs are necessary and have been a critical ingredient in the successful adjustment of millions of women following divorce or separation. However, as with any social problem, there is still room for improvement in the way we provide services for mothers and children.

How has our society fared in providing services to the final member of the family, the father? What do we know of the special issues and needs of the father following separation or divorce? What special programs are available to meet those special needs? Unfortunately, the answer to these questions is the same: Not very much. Research on divorce and separation adjustment has traditionally focused on the children and the mother, while only limited attention has been paid to the adjustment issues that fathers face following a divorce (Dudley, 1991c) or separation. As Kruk (1994) notes "there is a considerable body of literature concerning the impact of divorce on mothers and children; fathers' views and interpretations of the events surrounding divorce represent a significant lacuna in the research" (p. 18).

THE SPECIAL NEEDS OF FATHERS AFTER DIVORCE AND SEPARATION

Much of what we believe to be true about adjustment issues for divorced, separated, or never-married fathers comes not from scientific research, but rather from myths and stereotypes perpetuated by TV, radio, movies, newspapers and magazines. If we were to believe the images presented to us by the media, we would generally hold that nonresidential fathers have very little problem adjusting to less frequent contact with their children. These fathers are the so-called runaway dads, the disappearing father, and the deadbeat dad. How could men who engage in such irresponsible behavior be experiencing any sort of pain as a result of a breakup and spending less time with their offspring—isn't that what they really want? In fact, we could be led to believe that men really don't desire the responsibility that comes with fathering and that given the opportunity they will jump for joy once this burden is removed. If we are seeking the true story of what life is like for nonresidential fathers, we need to turn off the TV for a while and review the literature.

One of the earliest studies of fathers after divorce was completed by Hetherington, Cox, and Cox (1976). In their study they were able to identify three primary problem areas for fathers after divorce: (1) those related to the practical problems of daily living; (2) interpersonal problems in the areas of social life, intimate relationships, and in relating to the children and former spouse; and (3) problems related to self-concept and identity. This study was one of the first to suggest that divorcing fathers often experience their own form of stress and pain. The study also challenged many of the stereotypes that exist about divorced fathers, such as the one that fathers of divorce thoroughly enjoy their "wild" new single life and that fathers of divorce feel little loss over reduced contact with their children. Perhaps the most surprising aspect of this study is that despite its shedding light more than 30 years ago on what nonresidential fathers really go through, many of the myths and stereotypes persist today.

In a review of the literature on adjustment of fathers after divorce, McKenry and Price (1990) found there was increasing evidence suggesting that because of their traditional sex role socialization, men are particularly vulnerable to many negative consequences of divorce. It was their belief that men are often less able to cope with the emotional consequences due to their limited socialization for how to deal with such losses. For example, a common expectation of men is that they not show their painful emotions; i.e., real men don't cry. However there are certain types of situations in which relief and moving on psychologically can be accomplished only by working out painful emotions. In a sense, the socialization mechanisms that work to make men tough could eventually make a man uniquely vulnerable to catastrophic losses. McKenry and Price (1990) also point out that fatherhood itself may increase the problems that men experience after divorce. Since the vast majority of fathers (around 90%) will lose physical custody of their children (like Tom in our case example), divorce for men often means the loss of their relationship with their children. As one recently divorced father stated,

> I was completely devastated by the loss of day-to-day contact with my kids. Maybe I wasn't the perfect husband, but I am a great father. Why am I being penalized for what I can't do as a husband? Why am I only a "visitor" now?

It is evident from this father's statement and from the case example that for the noncustodial parent, divorce and separation will usually lead to multiple losses. After the breakup, the father will usually lose his home and neighborhood, his daily routine, his typical social supports, and unfortunately he often will experience the loss of a meaningful relationship with his children (McKenry & Price, 1990). As a result it is quite common for fathers to experience social isolation, loneliness, and depression. The importance of the research by McKenry and Price is that it was one of the first to suggest that not only do men experience pain as the result of divorce, but also in some ways their adjustment may be more difficult at times because they are men.

Further "myth-busting" concerning men's adjustment after divorce and separation can be found in Braver and O'Connell's book, *Divorced Dads: Shattering the Myths* (1998). Although the primary emphasis of this book was to dispel myths about father-child contact and fathers' financial support to their children, Braver did devote a chapter to the notion that divorced fathers have it easy emotionally after divorce, that only their ex-wives and children are distressed. The case study at the beginning of this chapter provides an excellent example of what life is really like for many men after separation or divorce. The fictional character Tom in the case example demonstrates many of the adjustment issues that Braver (1998) notes in his book. For example, he notes that one study (Price & McKenry, 1988) found that the suicide rates for divorced men were 5 times higher than for married men and significantly higher than the suicide rates for divorced women. Perhaps an explanation for this difference can be found in Weitzman's observation (1985) that women "are likely to find their lives after divorce better and more satisfying" (p. 345). Weitzman suggests that in general women feel better about themselves, their work, and their parenting skills after divorce than men.

The evidence seems clear that fathers do need special interventions following separation or divorce, yet little guidance exists in the professional literature on how to treat the nonresidential father who is going through the pains of separation from his children. The intent of the rest of this chapter is to explore issues related to the assessment and intervention with nonresidential fathers.

Reflection
Do you think that fathers may have more difficulty adjusting to divorce than mothers? If so, why? If not, why not?

ASSESSMENT OF NONRESIDENTIAL FATHERS

Overarching Conceptual Framework: Ecological Systems Model

As any good human-service practitioner will tell you, a thorough assessment must precede any intervention efforts. In dealing with nonresidential fathers, we believe that a holistic assessment of the father and his family is needed early in the helping process. This type of assessment is best developed through the use of an *ecological systems model*. Within an ecological systems model, practitioners are able to identify the various system levels in need of intervention (individual, family, group, community, etc.) and develop the specific strategies to be employed. In an ecological systems assessment, all of the factors relevant to a father's involvement with his children are to be identified along with an understanding of the relationships among these factors.

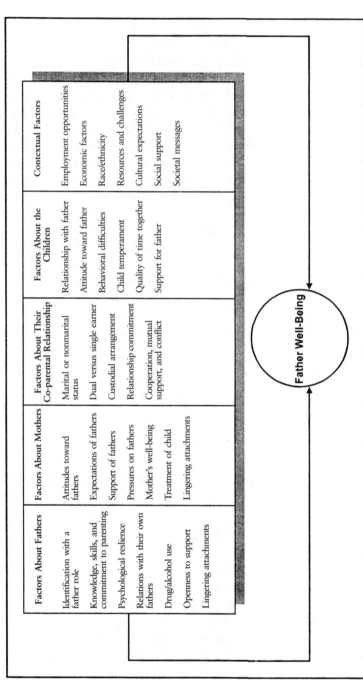

FIGURE 5.1 Model of father psychological well-being (derived from Doherty Model).

Note: From "Responsible Fathering: An Overview and Conceptual Framework," by William Doherty, Edward Kouneski, and Martha Erickson, *Journal of Marriage and Family, 60*(2). Copyright 1998 by the National Council on Family Relations, 3839 Central Ave. NE, Suite 550, Minneapolis, MN 55421. Reprinted by permission.

Although an assessment may focus primarily on the father, it is important to examine past and present environment factors. For example, his relationship with the child's mother, whether they actually lived together, and his relationship with the maternal grandparents can be extremely relevant in understanding the father's current attitudes, behavior, and circumstances.

Doherty's model for responsible fathering mentioned in chapter 2 provides a rudimentary understanding of the multiple factors that influence a father's well-being after divorce and separation. Figure 5.1 represents a reconfiguration of Doherty's model to reflect father adjustment. There is justification for linking the father's well-being after divorce or separation with responsible fathering, as some studies have shown a connection between the two (Stone & McKenry, 1998).

As can be seen in the figure, numerous factors can affect the psychological well-being of fathers following divorce or separation. The model provides a useful tool for gathering relevant information across various system levels to determine the factors that may be influencing the father's current level of functioning. Practitioners would need to assess the father's own psychological factors, as well as the influence of the child and the child's mother. The model also points out the need to assess societal and community issues that might influence the father's psychological well-being (see the issues under Contextual Factors in Figure 5.1). While this is by no means an exhaustive list of all the factors that might affect father psychological well-being, it does provide a useful list of topics that could be explored in an assessment of a nonresidential father.

Developmental Perspective

It is our belief that it is vitally important for those working with nonresidential fathers to remember that relationships develop over time and often go through a series of stages that affect those involved in the relationship. Fathers may have differential adjustments based on the type and stage of relationship they had with the mother of their children. In addition, the age of the child at the point of separation or divorce can be a critical factor in determining the child's adjustment and the quality of the father-child relationship. Children view and handle divorce in different ways based upon their stage of development.

Bray and Berger (1993) recommend using a developmental family systems model of divorce and remarriage for conducting assessments.

Although not all fathers will be married to the mother of their children, there are still merits in using the model developed by Bray and Berger. They remind us that the factors affecting a father's involvement with his children will vary depending upon the stage that the family is currently in, what has occurred in the past, and what will happen (or is expected to happen) in the future. In conducting an assessment of a nonresidential father, relevant factors need to be considered during several stages including the marriage (or coupling), the process of separation and divorce (or uncoupling), after divorce (or uncoupling), and during remarriage if either parent remarries (recoupling). It is important to remember that the relationships among family members can change over time, sometimes dramatically and that the circumstances of one stage are likely to affect attitudes and behaviors in later stages.

Emphasis on Strengths

We have repeatedly called for a strengths perspective in viewing the role of fathers in the families. It is our belief that it is important to use this perspective when completing an assessment with a nonresidential father as well. Just because he may be at a point in which the problems seem overwhelming does not mean that we focus completely on the litany of presenting problems. In contrast to a problem-based approach, many workers helping families are adopting a strengths perspective. In regard to assessment, this perspective moves workers away from focusing on deficits and redirects them toward "eliciting and articulating clients' internal and external resources" (Saleeby, 1992, p. 3). In essence, the worker begins to highlight what is right in a client's life rather than the traditional focus on what is wrong. Many see the shift from a deficit model to a strengths perspective as a necessary step to empowerment.

When we apply the strengths perspective to assessment of nonresidential fathers, the worker's actions are guided by these specific purposes: (1) clarify the unique capacities, skills, motivations, and potential of the father; (2) clarify the characteristics of the environment that influence the father's coping and adaptive patterns; and (3) clarify what needs to be changed in the father or the environment in order to make the fathers' transactions more mutually satisfying and growth-producing (adapted from Libassi & Maluccio, 1986). Furthermore, empowering assessment means looking for resources, both outside the father as well as within.

Assessment Questions

In summary, numerous questions can be important to ask in a holistic, developmental, and strength-based assessment. Questions should take into account the past as well as the current stages of the family's life. Whenever possible, these questions should be asked of both parents and in some cases it may be appropriate to involve the children. Some types of questions—such as ones about the quality of the relationship between the parents and the extent of the father's involvement in parenting—are asked at every stage (Bray & Berger, 1993).

1. During the marriage/coupling period:

- What were the strengths and weaknesses of the relationship?
- How long did the relationship last? What was the extent of the parents' commitment to each other and to the children?
- How old were the children when the separation occurred?
- What were father-child and mother-child relations like?
- How involved were the father and the mother?
- What parental roles did each play?
- How did the father perceive his role? What did he consider the most important aspects of his role as father (e.g., guidance, emotional support, recreational, etc.)
- What cultural or other diversity issues are important to consider? (e.g., religious factors, gender roles, cultural meaning of marriage and divorce, economic factors)

2. During the separation or divorce process:

- Did one parent leave the other or was it a mutual decision?
- How well did the nonresidential father adjust to no longer living with his children?
- If there was a divorce, what type of divorce proceedings were followed?
- What legal decisions were made about custody, visitation, and child support?
- What other legal issues were important?
- If there was a divorce, how did the legal proceedings and decisions of divorce affect cooperation between the parents?
- How did the separation or divorce process psychologically affect each family member?

- What were parent-child relations like during this period?
- What was the nature of the father's and mother's parental involvement?
- What parental roles did each assume?
- To what extent does the children's mother value the father as a parent and value his parenting ability?
- To what extent does he value the parenting ability of the children's mother?
- To what extent are the father and mother able to set aside their personal feelings for each other as former intimates and still evaluate each other objectively as parents?
- How does the father perceive his role as changing? How is he adapting to these changes?
- How does the father's culture view divorce? Is his culture accepting and supportive or more disapproving and blaming?

3. After separation or divorce:

- How have parent-child relations and the extent of parental involvement changed?
- How well has the nonresidential father adjusted to living separate from his children?
- If there was a divorce, have the divorce proceedings and decisions continued to affect the father and his relationship with his former spouse and his children?
- Have other legal issues affected the father and his relationship with his children?
- How has he psychologically adjusted to the separation or divorce?
- How have the two households been arranged? To what extent does it reflect a bi-nuclear family system?
- How are the grandparents and other extended family members involved and how do they affect the family system?
- What is the state of each parent's emotional health? Any evidence of depression, addiction, violence, etc.?
- What is the state of the children's mental health? Any evidence of school, sexual, interpersonal, or other problems?
- What is the economic status of each parent? Do they have stable, well-paying employment?
- How have the father's roles changed as a result of the separation? How committed is he to his various parenting roles (e.g.,

provider, disciplinarian, nurturer)? How satisfied is he with his current father roles?

- How important are these roles to him in relation to his other roles (e.g., worker, new husband, stepfather)?
- To what extent does his view of his fathering correspond with the views of his former spouse and others who are important to him? (Others could include his children, a new lover or spouse, coworkers, etc.).
- To what extent does he receive positive encouragement for his parenting behavior from other people in his life, such as a lover or new wife, his friends, coworkers, employers, etc.
- Is there considerable distance between the parents' households? Was the change in the location of households worked out cooperatively?
- What special supports (if any) are offered by the father's culture?

4. Remarriage or recoupling of either parent:

- Did either parent get remarried or begin to cohabit with someone?
- How well did family members resolve psychological issues in the previous relationship and to what extent were unresolved issues brought into the new relationship?
- How has the remarriage or recoupling affected other family members?
- How did family members adjust to their new roles in the step-family?
- How did the new stepfamily affect the other parent's involvement with the children?
- How did the parenting roles change after the remarriage or recoupling?
- How does the father's culture view remarriage and recoupling? Is his culture accepting and supportive or more disapproving and blaming?

Reflection
How would you work to establish a good rapport with a father during the assessment phase? What methods would you use to increase his willingness to respond to very personal questions? How will you keep from getting frustrated if your questions are not answered initially?

Special Assessment Topics to Explore With Divorcing and Separating Fathers

In addition to the broad-based assessment questions discussed in the previous section, it is also critical for workers to explore two areas that are of particular concern when dealing with fathers who are attempting to cope with the ending of a relationship: suicide and chemical abuse. We will discuss each of these issues and provide suggestions for assessment in this section.

SUICIDE

There is strong evidence that men who are undergoing an intense breakup of their families are much more likely to commit suicide. One study found that divorced men have suicide rates that are 5 times higher than for married men and that divorced men have significantly higher suicide rates than divorced women (Price & McKenry, 1988). These findings present an interesting challenge to the myth we discussed earlier, that is, that divorced men have an easy time with the breakup. In reality, it seems that fathers often may have higher levels of difficulty with the separation or divorce than the mother. Why would this be? Some authors, like Hall and Kelly (1996), suggest that the distress fathers experience is not so much over the breakup with the partner as it is with the loss of their children. Based on this perspective, it seems imperative that workers assess the degree of loss that the father is experiencing as a result of the separation from his children. Following are some assessment questions that might help explore this topic:

- How has the divorce or separation affected the amount of time that you have with your children?
- How are you coping with this reduced contact?
- Sometimes when fathers have less time with their children they start to feel a little down or depressed. Have you experienced any of these feelings?
- How would you rate the depression that you have experienced recently on a scale from 1 to 10, with 1 being not very depressed and 10 being very depressed?
- How do you deal with these depressed feelings? What helps you?

- Sometimes when people feel very depressed they start to have all kinds of thoughts about what do to in order to make things better. Sometimes people even have thoughts about hurting themselves. Have you had any thoughts like that?

If the father says yes to thoughts about suicide, then the worker should explore the issues with the standard questions regarding frequency of thoughts, seriousness of thoughts, whether the father has a plan, whether he has the means to carry out such a plan, etc. You can assess issues of anger and anxiety related to suicide in the same manner. These same questions are addressed when assessing for chemical abuse and addiction.

CHEMICAL ABUSE AND ADDICTION

There is also concern that men are much more likely to engage in a wide range of risky health behaviors, including chemical abuse following the break up of their family (Umberson, 1987). Some believe that this increase in chemical abuse is related to the parental role strain that results from being a nonresidential father (Umberson & Williams, 1993). In essence, the theory is that nonresidential fathering has built-in challenges that create stress. For example, nonresidential fathers no longer have a wife available to facilitate father-child interactions. Many men may not be prepared to take on sole responsibility for supervision of their young children, and there are no widely accepted norms or guidelines for nonresidential fathering (McKenry & Price, 1990). Fathers may be unclear about how to parent from a distance, particularly if their fathering behaviors were predominately shared activities (for example, the recreational fathering role). These types of shared activities become more difficult, if not impossible, when the father is relegated to a visiting role. This type of role strain and role confusion can lead to increased stress and potentially reduced contact between father and child (Stone & McKenry, 1998). Umberson and Williams (1993) also suggest that role strain can develop because of the need for continued contact between the nonresidential father and the child's mother in order to maintain contact with the child. If there are unresolved conflicts between the parents, the ongoing contact can become a source of additional stress. Finally, nonresidential fathers may feel a sense of guilt as a result of their own perception that they are not performing their role adequately (Umberson & Williams, 1993). These various stressors can create a situation in which fathers may turn to self-destructive ways of coping. We discussed suicide in the previous section as one dysfunctional way of coping with loss. Fathers may also resort to chemical abuse or addiction. As one father responded in the study by Umberson and Williams (1993): "I drink more now that I'm divorced. . . . I go out to a honky-tonk every other Sunday, I guarantee, after my kids leave, because I'm depressed. I mean, it's hard to see 'em go" (p. 395).

This father's comments provide us with some direction for the types of assessment questions we want to ask in order to evaluate whether the father may be having a problem with chemical abuse or addiction. The questions that we asked initially to assess for suicide potential will also be helpful in assessing chemical issues:

- How has the divorce or separation affected the amount of time that you have with your children?
- How are you coping with this reduced contact?
- Sometimes when fathers have less time with their children they start to feel a little down or depressed. Have you experienced any of these feelings?
- How would you rate the depression that you have experienced recently on a scale from 1 to 10, with 1 being not very depressed and 10 being very depressed.
- How do you deal with these depressed feelings? What helps you?

In addition to questions about depression, it is also important to inquire into issues of anxiety and anger:

- Sometimes fathers talk about feeling anger over how things are going in their lives, especially when it comes to limited access to their children. Have you experienced any feelings of anger? How do you deal with these feelings?
- Sometimes fathers say that they feel very tense or nervous about their life as a nonresidential father. Have you experienced any feelings like this? How do you handle them?

Once a baseline level of information is gathered about levels of distress, the worker can focus on issues specific to chemical abuse:

- Sometimes when people are under a great deal of stress they look for different ways to find relief. One way is to use alcohol or drugs. Have you tried to deal with any of your stress this way?

Once it is established that the father is using chemicals to deal with the stress, a traditional assessment can take place. Questions can be used to explore the types of chemicals used, the extent of the use, ability to control their use, degree that usage interferes with other aspects of their lives, family history of chemical use, etc.

In summary, nonresidential fathering has built-in stressors and challenges that can lead men to cope in self-destructive ways. These periods can be especially challenging for men because of the socialization process they undergo that stifles open expression of pain and asking for help. As Rubin (1983) noted, women are expected to express their emotions; men are expected to control and smother their feelings. For many of these fathers, their efforts to avoid dealing openly with their sadness, loss, anger, and fear may ultimately lead them to engage in various risky and self-destructive behaviors. It is the role of the worker to assess these issues and develop appropriate intervention plans.

Diagraming an Assessment

"Eco-maps" are widely used visual aids to assist in assessment. An eco-map is comprised of circles, each representing systems that transact with a client, which may be sources of support or conflict. Systems with which the client has no contact may also be included in an eco-map if the client needs to develop a relationship with the system. Information about the client's relationships with agencies, employers, church, school and other organizations, relatives, friends, and neighbors is plotted on a one-page circular chart. The lines from client to outside individuals and groups are drawn to indicate supportive or conflictual relationships. A graphic picture of our case example of Tom's support system is illustrated in Figure 5.2. As the figure shows, Tom is involved in a stressful relationship with his former spouse, Mary. Work is also a source of stress as well as his relationship with his parents and the maternal grandparents (Mary's parents). There are sources of support in Tom's life, including his church, his daughter, and his best friend, Jeffrey. The relationship with his own grandparents is skewed in the sense that he gives more than he receives in that relationship. As can be seen through this example, information gained

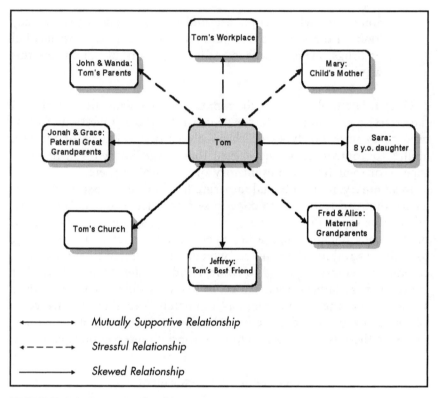

FIGURE 5.2 Eco-map for Tom.

from Tom's eco-map can be used to identify problematic relationships that could be improved and to identify the need for making new supportive relationships. The map also shows the relationship strengths that exist for Tom's use as he attempts to adjust to the separation from his children.

In addition to eco-maps, practitioners may also find it helpful to use the Social Network Map developed by Tracy and Whittaker (1990), which is another tool for assessing social support. Workers assist clients in developing a picture of their social support network based on a self-report. To use this tool, fathers would first identify their support network (including family, friends, neighbors, workplace, etc.). Next, by using a sorting technique and responding to specific questions, fathers would describe how they perceive the support they receive from others. For example, we explore Tom's report that his best friend,

Jeffrey, was a source of support by asking more specific questions about the type of support that Jeffrey offered. Types of support to explore include emotional, concrete, and information or advice. Tom would then need to specify the degree of support in each category. For example, we would ask Tom to characterize the degree of emotional support he received from Jeffrey as: (1) hardly ever supportive; (2) sometimes supportive; or (3) almost always supportive. It can be seen from this example that the Social Network Map can give much more detailed information about Tom's support system. Practitioners wishing to explore this method in more depth should see Tracy and Whittaker (1990).

Reflection
Construct an eco-map of your own life. What areas are truly a source of support? What areas drain energy from you? Consider how to use this type of assessment tool with your clients. How might it be helpful?

GENDER ISSUES IN ASSESSMENT AND INTERVENTIONS

It is generally accepted that clinical interventions often function to enforce the status quo as it pertains to women. More specifically, many have charged that counseling therapy has attempted to constrain changes in social and vocational roles for women. Chesler (1972) was perhaps the first to suggest that therapy functioned in many ways as an agent of social control by which women were rewarded for passivity and punished for social deviance by being labeled as sick. For example, women are socialized to believe that they are responsible for almost everything that keeps a family operating smoothly, such as housework and child care (Eichler, 1997). When a counselor intervenes with a family she or he may place this expectation on the mother inadvertently or intentionally. It may be in the form of how questions are phrased or who is asked certain questions. The worker may look only to the mother to respond to questions about the well-being of the children or about the general emotional atmosphere of the family. The woman may be labeled as an unfit wife or mother if she is unable to respond adequately to these questions. This type of questioning can serve to reinforce the notion that women are to be viewed only as the nurturer or the communications gatekeeper in a family. It may detract from the woman's other roles outside the home, such as provider. These types of counseling behaviors can best be viewed as gender-biased and certainly are not examples of gender-sensitive practice.

Collins, Jordan, and Coleman (1999) note that gender-sensitive practice with families "advocates sensitivity to the problems created when rigid, traditional gender roles are assigned to family members" (p. 201). It seems clear from the previous examples that women have long been victims of gender-*insensitive* practice. It is only recently that researchers and practitioners have started to consider the ways in which traditional counseling and therapy interventions may also be gender-insensitive toward men. In a study by Robertson and Fitzgerald (1990), practicing counselors and therapists were randomly assigned to view one of two versions of a videotaped role-play of a depressed male client, portrayed by a professional actor. The tapes were identical except for the client's occupation and family roles, which were depicted as either gender-traditional or nontraditional. After viewing the tapes, the practitioners evaluated the client on various dimensions, specified a diagnosis, and generated a treatment plan. The researchers found that practitioners were much more likely to diagnose severe psychopathology when a male chose not to engage in the stereotypical good-provider role. Clearly, practitioners in this study may have been applying rigid, traditional gender roles to these men, a practice not conducive to the type of gender-sensitive practice advocated by Collins and associates (1999).

What would gender-sensitive practice look like when applied to men? What would be the key elements, and what strategies would be used? What pitfalls should a worker try to avoid? What special treatment issues exist for men who are nonresidential fathers that might be overlooked due to gender-insensitive practice? In the following sections we will attempt to address these and other questions.

A Gender-Sensitive Model

Norman and Wheeler (1996) propose a practice model for social work practitioners that perhaps is applicable across disciplines. They maintain that much of the theory and practice literature is filled with unidimensional models of assessment and intervention. This one-size-fits-all mentality of assessment and intervention is not appropriate for gender-sensitive work with women or men. As they state:

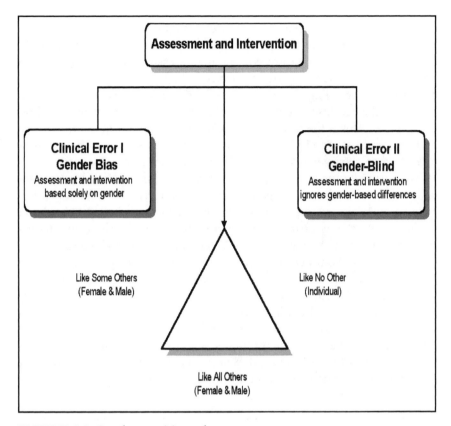

FIGURE 5.3 Gender-sensitive schema.

Note: From "Gender-Sensitive Social Work Practice: A Model for Education," by J. Norman and B. Wheeler, *Journal of Social Work Education, 32*(2), pp. 203–213. Copyright 1996 by Council on Social Work Education, Alexandria, VA. Reprinted by permission.

Neither females [n]or males should be subjected to unidimensional, inflexible models of psychosocial assessment and intervention. . . . Practitioners must keep in mind that each individual is unique, with unique experiences, perceptions, feelings, and behaviors, and yet has much in common with other human beings. (p. 208)

Figure 5.3 illustrates their schema and provides an initial conceptual framework within which practitioners can adapt their current assessment and intervention models. As the figure clearly demonstrates, there are two fundamental errors that workers might make with clients. The first, *gender bias,* refers to the tendency of some workers to see only gender issues when they are completing assessments and intervention plans. Using this lens exclusively leads the worker to make erroneous assumptions regarding the basis of a client's behavior by attributing the origins of the actions to gender differences when in fact they are based on other issues. This is the factor that was probably at work in the Robertson and Fitzgerald study (1990) in which practitioners evaluated men pathological when they were engaged in nontraditional role behaviors.

The second type of error, *gender blind,* is failing to take into account those situations in which the client's concerns stem from gender-based issues. An example of this view can be found in the work on intimacy and the assertion that perhaps there is more than one definition of intimacy, a female-defined version and a male-defined one (Baumeister & Sommer, 1997). Practitioners often apply the female intimacy yardstick in assessing male behaviors, when in fact we may be dealing with true gender differences about what constitutes intimacy rather than a "healthy" versus "unhealthy" typology. These two types of clinical errors lead to misunderstandings and inappropriate interventions. They have a rippling effect throughout the three dimensions discussed by Norman and Wheeler (1996). We will explore each of these three dimensions and the issues related to gender-sensitive work with fathers within each.

Reflection 5.4

Consider your own gender biases and how they might affect your work with fathers and with mothers. What will you do in order to overcome these biases?

Within the model, practitioners should remember that an individual is (a) *like no other* human being, (b) *like some others* (other females or other males), and (c) *like all others* in the human community (female and male). These three concepts form the basis for their three-dimensional approach to working with females and males.

LIKE NO OTHER

One of the first issues to consider when assessing and intervening with fathers is to remember that they are unique individuals with their own issues and perceptual realities. A father's life may be more different than similar to the lives of others (nonfathers, mothers, children). The fact that the client is a father does not mean that he shares the same opinions, views, perceptions as other men or even other fathers. Norman and Wheeler (1996) assert that workers must "personalize assessment data and avoid the pitfalls of categories, stereotypes, and classifications" (p. 209). Unfortunately, the research and practice worlds are filled with negative stereotypes about men in general and fathers in particular. For example, one need only review recent literature related to fathering to understand the problem. One of the more frequent portrayals of fathers in research is that of victimizer. The common theme within this type of research is to describe situations in which fathers are perpetrators of incest and physical and emotional abuse (Fong & Walsh-Bowers, 1998; Veach, 1997; Wyndham, 1998). This is not to say that these events do not occur or that they should not be researched. Every effort should be made to eliminate these types of harmful behaviors. The problem is that until very recently very little was offered as a contrasting view of men and fathers presented in the literature.

In 1996, Raffoul and McNeece edited a book entitled *Future Issues for Social Work Practice*. This book contained 27 chapters of practice concerns for the new millennium; seemingly a perfect opportunity to advocate for a new role for men in families. Unfortunately, the most visible way that men were discussed within this book was in a chapter entitled, "The Single Greatest Health Threat to Women: Their Partners" (Nurius, Hilfrink, & Rifino, 1996). Again, it is not our intention to dispute statistics that clearly document the harm that some men inflict on some women. Rather, it is a question of balance and of recognizing that each of our clients is "like no other" (Norman & Wheeler, 1996), that individual fathers do not necessarily resemble the men portrayed in the literature and the popular media. Each is unique with his own set of issues and strengths. Regrettably, it may be too easy simply to overgeneralize from such studies and come to believe that most fathers who are attempting to stay involved with their children after separation or divorce are doing so because of unhealthy reasons. A worker who desires to provide the best possible services to fathers will need to put aside such preconceptions and realize that it is vital to listen to the father's concerns with an open mind and open heart.

Other researchers have attempted to focus on actual fathering behaviors in order to demonstrate that a wide range of variation exists in how each individual father engages in fathering and therefore is like no other. In a study by Jain, Belsky, and Crane (1996) four different types of dads were identified: caretakers, playmates-teachers, disciplinarians, and disengaged fathers. Caretaker fathers engaged their children mainly in routine basic care activities, including dressing, feeding, and comforting. The playmate-teacher father focused on playful interactions and engaged in instrumental activities such as labeling and demonstrating things to the child. Disciplinarian fathers engaged more in correcting their children's behaviors, controlling, and socializing the child than in any caretaking, playing, or teaching activities, while the disengaged father remained detached and failed to participate in any activities with the child. Stone and McKenry (1998) noted how different fathering types could be linked to ongoing father contact with their children after divorce. In their typology, nurturing nonresidential fathers who de-emphasized the recreational components of fathering were more likely to maintain contact with their children after divorce. It seems critical for the worker to complete a thorough assessment regarding the type of fathering behaviors enacted by the father-client and how each is different from the others. Strengths and areas of need can be determined that could lead to a wide range of intervention strategies.

Reflection
A considerable amount of time has been spent discussing the need to assess areas of strength within fathers. How will you ensure that you spend an adequate amount of time discussing father strengths? How will you deal with fathers who feel as if they have no strengths?

LIKE SOME OTHERS

According to Norman and Wheeler (1996), all people belong to subgroups or categories. Gender is one of those categories and it is therefore appropriate and necessary to consider it in assessments and interventions. In essence, we can make some generalizations based upon gender, biological and socialization factors which contribute to commonalities among men. Of course, the debate is which ones and to what degree. When we engage in such generalizations we must be constantly aware that there is a thin line between helpful generalizations and unhelpful stereotyping. It is a difficult process to master, but it has its place in individual work with fathers.

Some of these commonalities can be observed in how fathers tend to enact their parenting role as compared to women. Research has shown that fathers tend to interact with their children in a way that is different than mothers' interactions. Fathers tend to spend a greater portion of their time with their children in playful interactions, even when conducting caretaking activities (Fish, New, & VanCleve, 1992). In essence, fathers are much more likely to serve in a playmate role with their children (Tiedje & Darling-Fisher, 1993). Snarey's (1993) multigenerational research identified several commonalities in the way that fathers related to their children. These similarities included such behaviors as playing games, going on outings, providing enrichment programs and lessons, teaching athletic skills, and verbal play. In practical terms, a worker may find it necessary to think twice before judging a father harshly for only playing with the kids.

LIKE ALL OTHERS

Finally, we must acknowledge that as human beings we share common issues that make us like all others. There are commonalities that connect us all. Norman and Wheeler assert that most assessments and intervention models do an adequate job of addressing this third dimension. Whether we are talking about psychodynamic models of intervention or cognitive-behavioral models, most theoretical orientations are quite adept at pointing out ways in which we are similar.

When we apply this concept to the special case of the nonresidential father, we recognize that he is like all others in his need for support, resources, and hope for the future. Nonresidential fathers and residential mothers can share a common love that they have for their child. This common love may very well be the starting point from which a worker can begin to make headway in establishing an effective co-parenting relationship between the father and the child's mother following separation or divorce.

In summary, Norman and Wheeler's framework for establishing gender-sensitive practice is an important starting point for workers to consider before they begin working with nonresidential fathers. The framework reminds workers to keep an open mind about their own gender biases and preconceptions that might interfere with their work

---

Perspective: Gender Biases in Services

What would you do if you worked at a homeless shelter and saw another worker tell a woman that she could not come into the shelter with her 4-year-old child unless she had a verifiable birth certificate or other documented proof that the child was related to her? Rasheed (1999) reports that while this would never happen to a mother attempting to enter a Chicago-based shelter, it is the standard procedure for fathers. Rasheed reports that there is only one shelter in the Chicago area that would accept a father without this type of documentation. Rasheed calls such biases gendered obstacles and asserts that they can actually interfere with the parental role of poor, residential and nonresidential fathers. Can you think of any other examples? What do you think could or should be done about such obstacles?

---

with fathers. It also provides a useful framework for developing highly individualized assessment and intervention strategies for fathers. Once a thorough assessment has been completed, workers can pursue an effective intervention strategy. Practitioners can use a variety of techniques to complete this assessment; however, there is a need for workers to avoid focusing only on the father's problems, but to include a review of his strengths. Chapter 6 discusses the various general intervention strategies that could be used with fathers including individual, family, and group interventions.

Questions for Discussion

1. Locate a nonresidential father and complete an eco-map with him. What did you learn from this experience? What did the father learn from the experience?

2. What strengths would you anticipate finding when working with nonresidential fathers? How would you explore these strengths?

3. What types of cultural beliefs could ease a father's transition during the separation process? What types of cultural beliefs might impede the process?

4. In your own words, describe what is meant by an ecological systems assessment with nonresidential fathers.

6

Individual, Family, and Group Services for Nonresidential Fathers

I can't go for counseling, people will think I'm weak. . . . and I already feel like a failure because of the divorce. (Tom, case example from chapter 5)

This chapter will help the reader gain a clearer understanding of the basic principles and skills involved in helping nonresidential fathers in individual counseling, family work, and groups. Special issues relevant to providing services to men will be explored with suggestions on effective programming and techniques that are useful when providing services to fathers. The purpose of this chapter is to help readers

- Increase their knowledge of biases that exist in working with fathers
- Apply a gender-sensitive approach to practice with fathers
- Increase their knowledge of working with fathers individually, in families, and in groups
- Apply theory to practice with fathers

In the following chapter we will explore various types of intervention techniques that may prove useful in working with nonresidential fathers. It will also become obvious that many of these strategies may prove beneficial to men in general. Once again, we will try to incorporate a strengths perspective in the intervention programs that we will discuss. Because only one chapter in our book deals with the overall intervention strategies to use with men, there is a limit to the depth of information that can be provided. This section should be viewed as an effort to provide a broad overview of some of the basic ingredients that go into successful interventions with nonresidential fathers.

INDIVIDUAL WORK WITH FATHERS

In this section we will identify the various challenges that a worker will experience when attempting to provide services to fathers. In chapter 1, we discussed the binds that men experience as they attempt to enact their roles (Goldberg, 1976). Many of these binds are reflected in the challenges that men face as they consider pursuing help from professionals. In the following pages we will explore several of these challenges and discuss various techniques that might help overcome the particular challenge.

Challenge 1: The Fear of Being Seen as a Failure

A typical obstacle for men and fathers seeking help is the perception they have that others may view them as failures (Jordan, 1992). It is often the case that the father will simply hold the view that it is unacceptable even to admit to having problems and that it would be unmanly to seek help from anyone (Heppner & Gonzales, 1987). Some have suggested that male clients may have a more difficult time asking for help from a male worker, as this would mean admitting one's inadequacies and unmanliness to another male.

Efforts to overcome this barrier to treatment may involve helping the father to save face. Scher (1979) notes that it is imperative for workers to be sensitive and to understand the pride of the male client. In social work practice, we call this starting where the client is. Every effort should be made to encourage the male client to talk about the fear of being seen as weak or as a failure. It is especially important to allow the father to talk about strengths as well as areas in need of improvement. As we have discussed throughout this book, the strengths perspective is a way of equalizing the helping relationship and of encouraging fathers to look inward to discover their own resources. As a practitioner, it is quite possible to identify strengths that the father may possess and make it a point to allow the father to expand on these strengths in order to lessen his feelings of inadequacy. For example, one father who entered counseling owned an auto repair shop. The social worker made a point early on to acknowledge this strength and even posed a hypothetical car-problem question to the client. Allowing the client to feel helpful reduced his sense of failure and allowed a degree of face-saving that made further work possible. Furthermore, it is quite possible that when men help men a degree of modeling can take place in which the father-client is able to observe effective and appropriate ways to deal with painful emotions (Heppner & Gonzales, 1987). Goldberg (1976) identifies this as an issue connected with a man's need to appear autonomous and not need assistance from others.

Challenge 2: Difficulty in Identifying and Expressing Emotions and Emotional Processes

It could be said that the male socialization process has been very successful in producing men who can achieve at business, sports, and other competitive activities. However the trade-off is that men often learn not to feel, or to deny or to repress their emotional responses to life's events, in essence men experience an emotional bind (Goldberg, 1976; Heppner & Gonzales, 1987). There is a degree of functionality in not feeling when it comes to beating out another competitor for a top-paying job in the company. Feelings of empathy might be viewed as unnecessary baggage that could hold the competitive male back from advances in his career. However, not feeling can take its toll in the interpersonal domain of the father's life. Being taught not to feel and that it is wrong to express so called weak emotions (sadness, compassion, warmth) can certainly reduce a father's capacity to adjust to the multiple losses that a family breakup can bring. He may not have the words to express his loss or the tools to even process the loss. Levant (1992) discusses this problem as a mild form of *alexithymia*, which literally means "without words for emotions." For example one father in treatment talked about his suicidal thoughts over a recent event at work in which he was passed over for promotion. Upon further exploration, the social worker was able to discover that the father's job performance had been slipping as the result of a debilitating depression related to reduced contact with his children following a divorce. If the worker had taken the client's concerns at face value, they could have spent the entire session talking about the workplace. The skilled worker was able to help the father express his emotions and process how his depression was affecting his job performance.

Reflection

What is your opinion of Levant's concept of alexithymia? Do most men have problems using words to describe emotions? What has been your experience with this issue?

Efforts to help men deal with their emotional issues can be a challenging task for the worker. At times, it may be necessary to help men establish an affective vocabulary due to their limited ability to express emotions. To facilitate the learning process some workers actually provide their clients with handouts describing various emotional states. It has also been our experience that men may channel all their emotional energies through only two or three affective responses. A faculty member used to joke with his students in practice class that men are socialized to believe that there are only a few acceptable male emotions: anger, lust, and happiness. The handouts discussed earlier can be helpful in this area. It is also important that the worker be skilled in exploring underlying issues that men may carry with them. For example, one father was referred for counseling due to his problems with anger toward his former spouse. After developing a rapport and level of trust with the father, the worker was able to help the father discover that beneath his anger toward his former spouse there existed a deeper fear that he might be hurt and rejected by women in general and that these feelings were longstanding for him. A less skilled worker might have simply focused on anger-reduction techniques that did not address this father's deeper, more meaningful struggles.

Challenge 3: Reactions to Increased Intimacy in the Helping Relationship

This particular challenge results when the worker has been successful in his or her efforts to develop a working relationship with the father (Heppner & Gonzales, 1987). This represents something of a paradox in that the relationship is jeopardized *because* of the success. The father may experience a sense of fear related to this newfound closeness. In the case of male client–female worker situations, the father may confuse this intimacy with sexuality. This should not be a surprise given the socialization process for men and their tendency to believe that this type of closeness is reserved for sexual partners. In the case of male client and male worker, Heppner and Gonzales (1987) suggest that high intimacy levels between males may lead to a range of homophobic reactions. There is little documented evidence available to support this claim, but it seems worth noting.

In general, the best way to deal with intimacy issues within the client-worker relationship would seem to be a direct and honest discussion before they even become an issue. These types of discussions can be framed in a way that will lessen the sense that there is something wrong with them if clients start to experience these reactions. For example, one worker talked with her client about how oftentimes clients in counseling relationships may begin to have sexual feelings toward their worker. By normalizing and universalizing the feelings, this worker was able to have a productive talk with her client about worker-client intimacy versus sexual intimacy. It was helpful for the client because he was able to learn from her perspectives and was able to identify healthy ways to deal with his emotional reactions as well as learn ways to avoid sexualizing all male-female relationships.

Challenge 4: The Involuntary Father Client

Sometimes many fathers and men in general seek help because their friends, children, former spouses, or current lovers have threatened in some way that the father will lose that relationship if he doesn't change (Carlson, 1987). The threat may even come from an authority figure such as a court system that has mandated counseling. In any of these situations, the father may feel coerced into seeking help. Fathers in this position may show opposition to helping efforts. Many helping professionals are inclined to label as resistance client behaviors that outwardly seem to oppose the course which the practitioner desires (Hepworth, Rooney, & Larsen, 1997). The key factor for the worker is that they sense the client is deliberately refusing to cooperate. Unfortunately, workers have been too quick to apply this label and attribute failure of intervention to client resistance, when in fact the failed intervention may be the result of inappropriate or ineffective helping methods (Hepworth et al., 1997).

Rather than taking a blaming stance, workers could better serve fathers who are clients by remembering that resistance is to be expected in all clients. Anderson and Stewart (1983) remind us that resistance to change in general and resistance to being influenced in particular always occurs when individuals, groups, and systems are required by circumstances to alter their established behaviors (p. 1). We should also question what we really mean by resistance. Do we mean that fathers are resisting change or that fathers are resisting what workers want them to do? If the worker wants to go in one direction, and the father in another, who is resisting whom (Miley, O'Melia, & DuBois, 1998)? Resistence may be more an indication that the worker and client are not on the same page. It may reveal that the father is motivated to move in another direction.

Reflection

What are some possible ways that a worker may actually be responsible for the level of resistance a father evidences in a helping relationship? How could issues of the gender bias discussed in chapter 5 play a part in this problem?

Egan (1990) provides some helpful suggestions for workers who find themselves in a situation in which resistance is being communicated. We have adapted these to fit the father-as-client:

SEE RESISTANCE AS NORMAL

The worker should remember that it is quite understandable for fathers to exhibit seemingly resistant behaviors, given what we have discussed about the male socialization process. Rather than seeing this as an obstacle, the worker could use this as an opportunity to deal with some of the confining and restrictive teachings that the father may have endured as a male in this society. For example, we could talk with Tom (our father in the case example) about how very normal it is to be reluctant and uncomfortable talking about his problems since men aren't supposed to even have problems. This could be a significant point for building rapport in the relationship.

SEE RESISTANT BEHAVIORS AS AVOIDANCE

Rather than quickly attributing the resistant behaviors to some underlying bad feeling the father has toward the worker, it would be better if the worker saw the possible elements of avoidance in the actions. When we avoid painful situations we are trying to protect ourselves from the bad feelings that may come with dealing with problems.

These bad feelings can almost feel like a form of punishment for the father. Why talk about the problem or do something that makes you feel worse? Egan (1990) encourages workers to help clients find concrete and specific ways in which taking part in a helping relationship can be rewarding rather than punishing. Workers need to help the father find incentives for engaging in the sometimes painful process of making changes. In the case of Tom, the worker might help him to see that working on his depression might ultimately help him have a better relationship with his children.

EXPLORE YOUR OWN RESISTANT ATTITUDES, BEHAVIORS, AND BIASES

It is not uncommon for workers to have their own personal feelings about their clients, beyond their professional stance. Most workers have had fathers or some significant father figure in their lives while growing up. Workers need to examine their own feelings, beliefs, and attitudes about father figures before intervening with fathers. It is very easy to fall into the trap of expecting resistant behaviors simply because that is the stereotype of men in general. Workers who prejudge in this way may very well get what they expect by inadvertently provoking that response from the client.

EXAMINE THE QUALITY AND APPROPRIATENESS OF YOUR OWN INTERVENTIONS

You may need to take stock of yourself as a practitioner when faced with patterns of resistant behaviors. Do you find yourself having problems dealing with one type of client? Are you able to adjust your style and intervention methods from case to case or must clients adjust to you? Are you aware of any gender-insensitive behaviors you might exhibit in your practice life? Do you have a tendency to over personalize what clients do in response to your suggestions and interventions? These are just a few of the questions that workers can ask themselves in order to become more effective practitioners with fathers or with any client population.

ESTABLISH A "JUST SOCIETY" WITH YOUR CLIENT

Arendell (1995) said that many of the men she interviewed in her study of divorced fathers talked about their feelings of unfairness in the breakups with their spouses and subsequent court proceedings. Jordan (1988) found that many fathers involved in a divorce felt that they had lost power over the continuance of their relationship with their former spouses and children. Some of this sense of unfairness may be ungrounded while other aspects may have merit. For instance, after divorce mothers receive custody of the children approximately 90% of the time, and Braver (1998) notes that nearly 75% of the fathers in his study felt that the divorce process favored mothers. Perhaps more telling, he found that a large number of mothers felt the same way. The point we are making here is that fathers will often come into the counseling situation with a sense of inequity in how they have been treated by the court system, their former partners, and perhaps their friends and families. It is the worker's responsibility to create a safe and accepting atmosphere for the father. However, safe and accepting may not be sufficient. Workers may also need to emphasize that while other segments of society may be unfair and unjust, it is the worker's goal to create a relationship with the father that is characteristic of a just society, in which there is mutual trust and respect within their relationship. What this means is that the father will have a place in which he can talk about his feelings of loss and powerlessness without fear of being judged or belittled. It means he can express his fears, anger, and sadness over the inequities he has perceived in the ordeal of separation or divorce. For the worker, creating a just society means making consistent efforts to reassure the father that while other areas in society may not be fair, the worker-client relationship is a place in which the father can be understood, supported, and treated fairly. Of course, this does not mean supporting a father's claims of unfairness that merely come from anger and vengeful feelings toward his former partner. But it does mean that the worker should keep an open mind to inequities that may exist in the separation or divorce process and be able to help the father work through the negative effects such inequities can provoke.

Reflection

Fairness seems to be an important clinical issue for nonresidential fathers seeking help. How could you work to establish a just society with your clients?

TAP INTO SIGNIFICANT OTHERS AS RESOURCES

Research has been fairly clear on the importance of the support and encouragement from others in helping fathers adjust to separation and divorce (Stone, in press; Tschann, Johnston, & Wallerstein, 1989). If this is true, then it makes sense that workers may find it valuable to tap into these significant others as a resource for the separating or divorcing father. Others may be able to help the father see the value in working on his individual issues within the counseling relationship. For example, a father's lawyer may help him see the value of fulfilling the obligations of the court.

BUILD A COLLABORATIVE RELATIONSHIP

We should make every effort to assist fathers to help themselves in the context of the relationship. It may be useful to have the father engage in a role-reversal with the worker. This would allow the father to experience increased feelings of control over the helping process as well as improve his ability to identify and resolve feelings of resistance and reluctance connected with the helping process. For example, Tom could take on the role of the worker and model more effective ways to address his own personal reasons for his resistance or reluctance. Groups can also provide an excellent opportunity for fathers to be helpers and to gain a level of self-esteem from this activity. (Group work will be discussed in more detail later.)

In summary, individual work with fathers can present numerous challenges to the worker. If the worker is willing to learn more about the male socialization process and how to practice gender-sensitive approaches, there is an increased likelihood of building rapport with the father and engaging him in the helping process. Workers must take a look at their own biases and pre-conceptions about men and counseling, and work to overcome any stereotypes they might hold. The worker must also be prepared to deal with levels of resistance that may at first appear impenetrable, but which with time can be overcome.

WORKING WITH NONRESIDENTIAL FATHERS IN FAMILY SYSTEMS

Goldsmith (1982) suggests that General Systems Theory provides an excellent vantage point from which to view and understand the family undergoing divorce or separation. She points out that although divorce or separation alters the system, it does not terminate it. Therefore, even though the father no longer resides in the household, the roles and relationships that make him a significant part of his children's (and former partner's) life continue. However, fathers are very often left out of intervention efforts to assist families adjust to divorce or separation. For example, let's consider our opening case vignette. Let's speculate that Tom's daughter, Sara, began to experience adjustment problems related to the divorce of her parents. In all too many cases, the worker would schedule an appointment with Sara and her mother and conduct an assessment and design an intervention plan with little or no input from Tom. Is it possible that the worker might be missing important assessment information, might be overlooking a valuable resource? It should come as little surprise that fathers would be absent from postseparation intervention efforts as they have been absent from treatment efforts with intact families as well (Hecker, 1991; Phares, 1996). It should be noted that sometimes the absence can be associated with the father's resistance to counseling. Others have viewed fathers as disengaged from intervention efforts (Brannen & Collard, 1982), but Phares (1996) asserts that some of the reasons fathers have not been included in treatment efforts are due to a worker's bias toward fathers. She asserts that workers may have some misconceptions:

- Assuming that fathers are not involved in the lives of their children
- Assuming that fathers would not participate in prevention or intervention efforts
- Using sexist theories that attribute an inordinate amount of importance to the role of mothering in child outcome
- Assuming that fathers are not important factors to child outcome
- Assuming that divorce or separation means that fathers no longer have much contact with the children

Perspective
Jemma brought her 7-year-old son, Kareem, into the Family Services Agency as a result of school problems. The school personnel had recommended counseling for Kareem in the hope that it would help him learn to handle his anger better. Kareem had been involved in several angry outbursts at school in which he had punched other kids and even shoved the teacher. The worker learned that these episodes had started about 3 months after Kareem's father left Jemma. The worker inquired about the father, but Jemma said that the father was more trouble than he was worth. The worker considered asking about involving the father but decided against including him because of Jemma's descriptions of the father. He sounded like another unmarried, deadbeat dad who wouldn't help out.
What do you think of the worker's decision? Is it possible that Jemma is inaccurate in describing the father? How could you explore this situation in more depth to gain a clearer sense of the value that the father might bring to the counseling effort?

When workers hold these assumptions about fathers—and in combination with real instances of fathers' reluctance to engage in treatment—it is little wonder that fathers have not been a part of traditional family intervention strategies, and even more understandable why they are not part of most postseparation family intervention efforts.

The truth is that treatment outcomes tend to be better when fathers are involved in family intervention efforts (Dadds, Sanders, Behrens, & James, 1987; Mann, Borduin, Henggeler, & Blaske, 1990). Of course, there are exceptions (O'Brien, 1988), but there still seems to be ample evidence that more vigorous efforts are needed to include fathers in family interventions (Phares, 1996), whether with intact families or postseparation families. The following are some suggestions for including fathers in family interventions following divorce or separation.

Engaging the Father in the Intervention

1. *Include fathers from the beginning.* Feldman (1992) suggests that workers should always include fathers in the initial intake meeting and the initial stages of intervention, rather than attempting to engage them at a later point in the intervention process.

2. *Make direct contact with the father.* Hecker (1991) suggests that workers should talk directly with the fathers who are reluctant to participate. This can demonstrate that the worker genuinely believes that the father's presence is important. The worker can also explain the benefits of intervention and if the father sees how it may help his child in the long run, he may be more willing to participate.

3. *Outline the rationale for including the father in the intervention.* Carr (1998) notes that it has been found that fathers respond positively to intervention requests if they are clear about what is expected of them within the treatment effort and why they are important. Fathers may be suspicious of the worker's motivation for asking them to be involved. They may fear that a blaming session will occur in which they will be targeted. This may be particularly true in divorce or separation situations in which passions still run high. If fathers can be helped to see that they are a valuable part of the treatment team and that fault-finding is not part of the process, they may be more likely to engage in the process.

Specific Intervention Skills to Use with Postseparation Families

Once the father has been invited and is willing to attend the family intervention effort, the worker needs to consider what specific skills will be needed in order to best meet the needs of all involved. Facilitating a family session that will include divorced or separated partners can be an extremely challenging task. It may be helpful to incorporate techniques from conflict resolution strategies and divorce mediation efforts. Combining techniques from these two areas leads to the following suggestions for working with the postseparation family.

SET GUIDELINES EARLY REGARDING APPROPRIATE AND ACCEPTABLE BEHAVIORS

It is very appropriate for workers to be direct when dealing with conflicting participants in counseling. It should be clear from the start that yelling, name-calling, and blaming are not part of the helping process. Nonresidential fathers may be quite angry about their situation, but will appreciate clear and consistent guidelines, especially when the guidelines are framed in a way that ensures fairness.

REFRAME

Brown (1997) suggests that workers can take statements that either or both former partners have made and translate them into a more positive context. Reframing may highlight the shared aspect of an issue between the two parents. For example:

Tom: She just doesn't make sure that Sara gets enough rest during the school week!
Mary: Well, he loads her up on junk food over the weekend!
Worker: It's obvious from your comments that you both care about Sara's well-being and want to make sure that she is doing ok."

ACKNOWLEDGE STRONG EMOTIONS

When we acknowledge the strong emotions that either parent may be expressing, we are telling them that they have been heard without inviting expansive exploration of the emotions (Brown, 1997). This can let a father know that his angry or hurt feelings have been heard but that the session time will not be spent trying to resolve all of these reactions.

CONTROL THE COMMUNICATION

Whereas traditional interventions may offer a wider range of free expression of thoughts and feelings, workers involved with conflictual clients often must take a more direct approach to controlling content. The worker should feel free to limit what is said and by whom. The ability to make this type of decision can cut off potentially destructive or unproductive comments within the session (Brown, 1997).

CONTROL THE EMOTIONAL CLIMATE

This tactic is directly related to controlling communications. Brown (1997) suggests that by controlling the emotional client, the worker can change the focus or even the emotional tone of the session. For example, the worker can slow the pace and speak quietly in order to offset an increasingly intense session.

MUTUALIZE

This tactic is closely connected with reframing. Workers assisting former partners should help them continue to see commonalities in interests that they will have (Brown, 1997); most commonly it will be the love for their children.

CAUCUS

In traditional family interventions, workers are discouraged from meeting individually with family members. However, in cases where there is still a great deal of conflict or the potential for physical or psychological harm, it is highly appropriate for the worker to meet with each family member separately (Brown, 1997). It has been our experience that if an individual meeting is scheduled for one partner, it is best to set up individual time for the other partner. It has been our experience that when a worker sees only one client individually, the other can become suspicious that perhaps an alliance is being formed between the worker and the former partner. The individual meeting can be used to help identify why the individual is "stuck" (i.e., unable to work out an agreement with the partner) and to develop a plan on how to get "unstuck."

SPECIFY THE GOALS OF THE INTERVENTION

Although this was mentioned as a tactic for engaging fathers in the intervention process, it also is an important ingredient for enlisting the ongoing participation of the father in treatment. Research has shown that fathers appear to appreciate workers' structuring behaviors during sessions (e.g., task-oriented and controlling behaviors) more than mothers do (Newberry, Alexander, & Turner, 1991).

DEAL WITH THE MOTHER'S RESISTANCE

There is indication within intact families that mothers may directly or indirectly block fathers from joining the treatment process (Sachs, 1986). If this is true for intact families, it would seem reasonable to assume that mothers may be even more inclined to resist efforts to include the nonresidential father in the intervention process. This is one reason why it is important for workers to talk directly with the father. It is possible that if the worker leaves the responsibility to the mother of contacting and enlisting the nonresidential father into the sessions, it will not happen because of the mother's resistance to such an effort. Beyond contacting the father directly, the worker also needs to talk about the mother's resistance with her. It is important that she have a chance to voice her concerns. There are certainly cases in which it would be dangerous to the mother to be in contact with the father, and that is not the intent of these intervention efforts. However, under most circumstances the resistance has less to do with physical danger than to lingering anger and resentment that may exist between the mother and father. It is the worker's responsibility to assess the reasons for the resistance and to intervene accordingly. If it is not a case of physical danger, then the mother may need help understanding why it is important to include the father in the sessions. She may hold some of the erroneous assumptions that we attributed to some workers earlier (e.g., assuming that a father's ongoing relationship with children is of little importance to the child's well-being). If this is the case, the worker may need to help the mother clarify these misunderstandings.

Reflection

Recall the example presented in the Perspective presented on page 139. What biases might the worker hold toward Kareem's father? How would you deal with these types of biases in yourself? How would you deal with a co-worker demonstrating these types of biases?

In summary, the inclusion of father in postseparation intervention efforts is a goal worth pursuing. A thorough assessment of the situation must ensure that women are not at risk for physical harm if the father is included. Once this is determined, there are specific techniques that can be used to increase the likelihood that fathers will at least show up for the first session. Once the father arrives, workers can employ strategies from conflict resolution and mediation practices to ensure a safe and productive session for all. Given the evidence that suggests that including fathers can improve intervention outcomes it seems even more important to make every effort possible to reach out to the nonresidential father.

GROUP WORK WITH NONRESIDENTIAL FATHERS

Workers wishing to help nonresidential fathers through a group format will need to remember the issues related to gender-sensitive practice that were discussed in the previous section. Workers will also be faced with the same kinds of challenges in dealing with fathers in groups that we discussed related to individual interventions (issues of resistance or reluctance, problems identifying emotions, etc.). Andronico (1996) believes that groups provide the ideal setting for men to deal with life's transitions. He notes that groups provide a unique opportunity for men to deal with the problems of being male in these changing times. Andronico sees groups as providing men special assistance by

- Helping to fight feelings of alienation that modern men may experience
- Providing men with a sense of community
- Helping men to feel less isolated in the divorce and separation process
- Providing protection from compensatory behaviors (e.g., chemical addictions)
- Providing an opportunity for men to emulate healthy models of masculinity (e.g., not based on the misuse of power)
- Exploring spiritual issues and other men's issues

Greif (1997) notes how group work with noncustodial parents can help to ease their pain and provide a safe place for them to explore their relationship with their children.

Based upon research and our own practice experience, several common themes seem to emerge when nonresidential fathers are served. Some of these themes apply to all types of interventions with nonresidential fathers (i.e., individual, group, family) while others are particularly pertinent to group work with fathers. Following are those themes that workers may want to address when serving nonresidential fathers.

Theme One: Powerlessness

In previous chapters we discussed the importance of efforts to enfranchise fathers. As noted earlier, fathers who are left out of decisions concerning their children, can begin to feel alienated and powerless. Many researchers contend that men in general experience a greater sense of powerlessness and pain following divorce than do women, and therefore have greater emotional difficulty adjusting to divorce than do women (McKenry & Price, 1990). Some of this may be due to the fact that men generally initiate separation less often than women (Wallerstein & Blakeslee, 1989). In a sense they feel they were powerless to save the relationship.

Workers serving nonresidential fathers in groups will therefore need to assist these men in expressing their feelings of powerlessness and help group members become a support system for one another. It may be helpful to assist fathers in developing a consistent narrative that explains the reasons and circumstances for the end of the relationship (Wall & Levy, 1994). Such explanations may ease their sense of powerlessness and help them grapple with the *why* of the breakup. Group members can help one another in reaching this level of understanding. Effective narratives include attributing the responsibility for the breakup to both partners and accepting that the decision to separate made sense given the situation (Wall & Levy, 1994). The ability to establish such narratives may ultimately help the father develop a constructive relationship with his former partner. Such a relationship may ultimately help the father gain an increased sense of power and control in his life. For a father, constructing this narrative with the help of other men may increase his willingness to let go of some of the destructive views of masculinity discussed earlier in this chapter.

Theme Two: Rejection by the Children

Wall and Levy (1994) suggest that it is critical to help nonresidential fathers talk about their fears of rejection by their children. Greif (1997) found that some of these fears are based upon real experiences for the nonresidential parent. For example, in the groups that Greif facilitated, he noted that some children refused to see their parent. At other times, parents felt rejected if the child did not want to spend their prearranged visitation with them because it interfered with activities with their friends or other relatives. These types of rejections and perceived rejections can lead to feelings of hurt, anger, and depression in the father and may ultimately lead to the father's withdrawing from the relationship with his child.

The group can be an effective place for fathers to explore their feelings of rejection. Other members can offer support and comfort. It is also possible that other fathers may even be able to offer up an alternative explanation of the child's behavior that may lessen the father's sense of hurt and rejection. For example, a father discussing the rejecting behavior of his teenage son was able to gain a new perspective when another group member pointed out how such behaviors were typical developmental issues in teens, that is, that even in intact families parents deal with the individuation efforts of their teens. Groups can provide a unique opportunity for fathers to present their feelings and perceptions before other fathers for feedback and clarification.

Reflection

Often we forget the reciprocal nature of the relationship between parents and their children. In essence, parents give children the love that children need and in return parents (consciously or not) hope for some display of love in turn from the child. When this reciprocity breaks down, parents can become confused, depressed, even angry. Of course, this breakdown occurs in every family, but for the nonresidential father these lapses in reciprocity can lead him to erroneous conclusions. These fathers can attribute an off-base meaning to this breakdown that is detrimental to the relationship. Consider ways in which you can help a nonresidential father normalize the ups and downs that come with parenting. Consider how you can help the father and the child adjust to their postseparation relationship.

Theme Three: Negative Feelings Toward Former Spouse

As was discussed in an earlier section, men are less likely to be the ones to initiate the separation process. It is quite common for them to engage in a blaming game in which the former partner is painted as the victimizer. This is further exacerbated by the gatekeeping role that many mothers take after divorce or separation (see chapter 2 for an expanded discussion of this topic). Fathers can grow to resent this type of power and act in ways that could jeopardize the relationship with their children (e.g., putting the child in the middle of conflicts or creating loyalty conflicts for the child). Many of the intervention issues we discussed about feeling powerless would be helpful for reducing these negative feelings. Once fathers can begin to take ownership for the failed aspects of the relationship, they can move on to accepting the breakup and learning from it. Some workers encourage fathers to examine what they can learn from the failed relationship that may help future relationships succeed. Once again, the group format can offer unique opportunities for fathers to talk about their angry feelings, develop a realistic narrative to explain the breakup, and assist one another to move on in the process.

Theme Four: Loneliness, Alienation, and Loss

Some researchers assert that men may benefit more from the socioemotional features of their intimate relationships than women do, and therefore they may have more difficulty replacing what a partner and family provided. This can lead to expressive hardships for men (Reissman, 1990). Men may have become dependent on their partners for initiating and planning most of their social activities, whether it was going out to movies, dinner with friends, or a picnic with the family; fathers may be at a loss regarding how to establish their social lives without their partners. The former partner may also have played a vital link between the father and his children. With her gone, fathers may be at loss to relate effectively with their own children. In addition, most men are dealing with the real losses of home, family, and time with their children.

Groups can offer fathers the opportunity to form new relationships and friendships. Through role playing and rehearsal techniques, fathers can experiment with new ways of relating to their former partners and their own children. If a safe environment has been created by the worker, fathers will be able to explore these very painful experiences. They can discuss the emotional reactions to their losses and receive support and guidance from other fathers.

Theme Five: Emotional Triangulation

Greif (1997) noted how some nonresidential parents put their children in the middle of disputes that they have had with the child's mother and vice versa. For example, some parents would explode at their child because of the behavior of the child's other parent. Other writers have noted the dysfunctional games that parents sometime play at the expense of their children. Games like "spy" in which children are asked to tattle on the other parent, or "messenger" in which the child must relay adult-level messages back and forth between parents because of the parents' inability to communicate only serve to harm the child and adversely affect his or her adjustment to the separation of their parents.

Group leaders can offer members basic information about these types of games and the harmful impact they have on their children. Leaders can even show films (for example, *Tender Places*) that help fathers to empathize better with the plight of their children. Many fathers will change their behaviors if they recognize the long-term harm it may have on their children. Group members can role-play alternative behaviors in terms of dealing with their former partner. Role reversals can also help fathers understand their children's emotional issues, as well as those of their former partners. Members can also effectively challenge one another when they hear examples of these types of behaviors by group members.

Theme Six: Lack of Role Clarity

It has been pointed out that the role of nonresidential father is an ambiguous one without clear guidelines (McKenry & Price, 1990). Stone and McKenry (1998) found that fathers who did not have a clear sense of the expectations and norms for nonresidential fathering were less likely to stay involved with their children after divorce. Therefore it seems reasonable that this should be a group (as well as individual) theme in treatment. Armando, the recently divorced father of two children, put it this way: "I'm just not sure how I'm supposed to act and what I'm supposed to do. . . . I'm confused about how to be their dad when I can only see them on the weekends."

As Armando's comments indicate, nonresidential fathers can go through a period in which they feel lost about the parameters of their new role, a role which has very few clear guidelines. It is possible that the legal system has specified some aspects of the nonresidential role, but most likely the court has spoken only to visitation rights and support obligations. Obviously there is much more to fathering than paying child support and showing up for visitation.

The group format can offer an excellent opportunity for fathers to explore the role of nonresidential fathering. Changing role expectations can be explored and processed. Fathers can talk about successful ways to transition into nonresidential fathering. It can be helpful for members to assemble a list of the specific ways that they can enact the role of nonresidential fathering. It can be expected that some fathers may have difficulty believing that they can still have a significant impact on their child's life when they only see their children during visits. Groups can serve as a helpful place for fathers to share ways to be involved in a child's life that do not require face-to-face contact (e.g., phone calls, cards, letters, e-mail, etc.). It is also possible that members need to discuss the changing child custody standards in their states. They may find that shared parenting (discussed in chapter 12) is a viable option for them. Sometimes lawyers are reluctant to pursue this option. It is possible that group members can offer alternative custody arrangements that lead to more time being allocated to them with their children.

Theme Seven: Reflection With Their Own Fathers

Sternbach (1996) suggests that whether spoken or not, men involved in group work begin dealing with issues about how they were fathered. Sternbach suggests that workers deliberately introduce this theme after the first few sessions rather than ignoring it. Men often hold very strong feelings about the way they were fathered. Whether trying to live up to the high standards of excellent fathering set by their own fathers or trying to avoid the mistakes their fathers made, men will often face an internal struggle to come to terms with how they father compared to how their own father did.

Sternbach (1996) employs a group exercise with men in which he suggests that the members go around the circle and complete this sentence, "When I think of my father, I feel _____," (p. 221). He notes that it is important that they say the complete sentence each time as it creates a cadence or rhythm, that in some ways resembles a chant. An example of a group member's response to this sentence completion task was, "When I think of my father I feel the tip of the iceberg—anger, abandoned, lonely, curious, emptiness, sad, confusion, my own death, unimportant, inadequate, cheated, pity, cold, uneasy. . . ."

Sternbach asserts that this exercise can lead to an "ah-ha" experience for some group members as they begin to see commonalities among themselves. Through these commonalities, Sternbach states that men can begin to "reach for connection across the emptiness and mistrust that otherwise separates them" (1996, p. 221).

Reflection

Use Sternbach's exercise to explore some of your own feelings about your father. Complete the sentence, "When I think about my father, I feel _____." Now consider how your response might affect the way that you interact with fathers in your work.

Global Guidelines for Group Intervention

Once the worker has a better understanding of the common themes to expect when facilitating a nonresidential fathers' group, he or she can begin to consider how to structure the group and what content to include within that structure. Hall and Kelly (1996) discuss the importance of structure to nonresidential father groups. They suggest that members be given a rough outline of what should be accomplished in each session and briefly discuss how the tasks for each session are expected to be accomplished. Within their structure the following topics are covered (p. 252):

Session 1:	Testing and screening—for pregroup assessment
Session 2:	Introductions: members, workers, group work itself, and work with nonresidential fathers
Session 3–5:	Power issues
Session 6–8:	Achieving personal and parenting talents
Sessions 9–11:	Address affiliation needs
Session 12:	Review and practice
Session 13:	Termination rituals

Each of these 13 sessions is divided into 3 therapeutic hours, which are used in different ways. The 1st hour is used for cognitive interventions, the 2nd hour for affective interventions, and the 3rd hour for behavioral practice. Hall and Kelly (1996) also suggest the use of two workers, a male and a female. The leaders divide leadership roles for each group; one is responsible for task leadership and the other for relationship leadership. These roles alternate.

In terms of content, Hall and Kelly suggest that when nonresidential fathers learn information that is relevant to them as a group, "they are less likely to feel alienated and as powerless and, therefore, are less likely to feel depressed" (1996, p. 252). They offer the following guidelines for determining if a particular content topic is worth presenting in group:

1. Is the information relevant to these fathers?
2. Is the information able to guide and direct their behavior toward healthy outcomes for the entire family system?
3. Is the information useful in legal interventions for continued involvement with their children?
4. Is the information useful in increasing their parenting skills?
5. Is the information a guide for building closer relationships with their children?
6. Is the information helpful in building a dual-parent relationship with their child's mother?
7. Is the information suggestive of ways to increase their sense of power, achievement, and affiliation as parents?

In summary, group work with nonresidential fathers can provide an excellent opportunity for fathers to explore topics that are relevant to them in the context of a supportive environment of other men. The content covered within group can help fathers gain new parenting skills as well as personal coping skills. It should be noted that a considerable degree of work needs to be put forth by researchers to evaluate the effectiveness of such interventions. Nonresidential father groups are still relatively new and little exists in the way of evaluative research.

Reflection

Is it better for fathers to be served by men or women? Does it even matter? It seems that there are risks and issues to consider with either gender. Myers (1989) reports that clients may either parentify or infantilize male workers. Wall and Levy (1994) suggest that female workers run the risk of identifying with the fathers' former partner, and thus align themselves against the father-client. What are your thoughts on this topic?

Special Issues: Self-Help Groups of Men Helping Men

Self-help/support groups have been a viable treatment option for men throughout most of the 20th century. Alcoholics Anonymous (AA) self-help groups have been in existence since the 1930s (Thoreson & Budd, 1987). However, it wasn't until the emergence of several of the predominant men's movements in the late 1960s that men began joining other types of self-help groups in numbers. Some of this may even be attributed to the women's movement and its emphasis on consciousness-raising support groups (Kauth, 1992). For example, the mythopoetic movement began quietly in the 1980s with a few men attending lectures and weekend retreats. By 1990, thousands of men had attended mythopoetic events, and Robert Bly's book *Iron John* was a best-seller (Messner, 1997). Self-help groups offer the opportunity for men to help men in a way that is potentially empowering and that encourages personal growth. Some have noted that men's support groups allow men to mentor men in developing a healthier sense of masculinity exploring ways to better fulfill their male roles such as husband and father (Horn, Jolliff, & Roth, 1996).

Kauth (1992) maintains that there is a slight difference between support groups and self-help groups. Support groups ". . . gather with more of a consciousness-raising, personal growth, feel-good focus, while self-help groups gather to deal with a specific problem and have a coping-better-with-the-problem focus (p. 4). However, he notes that the two groups very frequently become quite similar in that they proceed through a very similar process. They also typically share a belief in the importance of a nonhierarchical leadership structure, one in which members do much of the facilitation of the group. Because the two types of groups are similar in how they ultimately function we will refer to them interchangeably within this section.

Some writers have expressed concern that professional group leaders might interfere with the effective functioning of self-help support groups that are led by lay persons (Katz & Bender, 1987). Essentially the fear is that the professional might intimidate, interfere with, or take over the facilitation of such groups. Members themselves are sometimes apprehensive about professional involvement because they fear it will "compromise the autonomy and confidentiality of the group" (Toseland & Rivas, 1998, p. 23). It seems very important, therefore, that professionals working with self-help support groups be particularly sensitive to this fear and make every effort to develop a consultant role with these groups rather than a dominant leadership role.

It would seem that the facilitative function that a worker takes with self-help support groups should focus on assisting the group to develop the distinctive characteristics that will make it an effective group. Reissman's thoughts (1987) regarding the successful ingredients of a self-help support group were summarized by Zastrow (1993). A discussion follows of these areas and their application to father self-help support groups:

A NONCOMPETITIVE, COOPERATIVE ORIENTATION

Noncompetitiveness and cooperation would seem to be important norms to encourage within a father's group. Fathers may come into group with a great deal of anger about their breakup. Some may even have fallen victim to an urge to defeat their former partner by turning the children against her or other such harmful actions. Group could provide a place for fathers to help one another get past such destructive competitive urges.

AN EMPHASIS ON THE INDIGENOUS–PEOPLE WHO HAVE THE PROBLEM AND KNOW A LOT ABOUT IT FROM HAVING EXPERIENCED IT

Fathers could benefit from the opportunity to learn from more experienced fathers within the group. Horn and colleagues (1996) noted the importance of the role of mentoring in men's groups. Those who were further along in the separation process or who were successfully navigating their postseparation relationships with their children and former partners could serve as valuable mentors to those in the group who are stuck earlier in the process.

AN ATTITUDE OF "DO WHAT YOU CAN DO, ONE DAY AT A TIME. YOU CAN'T SOLVE EVERYTHING AT ONCE"

This ingredient has been a standard within the AA community since its inception. Perhaps you have seen the bumper stickers that proclaim ONE DAY AT A TIME. There is a great deal of wisdom in this single statement. Once again, the mentoring capacity within the father's group could serve a vital function because members would hear and see evidence that it is far better to take on challenges one day at a time than trying to tackle everything at once.

A SHARED, REVOLVING LEADERSHIP

This would seem to fit with the noncompetitive and cooperative nature of self-help support groups. By spreading leadership around, it may be possible to increase each member's sense of ownership and responsibility to the group itself.

An Attitude of Being Helped Through Helping

Many men who come to group may feel defeated and worthless as a result of the losses they have incurred from the separation. It could be a vital boost to their self-esteem if they were in some way able to help another within the group. As discussed earlier, feelings of powerlessness are common to fathers after separation. The self-help group experience could offer fathers an opportunity to regain some "power" by helping others.

An Understanding That Helping is not a Commodity to be Bought or Sold

It is not uncommon for those in our society to only associate quality service with a price tag. In the area of self-help support groups, the degree of help one receives is not contingent upon how much money one pays, but rather on how much of yourself you invest. Helping becomes what it is: the byproduct of a caring relationship.

A Strong Optimism About The Ability to Change

Fathers may also come into group believing what others have told them about change, that a person can change the way they are or that change will only be for the worse or that the woman they were with is the one who needs to change. None of these messages will prove helpful to the father who is dealing with multiple losses. Mentors within the group can model how change can occur, how it can be positive, and how it does not depend on someone else's changing.

An Understanding That Although Small May Not Necessarily be Beautiful, It Is the Place to Begin and Build On

Fathers may come into the self-help support group with expectations that they will feel better overnight. The mentoring aspect of the group will allow fathers to better understand that improvements will most likely occur in small increments, and that any change for the better, no matter how small, is something to appreciate. This perspective may be particularly important as fathers struggle with the postseparation visitation arrangements with their children. Fathers can explore ways to make the most out of their limited time with their children and how to build a quality relationship based on just a weekend together.

An Understanding That Helping is at the Center—Knowing How to Receive Help, Give Help, and Help Yourself

Fathers may come into the group needing to learn a great deal about nurturing. They may have trouble giving or receiving nurturing in their relationships. The self-help group can be a place for fathers to explore ways to both give and receive help and nurturing.

An Emphasis on Empowerment

Empowerment has been defined as a process by which people gain understanding and mastery over their own affairs and obtain access to the democratic processes of one's community and relevant institutions (Rappaport, 1987). A major goal of empowerment practice is to help individuals or communities change the situations that perpetuate problems (Guitierrez, 1988). These changes may lead to a more balanced apportionment of resources, nonexploitive personal relationships, and a sense of power through increased self-respect, confidence, knowledge, and skills (Rees, 1991).

For fathers in self-help support groups, this need not be limited necessarily to empowerment in their personal lives. The members of the group may decide that there are social and political issues they want to address. Fathers could decide to band together with other groups and petition their legislators for new policies that are father-friendly in the area of custody, support, or the workplace.

Are support groups helpful? It might be useful to read the following personal account by a participant in a self-help support group for men.

Perspective: What Goes on in a Support Group for Nonresidential Fathers?

We met weekly for 4 years. It was a long time to be together and to get close. And we did get close, which we thought we could only do by meeting in a structured men's group. We were six fathers from varied backgrounds—three of us were divorced and still single, one remarried, one single never-married father, and one gay father. We alternated our meetings at each others' houses and got to experience how each one lived.

The first year or so that we met together, we got thoroughly acquainted. We ended up talking a lot about our relationships with the women in our lives. A couple of us were in frustrating and self-destructive relationships; we needed help in getting perspective on what we were doing with our lives. The gay man was attempting to go straight, that is date women and try to become heterosexual. Of course, we all had advice for each other about finding "healthier" relationships, but we didn't always follow it. We also spent time talking about our children and how much we longed to spend more time with them. We talked about the barriers to spending more time with our kids, some the result of the child's mother, other reasons related to our life decisions.

A strange thing happened in our year together. We began to shift away from talking about our women (or men) and began talking more about our fathers. This became a passionate topic that absorbed us in countless hours of discussions. Somehow, it was an aspect of our lives that most of us had not considered before. Who were they to us and what were their strengths and shortcomings? We quickly realized that all of us but one had a father with a similar profile—an aloof father who was unavailable to us emotionally and physically. Our fathers didn't seem to know how to be nurturers, a concept that we were on to by this time in our lives. Nurturing was paramount to us, and we wanted to share it with our children! The one member that had a very close relationship with his father became our source of numerous questions like, "What was it like?" "What did you do together?" and "How did he comfort you?" This member began telling us stories of his times together with his dad. At times they cried together, and his father always seemed to be there when his son needed comforting or support. *(continues)*

> By the last year of our time together, we began to appreciate all of our fathers. None of them had abandoned us, and they were good providers and protectors. Further, we realized that they were not as fortunate as we were to be fathers during an era when nurturing was valued by society. Near the end of our last year together, we began to disengage and say good-bye. We had helped each other in very profound ways but we were ready to move on.

This account clearly indicates that the experience was very helpful to the participant. Borman (1979) suggested that there are at least five therapeutic factors that are effective for self-help groups:

1. *Cognitive restructuring.* Fathers within a group can have the opportunity to develop a new perspective on themselves and their issues. As the participant in the Perspective noted, members began to recognize the role that their own fathers had played in their lives.

2. *Hope.* Fathers in a self-help group can develop a sense of hope that their life will improve as they see the lives of other fathers in the group with similar problems have improved. As the participant in the example noted, the members turned to the one group member who had experienced a positive relationship with his father to answer their questions about healthy fathering. This hope was enlivened when some members of the group became fathers themselves and were able to father in ways that were better than the type of fathering they had received.

3. *Altruism.* Fathers within a self-help group can feel good about themselves for helping others. From the participant in the example, it can be implied that a sense of well-being occurred as a result of being in the group that was in part related to his own opportunity to help other men.

4. *Acceptance.* Fathers within a self-help support group can gain a sense of trust that they will not be rejected or blamed for their problems or issues. As the participant in the example noted, members gave each other advice on how to find healthier relationships that was not always followed. This would suggest that members felt free to talk about their problems as well as offer suggestions to each other without fear of being rejected or judged.

5. *Universality.* Fathers can gain the awareness that they are not alone in having the problems they face. As the participant in the example noted, "we quickly realized that all but one of us had a father with

a similar profile—an aloof father who was unavailable to us emotionally and physically." This type of realization can reduce feelings of alienation and help men to recognize that they have common areas of concern that can connect them in positive ways.

The combination of these 5 therapeutic factors will help to ensure that a self-help support group for nonresidential fathers is successful. Although the challenges are many for these fathers, such group efforts may offer significant assistance to them as they adjust to life after separation.

In summary, it is evident that fathers can receive assistance using a variety of intervention models. The foundation for any intervention plan is a complete, thorough, holistic assessment. Workers who wish to help these fathers will need to consider their own biases and prejudices when it comes to serving men in general, and fathers in particular. However, if they are genuine in their efforts and can employ a gender-sensitive practice approach they will find themselves quite capable of being a resource to nonresidential fathers.

Questions for Discussion

1. What are some of the ways that you could apply Goldberg's five binds (discussed in chapter 1) to your work with men?

2. Had you ever considered the different intervention approaches that might be used in working with men? After reading this chapter, how is your practice approach with men going to change—or not change?

3. How would you feel about leading an all-male "self-help group?" What special skills do you think you might need? What special challenges would this pose for you?

IV

Policies and Programs to Assist Fathers at Risk

7

A Place to Begin: Conducting a Community Needs-Assessment

Children give us something more important and meaningful than our-selves to work and sacrifice for. They help shape our personal, marital, and family priorities, and they inspire us sometimes to keep going. They need us, and in a real sense we need them too. Absent parents are disadvantaged and diminished because they may have little reason to think beyond themselves or to struggle for the sake of another. Indeed, they miss the satisfaction, pride, and rewards of being an involved parent or caregiver. Our philosophy that fathers need their kids as much as their kids need them—even if those dads don't know it yet—will underscore everything we'll be doing. (Meloy, 2000)

One decisive way to find out about the status of fathering is to con-duct a community-wide assessment of fathers' needs. Such an assess-ment can begin to document the extent to which fathering is at risk in a local community. This chapter will help the reader to consider, in some depth, a community needs-assessment as a tool for understand-ing the needs of fathers. The specific purposes of this chapter are to help the reader

- identify the pros and cons for conducting a community needs-assessment
- analyze a case study of a community needs-assessment con-ducted by a rural county in North Carolina
- describe a model for conducting your own community needs-assessment of fathers

PROS AND CONS FOR CONDUCTING A COMMUNITY NEEDS-ASSESSMENT

Many questions may be running through your mind about community needs-assessments.

1. Why conduct a needs-assessment?
2. Why focus on fathers' *needs?* Why not just continue to target their *problems?*
3. Why not focus on the family as a whole?
4. What good will a needs-assessment do anyway?

Why Conduct a Needs-Assessment?

A broad, systematic research effort like a needs-assessment can be highly beneficial in addressing community-wide needs and problems. Most important, such an assessment can provide valuable information for understanding a particular social problem that is troubling a local community. The alternatives—depending upon hearsay evidence, depending upon a few individual case examples, or having hunches about a problem—are not enough documentation if the problem is to be taken seriously (Marlow, 1998).

Needs-assessments are particularly useful if a new policy or program initiative is being considered or if an existing program is in the process of being changed or being considered for discontinuation. And if outside funding sources (federal, state, or local government, private foundations, or corporate support) are needed to support a program, the documentation produced by a needs-assessment can take on even greater importance.

A needs-assessment can answer several important questions. Some examples that could be asked about fathers and their families include

- To what extent are fathers in the community actively involved in raising their children?
- To what extent are they providing economically for their children?
- What problems do fathers face in their role as a parent?
- What trends are evident in teen pregnancy, unmarried parent-

ing, single parenting, and divorce? Are these family patterns increasing or decreasing?

- To what extent do services exist to help fathers with their parental roles?
- What are the demographic characteristics of fathers who use existing services?
- What barriers are there to access existing services?
- What service gaps are evident?
- What new policy initiatives could benefit fathers?

Why Focus on the Needs of Fathers?

Overlooking needs and focusing only on problems can pose serious limitations. One illustration of a problem-focused strategy is the Child Support Enforcement Law discussed in chapter 8. This legislative initiative and its more recent amendments are a genuine effort to hold non-custodial parents accountable for paying their child support. Yet the Child Support Enforcement Agency has predominately used coercive strategies such as garnishing the wages of non-compliant parents, withholding their driver's licenses, or putting them in jail to accomplish its goals. Voluntary measures are noticeably missing from this law; nor has there been an equally ambitious effort to enforce the noncustodial parents' visitation rights, a frequently heard excuse of many noncustodial parents for being noncompliant with child support.

We know that all people have basic human needs, yet we know too little about what fathers need as parents. Perhaps this lack of understanding can be partially explained by the lack of awareness that many fathers have of their own needs, which should come as no surprise because most of them have not received any preparation for becoming parents. Also, as we have noted before, many fathers tend not to be openly expressive and assertive about their needs because of the ways in which they have been socialized. In chapter 6, for example, we suggested that many fathers may even experience alexithymia, which means that they may not have the words to express their emotions and may need help in learning how to do this (Levant, 1992).

All fathers do not have difficulty communicating their needs, of course. For example, members of fathers' rights groups are often quite outspoken about their parental needs when they perceive that they have been overlooked by the court system. This attribute of fathers' rights groups is, in itself, a strength and has contributed valuable information about the perspectives and needs of many noncustodial and unmarried fathers.

Seeking the cooperation of fathers is essential if programs are to be effective in bringing about positive changes in their lives. Cooperation is most likely to be evident when we take their needs into account. Several studies have documented the expressed desire among nonresidential fathers to assist their families economically (Braver & O'Connell, 1998; Hawkins & Dollahite, 1997). Yet when we seek to involve them, we often find that they are faced with their own problems that can interfere with paying child support, including a lack of steady employment, unresolved communication problems with their children's mother, and difficulties in arranging and implementing regular contact with their children.

As part of a cooperative strategy for involving fathers, we need to listen to them more attentively. For example, how do they feel about their role in the family? What do they see as the obstacles to greater involvement and how can they make a greater contribution? Little of the literature so far has been able to capture their perspectives on these and related topics. The voices of noncustodial divorced fathers and teen fathers are beginning to become evident in the family literature, while unmarried fathers remain a largely invisible group. We still have a long way to go in understanding their perceptions of their family's needs, problems, and solutions.

Why Not Focus on the Family as a Whole?

This is a good question in that fathers are members of a family unit, and families are best served if they are viewed as a total system. As we have pointed out several times previously, however, fathers seem to be inadvertently left out of much of the program planning and development aimed at helping families. For many, "families" is synonymous with "mothers and children." Nonresidential fathers in particular are often the unnoticed or invisible family member, even when they are active parents. This is evident, for example, in the term single-parent families that is commonly used by all segments of society even when a nonresidential father is actively involved.

Reflection

Do you think that there are good reasons to conduct a special needs-assessment of fathers? Why or why not? What benefits would you see in having data on the needs of fathers in your community?

Many people believe that we are living in a critical time in our society's history because of what we perceive as a widespread epidemic of nonresidential fathering. The social conditions of these times may be calling out for a special mandate to investigate this ominous pattern and find ways to overcome it. Little is known about nonresidential fathering and even less is known about their firsthand views. In other words, the absence of fathers from so many families warrants a special investigation. We can call it an interim investigation that must be completed before we can get back to a focus on the family as a whole.

Our review of the literature on professional services to families suggests that new policy and program initiatives are needed to reach out to fathers, particularly those who are conspicuously absent or marginally involved as parents. In most cases, family agencies are primarily geared to serving mothers and children whether by intention or not. This is evident in such things as the predominance of female service providers, an emphasis on daytime service hours, the disproportionately low percentage of adult male clients, and the relative absence of services designed specifically to address fathers' needs. Chapter 6 addresses some of these issues in more depth and suggests that many family service agencies may have a gender bias when it comes to serving fathers.

It is important to note here that we are not saying that new family agency initiatives should emphasize fathers only. Along with individual counseling to men and support groups tailored specifically to fathers' needs, for example, we also need a variety of programs to promote improved communication and cooperation between mothers and fathers. Conflict resolution strategies, binuclear family therapy, and support groups for custodial mothers are examples. It is imperative that we attempt to help fathers in the context of the family system because fathers significantly impact and are impacted by other family members.

It is also essential that we devise effective outreach strategies for recruiting and sustaining the involvement of fathers in service provisions. In discussing fatherhood initiatives with many colleagues over the years, we have discovered that recruitment is a common challenge across numerous programs. We are aware of countless genuine attempts to help fathers that have failed because the fathers did not respond. And often when attempts to recruit fathers have succeeded initially, sustaining their participation did not. Suggestions for successfully recruiting men for fatherhood initiatives is discussed later in this chapter and in other chapters.

What Good Will a Needs-Assessment Do Anyway?

Of course no guarantees can be made, but we suspect that many positive benefits can emanate from a community needs-assessment of fathering. And the more organizational and institutional participants involved and committed to such an assessment, the more likely it is that positive benefits will materialize. Why? Because a genuine community-wide concern for fathering is being expressed. In other words, a needs-assessment means that the community cares about its fathers.

Perhaps an examination of the experiences of one community will be helpful in illustrating the possible benefits of a needs-assessment. This community is Davidson County, a largely rural community in North Carolina. Both the successes and shortcomings of Davidson County's efforts to address the needs of their fathers follows.

A CASE STUDY: ACT COALITION OF DAVIDSON COUNTY

This fatherhood initiative was started by the ACT Coalition of Davidson County that was founded to serve children (Innovative Program). One of its first victories occurred in 1995 with the successful placement of a severely disabled infant in a regular day care program. From there the staff decided that they wanted to serve more children with special needs within their regular day care facilities. Thus, the coalition's name was coined: ACT or All Children Together.

Begun by the local Baptist Children's Home, this special venture became a coalition of leaders from several local organizations concerned about families. These leaders were selected to represent many key organizations in the county, including county government, the departments of health and social services, family agencies, the mental health department, churches, the chamber of commerce, the school system and the head start program, second-language communities such as Mexican Americans, the local ARC (formerly "Association for Retarded Citizens"), and parents' groups.

Examining Available Data

Early on, ACT began to investigate its concern for children from a broader perspective of parent involvement. The group began to look at available statistics on how many children were living with both of their biological married parents, only their biological father, or with a step-father. It also sought statistics on the number of noncustodial fathers who were actively involved with their children and took a closer look at local indicators of family well-being. It discovered that their county had a high divorce rate, a large number of noncompliant child support cases, that more than a quarter of recent births were to unmarried parents, and that almost all births to women under 18 occurred outside of marriage. Some of the indicators it found were only estimates, which still provided a good beginning database for deciding what to do next.

Table 7.1 presents some of the details of the initial investigation and the likelihood of possible trends. As the table suggests, some of these trends from 1990 to 1997 have been positive while others have been negative.

TABLE 7.1 Relevant Social Indicators in Davidson County, 1990 and 1997

Social Indicator	1990	1997
Marriages	954	1,155
Divorces per 100 marriages	43	53
Children under 18	30,320	33,038
Births	1,883	1,736
Out-of-wedlock births	not avail.	475
Teen pregnancies	484	354
Teen pregnancies as % of total pregnancies	26%	20%

Source: ACT Coalition of Davidson County, NC (1999).

TABLE 7.2 Social Indicators of Davidson County and North Carolina, 1995

Social Indicator	Davidson County	North Carolina
Population—White	89%	76%
Population—Minorities	11%	24%
Divorce rate	55%	58%
15–19-year-old females with a birth	59%	64%
Abortion	12%	18%
Abortions (15–19-year-old females)	31%	27%
All births out of marriage	24%	31%
Teen births out of marriage	85%	83%
% White families with teen single mothers	12%	12%
% Minority families with teen single mothers	48%	40%

Source: ACT Coalition of Davidson County, NC (1999).

The coalition also gathered data on similar indicators in the state of North Carolina for comparison purposes. As Table 7.2 reveals, this rural county discovered that many or its rates are similar to the state as a whole. The table also reveals some differences that were helpful to know. For example, while births out of marriage and abortion rates were lower in Davidson County than for the state as a whole, out-of-marriage births and abortions for teenagers seemed somewhat higher. Also, minority teen births were higher for Davidson County than for the state. These statistics suggested that teen mothers and fathers were possibly an important at-risk group to consider as a target for intervention.

Consulting Other Organizations With Fatherhood Initiatives

After consulting several national fatherhood groups, ACT discovered that family trends in Davidson County generally paralleled national trends. The national fatherhood groups that were consulted by ACT had an influence on what ACT would do next. ACT found that more than one third of all children nationally live separate from their biological father and that about one third of all recent births were to unmarried parents. From a survey on one website (ACT Coalition of Davidson County, NC, 1999), it found that the vast majority of high-school dropouts who had serious behavioral problems or were in juvenile detention centers or prisons came from fatherless families. ACT also discovered the book *Throwaway Dads* by Parke and Brott and chose to use it as a resource in identifying what men can do to get more involved as parents, what women can do to get fathers more involved, and what government and the private sector can do (Parke & Brott, 1999).

ACT also discovered from a Gallup Poll (1996) that 79% of those surveyed felt that the most significant family or social problem in the U.S. was the physical absence of the father from the home. It also discovered a guiding principle of the National Fatherhood Initiative (ACT Coalition of Davidson County, 1999), which it decided to adopt: "The ultimate measure of success [of a project such as theirs] ought to be the number of children who have a close and enduring relationship with a loving, committed, and responsible father." After much deliberation, the ACT Coalition Board formally shifted its major focus to fathers; the Board voted unanimously to "begin repairing the collapsing base of fatherhood in Davidson County" (ACT Coalition of Davidson County, NC, 1999).

Reflection

The ACT Coalition Board is an excellent example of a grassroots effort to create change at the local level: citizens collaborating on a common concern to create meaningful change in their community. Rather than waiting for a top-down legislative solution (e.g., from the Federal government), local residents can determine their unique needs and develop a solution based on those needs. Are there other grassroots efforts with which you are familiar? Have you ever been involved in such an effort? What are the advantages and disadvantages of creating change in this manner?

The coalition continued its dialogues with several national consultants and organizations involved in fathering initiatives. In addition, it thoroughly familiarized itself with the recent professional literature, particularly writings that dramatize the unmet needs of fathers. Among other things, ACT discovered that a lack of available programs to meet the needs of fathers was not unique to Davidson County; it was a state and national phenomenon. Needless to say, these investigations informed, confirmed, and inspired ACT as it moved forward with its efforts.

Considering Funding Support and Proposal Development

Early in this process, the coalition realized that it needed substantial financial support if it were to succeed and decided to seek funds from a private foundation. The Duke Endowment, a foundation that supports innovative family programs sponsored by the Baptist Children's Home in North Carolina, was awarding short-term grants at the time to groups that were addressing family issues in the region. To ACT's delight, this foundation was interested in its efforts, particularly if the focus was on fathers.

The coalition prepared a proposal for a 3-year program, which was expected to be a model for other communities that were interested in establishing fatherhood initiatives. Writing the proposal enabled ACT to articulate several useful goals and objectives as well as to propose a variety of program initiatives.

The coalition proposed three overall strategies to strengthen fatherhood in the county, and it deliberately used language that was affirming of fathers and encouraged their cooperation. The strategies were (1) reconnect fathers and their children; (2) promote and celebrate responsible fatherhood, and (3) implement programs to help fathers reach their full potential as parents.

Several activities were proposed to implement these strategies and were articulated in father-affirming language:

- reaching out to fathers who feel excluded from their children's lives
- advocating for father-friendly employers and family agencies
- educating the community about the roles that fathers play in their children's lives
- providing training and support to fathers and families

Seeking a More In-depth Understanding of the Needs of Fathers

At this point, the ACT Coalition prepared to conduct its own assessment of the needs of fathers and the existing services to fathers in Davidson County. Fortunately, the Duke Endowment was willing to provide a small grant to complete this study. A strategic planning firm was enlisted to aid in this task. With assistance from this planning firm, ACT proposed to conduct a needs-assessment using five identified methods: (1) a series of focus groups with subgroups of nonresidential fathers; (2) one-on-one interviews with these fathers; (3) key informant interviews with pertinent professionals; (4) assessment of existing agency services to fathers; and (5) further examination of existing statistical data on fathers.

The focus groups were intended to find answers to several general questions, three of which were paramount (ACT Coalition of Davidson County, 1999, p. 4). First, they wanted to know what factors or experiences help fathers to attach or connect with their children. Second, they were interested in knowing whether the relationship with the child's mother helped or prevented the father from maintaining contact with his children. Finally, they wanted to know what types of activities or services were needed to meet the needs of fathers.

Unfortunately, these initial focus groups did not go as planned. Many fathers were invited to attend these groups with the help of the Child Support Enforcement Agency (CSEA), the school system, and numerous family agencies, but only one father came. It was difficult for the schools and family agencies to even identify who the nonresidential fathers were. The coalition was suddenly faced with its first major stumbling block—how to recruit and get feedback from the nonresidential fathers, which was a bigger challenge than expected.

The planning agency that was assisting ACT recommended a backup plan. A focus group was organized made up of 13 ACT board members and other interested citizens who had exposure to fatherhood issues to attempt to answer the questions on behalf of these fathers. This focus-group session was valuable in uncovering many likely responses to the questions that were to be asked of the fathers groups, but the absence of firsthand feedback from these fathers remained problematic. Why was *their* feedback so important? For beginners, fathers from these groups would be the only people truly able to speak directly to their needs and the types of programs that could help them. Furthermore, their participation would be essential to knowing what to do next. And of course, if these fathers could not be recruited for focus groups, how would they be successfully recruited into programs that would be offered to them at a later stage? This recruitment question had to be cracked before going much further if this was going to be more than business as usual in which nonresidential fathers were mere spectators.

Reflection
Do you agree that nonresidential fathers would need to be consulted before an effective program could be devised to help them? What might you suggest that the ACT Coalition do to crack the recruitment question?

Assessment of Existing Resources and Suggestions for New Programs for Fathers

A resource-assessment committee was established by the ACT Coalition to gain additional insight into current programs and services that were being provided to families and, more specifically, to fathers. Using a survey study, assessments were made of a family service agency, the correctional facilities, the mental health department, the hospital, other community health providers, local churches, the schools, and other agencies. The committee found that most of the programs and services offered in Davidson County were directed to mothers or both parents. The committee found few programs that focused on the needs of fathers. However, they felt that with some creativity many programs could be expanded to include components just for fathers. For example, they suggested that the mentoring program of the family service agency could add a component in which older dads could pair up and support teenage dads. Other suggestions included special classes for fathers of special-needs children as part of the early childhood intervention program of the mental health department, and more marriage counseling in the churches.

The resource assessment committee's primary recommendation was that new programs were needed to meet many of the needs of fathers, and a critical decision had to be made. Should they focus on helping fathers who want help or on fathers who need help the most? This issue was raised because of the low response rates to the focus groups. They wondered what the reasons were for these low responses, and whether the low responses should be interpreted as a lack of desire for help among fathers.

A Breakthrough on Recruitment

At about this point in time, ACT's new fatherhood initiative hired its first executive director, Stan Meloy. Almost immediately he began to shape the organization's purposes and strategies. Specific target groups of fathers were added: absent fathers not paying child support, incarcerated fathers, couples considering marriage, and blended families. New programs were instituted to help teen dads, noncustodial weekend dads, and fathers failing to pay their child support. A next step would be the one that had already plagued the ACT group—recruiting these fathers and sustaining their participation.

Meloy (2000b) explained that sending dads a letter followed up by a phone call was not an adequate recruitment strategy. This approach lacked a "sit down and get to know you" component, according to Meloy. His approach would be to visit fathers in their homes using a positive approach that seeks to get to know what *they* need as fathers.

Reflection

Why don't you think the mail and phone surveys worked? Do you agree with Mr. Meloy's point of sitting down with the father and getting to know him? What might be the challenges in this approach?

Partnering With Other Social Service Organizations

Meanwhile another critical strategy for recruiting fathers evolved—partnering with other existing nonprofit or social service organizations that were concerned about fathers. With regard to the teen dads, ACT negotiated a contractual agreement with a community mental health agency because they offered a program called MATCH that assists teen moms. Strategically, this agency was a member of the ACT Coalition. The intent of this agreement was to explore a teen fatherhood component that complemented their program, and working with this agency turned out to be an effective way of identifying teen dads through the teen moms participating in MATCH. MATCH was using a pretest/posttest evaluation tool that seeks the mom's perceptions of the impact of the program. The teen mom program agreed to add a couple of questions to this evaluation, such as "How do you feel about the father of your child?" and "Would you want him to be more involved in raising your child?" If the teen moms said that they wanted him to be more involved, the father's name, address, and phone number were sought. To ACT's delight, most of the teen moms said that they wanted the dad to be more involved.

A growing list of teen fathers who had the support of the teen moms began to develop. These fathers were approached by letter and follow-up phone calls, but the calls merely asked whether to visit the father at his home or at another more comfortable site. Fortunately, this new effort has not offended any of the teen dads who have been approached. The next step will be to involve these teen dads in a mentoring program with older, experienced fathers. Support groups will be offered separately to both the teen dads and the mentors to assist them in developing a mentoring relationship.

Partnering with other organizations has been a strategy used by ACT to build other programs as well. The family court and a local job-training center were approached to assist ACT in establishing a program for fathers who were noncompliant in paying support. The court was considered a resource in supplying fathers. The court agreed to give noncompliant fathers a choice—either spend the weekend in jail or attend eight weekly group sessions sponsored by ACT. In turn, ACT designed an Upbeat Dads group service to help these fathers talk through their various struggles so that they would *want* to pay support. The job-training program was also involved to help these fathers get jobs so that they could pay child support.

Next Step?

This case study is still a project in the making. Through a number of efforts, the ACT Coalition has already gathered an enormous amount of previously unknown information about the needs of fathers. Perhaps even more importantly, the coalition members had thoroughly educated themselves about the unmet needs of fathers. Because of their genuine openness and desire to learn about other perspectives on families, they were able to make positive changes in their attitudes about fathers. They were no longer espousing stereotypes and other types of ignorance about fathers, particularly about teenage and other nonresidential fathers. To the contrary, they began educating others in their community, including confronting the stereotypes, ignorance, and indifference to fathers' needs.

The coalition was also discovering and establishing new allies in their new efforts to help fathers. Early on they had turned to several national consultants and organizations that were experts on fatherhood initiatives, and they decided to continue to seek their counsel as they proceeded. They also became well versed in the literature about fathers and began incorporating these research findings and perspectives into their community presentations, program proposals, and daily conversations. Also, they were wise indeed to involve a broad-based coalition of agencies and organizations to accomplish their goals rather than one or two agencies going it alone. In addition, they succeeded in obtaining substantial financial support from a private foundation, a feat that many community groups in similar circumstances had been unable to do. And they were beginning to crack the difficult problem of recruitment.

A MODEL FOR CONDUCTING YOUR OWN COMMUNITY NEEDS-ASSESSMENT

DePoy, Hartmann, and Haslet (1999) identify several critical-action research principles that could be used in conducting a community needs-assessment. These principles overlap with many of the principles discovered by the ACT Coalition.

Reflection

Key critical-action research principles:

1. Collaborate with those affected by the problem to clearly articulate the problem, its scope, and all of the stakeholders.
2. Articulate the purpose of the change that the research is designed to accomplish.
3. Include both professional and lay researchers on the team.
4. Train the lay researchers in how to design, conduct, and use appropriate research methods.
5. Report findings in accessible formats for all stakeholder groups.

Which of the above principles were utilized by the ACT Coalition? How could some of the other principles be utilized to help the ACT Project? For example, how could lay researchers have helped with the initial needs-assessment? (DePoy et al., 1999)

Based on the critical action research principles of DePoy and colleagues (1999) and the experiences of the ACT Coalition, we offer a general outline for conducting a needs-assessment of fathers in other local communities:

1. Build a community-wide organization to sponsor your fatherhood initiative. Include representatives of all relevant agencies and organizations that have an interest in fathers and families on this organization. Also, include representatives of fathers' and mothers' groups, and make sure that you have included people with varying views about how to help fathers.

2. Based on extensive discussion within the organization, articulate a focus for your group, including identifying target groups of fathers that you wish to help, general goals for helping them and their families, and some initial assumptions about the causes of their problems and possible solutions.

3. Develop small committees to gather different types of information about these fathers in the goal areas that you have articulated. Committees can have several focuses such as

- collecting available statistics from the U.S. Census, special U.S. Census reports, health statistics, state studies, local studies, etc.
- reviewing the Web sites of several national fatherhood organizations to find out what they offer, and then calling the organizations that are most relevant to your project's goals (A list of such organizations can be found in the Appendix.)
- talking to the staff and clients of local agencies about these topics
- finding out more about existing programs that serve fathers

4. Organize and report on the material collected in the prior step. As you do this, try to make sure that it is in a format that is easy to read by all stakeholder groups.

5. Explore funding support for your project and involve the ideas of these funding agencies in your continued articulation of the problem and goals of your project. Also, begin articulating a program proposal for funding support. Possible funding supports could be identified earlier in the process in a general way.

6. Decide on the methods that you will use to conduct your own needs-assessment of fathers. This will likely be an in-depth, firsthand study of the community. Possible methods to consider are focus groups, informant interviews, surveys of existing agency resources and services, other surveys of public attitudes, etc. Be sure to include ample participation of fathers' groups that are of interest to your organiza-

tion in the needs-assessment study. Also decide if a professional firm or individual consultant are needed to help you develop your research methodologies.

7. Conduct your planned study as articulated in the previous step and compile an easy-to-read report of your findings.

8. Involve all of the participants in articulating an implementation proposal (sponsoring organizations, fathers that you have met in focus groups, funding agency, etc.). Develop this proposal by first supplementing and revising the earlier versions of your problem definition and goals. Then develop a set of general strategies and specific program proposals that could be implemented to achieve your goals. Be sure to develop a realistic time line for implementing your proposal.

9. Be sure to consider all of the following system levels of intervention in your general strategies:

- individual services to fathers and other family members
- group services to fathers
- mediation services to fathers and their families
- community education
- new family-agency policies

SUMMARY

We note that the efforts of this small rural county coalition are to be commended as they were both ambitious and successful within a fairly short period of time. So few counties or other governmental agencies have launched such courageous efforts. The successes of this project were many, including becoming more enlightened about the problems confronting fathers, establishing a broad-based community coalition to take appropriate action, securing funds for a 3-year project, and involving fathers and other men who would otherwise never have been reached.

Yet this small but mighty coalition has experienced the downside as well. During their initial efforts, for example, they discovered their first major challenge—how to get the fathers who need the help to want it when it is offered. This is an ongoing challenge for this coalition. If they succeed in reaching these fathers, they will likely have a good chance of reaching their ultimate goal of "increasing the number of children who have a close and enduring relationship with a loving, committed, and responsible father" (ACT Coalition of Davidson County, NC, 1999).

Questions for Discussion

Consider the possibility of conducting a community needs-assessment of fathers in your city or county. In this regard, attempt to answer all of the following questions:

1. What organizations and agencies should be invited to become involved in your fatherhood initiative?

2. How will you select representatives from relevant fathers' and mothers' groups?

3. How will you know if you have varying viewpoints from your organizations and parents' groups about how to help fathers and families?

4. How will you organize these various representatives into a community-wide coalition? (What will this coalition initially be called, how often will you propose that it meets, how will organizations and parents be notified about its proposed purposes, and how will you recruit them for an initial meeting?)

5. Plan an initial meeting for this new coalition. (Identify some possible purposes for the coalition, some possible target groups of fathers to help, general goals to consider for helping them, and some initial assumptions about the causes of their problems and possible solutions.)

6. In preparation for your coalition's initial meeting, review relevant U.S. Census reports and state and local studies. Summarize what you have learned that can be shared at the initial meeting of the coalition.

7. Review three of the Web sites of national fatherhood organizations listed in the Appendix of this book. Summarize what you have learned that can be shared at the initial meeting.

8

Policy Initiatives That Support Active Fathering

If you [nonresidential fathers] don't pay the child support you owe, we will garnish your wages, take away your driver's license, track you across state lines and, if necessary, make you work off what you owe. (President Bill Clinton)

This chapter will help the reader understand the policies that have been enacted in this society to address the issue of nonresidential parenting. A brief historical perspective will be offered as well as an exploration of more recent policy initiatives that have the potential for promoting active fathering. The purpose of this chapter is to help the reader

- Understand the historical policy initiatives directed toward nonresidential fathers
- Connect historical beliefs and stereotypes about nonresidential fathers with current beliefs, practices, and policies
- Identify key policy initiatives related to nonresidential fathers
- Describe the impact of policies on nonresidential fathers
- Identify helpful policies for nonresidential fathers

OUR PAST

Local, state, and national policies are critical in shaping the specific intervention programs that are developed and ultimately funded in our society. For example, Head Start was developed as a direct result of the polices that were enacted during the War on Poverty in the 1960s. It is important to recognize that programs that emerge to assist nonresidential fathers are also frequently enacted as a direct result of local, state, and national policies.

It is the intent of this chapter to explore the overarching policies that affect nonresidential fathers. Some of these policies create antagonistic and negative feelings toward nonresidential fathers, with programs to match those attitudes. These policies often *reflect* the negative societal views of these fathers. Other policies have sought to increase our understanding of the special issues faced by nonresidential fathers and lead to program efforts that truly assist these fathers.

How can we help nonresidential fathers become more involved with their children? What policies can we enact? What programs can we develop? Historically, efforts by society to assist nonresidential fathers in being responsible parents have led to policies that focus on finding better ways to collect child support payments from them. Child desertion and the subsequent lack of financial support were first raised as public concerns in the late 19th century when, in 1894, the National Conference of Charities and Correction led by Reverend E. P. Savage explored the issue. Savage (1895) conducted a study in which he documented the conditions of the more than 7,000 deserted children reported by 800 charitable agencies. Savage estimated that more than two thirds of these children had been abandoned by their fathers. He speculated that in 1895 more than 25,000 children had probably been deserted by fathers in the United States. Savage went on to complain about the lack of effort by the government to pursue these fathers and recommended that taxpayers be notified so they might understand the cost of such abandonment (estimated at $2 million a year). It was his hope to arouse the public to take action against these nonresidential, uninvolved fathers. Of course, Savage's research did little to explain the *reasons* for the absence of these fathers or their *reasons* for not contributing financially, but was driven instead by a political agenda to punish the offenders.

As you listen to Savage's plea for punishment, it is easy to detect similar sentiments that exist in our society 100 years later. President Clinton's quote at the beginning of this chapter reinforces the notion that the overriding concern seems to be on using punitive measures to make fathers more responsible. Clinton's words show little concern for the underlying reasons that might lead a father to be absent and uninvolved. The emphasis seems to be on treating a symptom rather than exploring the causes of absentee fathers. Examples of policy initiatives that have resulted from this punitive stance include such things as child support enforcement policies, the Family Support Act of 1988 (FSA), and more recently the Personal Responsibility and Work Opportunity Reconciliation Act of 1996. The consistent theme of policy initiatives throughout this century has been to find better ways *to punish nonresidential fathers to make them pay child support.* Each generation has seen increasingly punitive stances toward nonresidential fathers, from the $100 fine and 3 months in jail imposed in the early 1900s to sanctions of $250,000 and/or imprisonment for up to 2 years allowed by the FSA in 1988. Key issues continue to be overlooked, including the following:

- A consistent failure to consider the mitigating circumstances that might lead a father to become an absent father, such as health issues, lack of knowledge about how to be a visiting parent, and barriers imposed by the in-laws.
- The societal factors that may have led to absentee fathers, including harsh economic times, discrimination toward minority fathers, and male socialization issues related to fathering.
- The particular dynamics of the relationship with the child's mother that may impact a father's ability to carry out important paternal roles and responsibilities; in particular issues related to the gatekeeping role of the child's mother, continued hostility between the parents, and intentional blocking of visitation by the children's mother
- The special needs of the nonresidential father and the built-in challenges of trying to stay involved with their children on a visiting basis. For example, men may feel powerless in their role as visitor in their child's life, and children may not understand how to relate to their own father as a visitor in their life.
- The other important strengths that fathers can bring to the father-child relationship, social and emotional supports that are more vitally important than financial support. As was pointed out in chapter 3, father presence can have numerous positive effects on child development.

Reflection
It seems that efforts to involve nonresidential fathers with their children that focus solely on child support enforcement are doomed to fail. Why is this still the most visible policy stance in this society? What can be done to change this to include a more holistic view of the nonresidential fathering role?

Very few policy efforts have sought to assist nonresidential fathers in finding ways to contribute the nonmonetary types of assets that fathers possess. As stated in the opening to this chapter, policies guide program development and therefore it is no surprise that very few program initiatives during the past 100 years sought to involve nonresidential fathers in meaningful ways beyond financial support of their children. Fortunately, more recent policies and programs have experimented in helping nonresidential fathers to be active parents in every aspect of their child's life, not just the financial. Innovative programs are being developed that build on fathers' strengths as well as help teach nonresidential fathers how to nurture and be part of their child's life. The following sections will discuss the policies behind these programs, and later chapters in the book will give specific examples of such programs.

SUPPORTIVE POLICIES

Despite the historically harsh treatment of nonresidential fathers, many still stay involved. They pay child support, spend quality time with their children, and contribute to the development of their children in ways beyond financial measures. Occasionally, supportive policy initiatives are put forth and eventually lead to meaningful programs that actually assist and support nonresidential fathers in their efforts to stay active and involved with their children. Some of these programs even encourage and expand upon fathers' existing strengths in ways that actually improve their ability to parent. It is the purpose of this section to explore helpful policy initiatives directed at nonresidential fathers.

National Policies

TAX REFORM POLICIES

The Earned Income Credit (EIC) is a federal policy that was created to reduce the tax burden on workers who earn low or moderate incomes.

For example, in order to qualify for EIC in 1999 an individual's earned income and modified adjusted gross income must be less than $26,928 with one qualifying child, or $30,580 with more than one qualifying child. Further expanding the earned income tax credit would increase the incomes of poor families and potentially assist in self-sufficiency.

FAMILY AND MEDICAL LEAVE ACT OF 1993

In 1993, Congress passed the Family and Medical Leave Act (FMLA) of 1993 (P.L. 103–3). The FMLA requires businesses with 50 or more employees to provide 12 weeks a year of unpaid leave for birth, adoption, or personal or family illness. Employers must also continue to provide health care coverage during leave and restore employees to their jobs or equivalent positions upon their return. Mandated family leave is largely a result of unprecedented changes in the composition of the workforce and the nature of workers' family responsibilities, dramatically altering the traditional relationship between employees' work and personal lives. This conflict between work and family obligations has become an inevitable aspect of modern work life, often resulting in absenteeism, work interference, job turnover, and other deleterious impacts. While conflict between work and fathering responsibilities cannot be eliminated, family leave and other work/family policies can make it easier for fathers (and mothers) to fulfill their responsibilities as parents, family members, and workers.

Research has shown that mandated family leave apparently has not dramatically changed the number of fathers taking leave (Scharlach & Grosswald, 1997). For example, the increase of males who took family leave at AT&T increased only slightly after passage of FMLA, from 4% in 1993 to 6% in 1994 (as cited in Levine & Pittinsky, 1997). Without the availability of paid leave, utilization rates will likely remain low. Just as government mandates were needed to grant employees unpaid family leaves, they ultimately may be required to institute paid leaves.

Levine and Pittinsky (1997) point out that it would be a mistake to view the use of paternity leave by fathers as a barometer of social change in fathering. They suggest that we should avoid applying a "maternal" standard to the use of parental leave. There may be no reason for fathers to use parental leave in the same manner that mothers use it, especially if there is a significant loss of income as a result of his doing so.

Reflection

Roberto worked full-time as bookkeeper in a large department store. He and his partner had agreed upon joint physical custody following their breakup, but this was very difficult for him to carry out at times because of the special needs of his disabled child. His son required frequent visits to the doctor for blood work and other tests. The situation seemed hopeless for Roberto until the FMLA of 1993 was passed. Now Roberto can use the family leave policy periodically to take his child to the doctor and to attend group therapy sessions for family members of children with disabilities. Roberto reports that he has made noticeable improvements in bonding with his child and in his caretaking abilities.

What could you do to encourage other fathers to take advantage of the FMLA? How would you deal with their fears that it may hurt their careers?

Although family leave has only limited value for the nonresidential father (because it would most likely apply to the time period right after child birth), it is significant that fathers were included in the policy. In a sense, the inclusion of fathers serves a symbolic purpose by acknowledging the important role that fathers can and do enact with their children and families.

PERSONAL RESPONSIBILITY AND WORK OPPORTUNITY RECONCILIATION ACT OF 1996

Although the Personal Responsibility and Work Opportunities Act of 1996 contained many sections that were simply designed to get money from nonresidential fathers and put women to work who were on AFDC, there was an important provision included that provided for access and visitation programs for fathers. In an apparent effort to increase noncustodial parents' involvement in their children's lives, the policy included grants to help states establish programs that support and facilitate noncustodial parents' visitation and access to their children. This provision represents a minor revolution in the way the federal government has historically viewed the nonresidential father. It opens the door for states to explore creative ways to involve nonresidential fathers. This policy has been instrumental in getting several states to explore alternative ways of involving nonresidential fathers and their children, involvement beyond child support enforcement.

MINIMUM WAGE INCREASES

Mandatory federal increases in the minimum wage can have a positive ripple effect on all family members. With respect to fathers, increased wages can lead to increased resources available to provide essential items for his children. This may assist the father in paying regular child support and maintaining a more satisfying lifestyle in his own household.

State Initiatives

The National Center for Children in Poverty (NCCP) has identified five key strategies that are critical to increasing nonresidential father involvement:

1. Promoting public awareness about responsible fatherhood
2. Preventing unwanted or early fatherhood
3. Enhancing fathers as economic providers
4. Strengthening fathers as nurturers
5. Promoting leadership capacity

Numerous states have made efforts to implement policies and programs that address one or more of these five strategies. Based upon surveys conducted by the NCCP, state efforts to address these five areas are summarized below:

PUBLIC AWARENESS

NCCP conducted surveys in 1997 and 1999 to assess what was happening at the state level in relationship to these five strategies. Results from the 1999 survey found that all of the states responding to the NCCP questionnaire had at least one activity to encourage responsible fatherhood. The study showed that 38 of the 45 responding states reported current activities using public awareness to promote responsible fatherhood. Twenty-one states are implementing two or more public-awareness initiatives to encourage responsible fatherhood. There was an increase in the proportion of states that have public awareness initiatives compared to 1997. These strategies included (a) sponsoring conferences, forums, or summits on responsible fatherhood; (b) using sports teams to bring the message of responsible fatherhood to the public; (c) using public service announcements on posters, radio, television, or the Internet; and (d) using special publications on fatherhood.

PREVENTING EARLY FATHERHOOD

In 1999, 37 states indicated that they sponsor one or more initiatives to help prevent unwanted or early fatherhood. These strategies include (a) a school-linked strategy, usually a curriculum to help young men prevent unwanted fatherhood; (b) community-based programs funded or entirely run by the state; (c) federally funded abstinence programs; and (d) specialized direct-service programs that teach father responsibility through either case management, mentoring, or peer education. Other means, include working with incarcerated youths, developing a task force on unintended pregnancies, developing plans for interagency collaboration for preventing unwanted or early fatherhood, encouraging state service agency staff to speak with and help young fathers, and working with businesses to promote positive youth development.

ENHANCING FATHERS AS ECONOMIC PROVIDERS

Given the low national child-support collection rates (nationally, Child Support Enforcment [CSE] agencies collect in about 21% of the cases) and the large numbers of low-income fathers, strategies to promote economic family sufficiency among fathers is crucial. Forty-three states reported strategies to help fathers be better economic providers for their children, either by assisting low-income fathers with employment and training or by improving child support enforcement. These strategies include (a) an employment and training program for low-income and unemployed fathers, often funded by Temporary Assistance for Needy Families (TANF) or Welfare-to-Work funds; (b) improved methods for determining paternity; (c) training staff at state and local service agencies, including Head Start, in CSE procedures; (d) continuing child-support pass-throughs[1];

---

[1]Pass-through is a technical term referring to an effort to encourage cooperation between Aid for Families with Dependent Children (AFDC) recipients and the child support enforcement agency. New laws have required states to disregard the first $50 paid by the father in child support each month, and allow that money to "pass through" directly to the child. In the past AFDC merely used father contributions to offset their costs.

and (e) a state earned income tax credit (EITC) to low-income families.

STRENGTHENING FATHERS AS NURTURERS

In 1999, 36 states indicated they were implementing one or more initiatives to promote fathers as nurturers. Strategies include: (a) using access and visitation projects supported with federal funds from the welfare law, (b) sponsoring divorce and conflict mediation or counseling for divorcing or never-married couples, (c) providing programs for incarcerated fathers, and (d) promoting father-friendly workplace policies. Other methods include establishing a putative father registry for men to volunteer paternity, providing public assistance to mothers who marry the father of their child, and outreach and parenting classes to new fathers.

Perspective: Innovative Programming

An example of a program that came about as a result of the changing direction of policy related to nonresidential fathers is It's My Child, Too, a parenting program aimed at young, unwed fathers in Indiana (Innovative Program). The goal of the program is for fathers to recognize the important role they play in the lives of their children as well as to become better parents. The fathering course was developed by Purdue University's Center for Families and is administered by the Purdue Cooperative Extension Service. It is partially funded by the Restoring Fatherhood Initiative, an effort by the Family and Social Services Administration of Indiana that diverts funds that would have gone to welfare into fathering programs. It's My Child, Too is being implemented in schools, community centers and detention centers. Most fathers attend the program once a week for 6 weeks. The program focuses on

- The father's role in children's lives
- The basics of child care and development
- The strategies for proactive parenting
- The ways to recognize and cope with stress
- The need for parental cooperation

Initial feedback from participants has been very positive.

BUILDING STATE AND LOCAL LEADERSHIP AROUND A FATHERHOOD AGENDA

A focus on leadership is a key to promoting a policy agenda in the context of multiple state and local priorities. There are three clear ways of indicating leadership around a fatherhood agenda: (a) creating a state-level focus for engaging a broad group of stakeholders; (b) developing fiscal strategies to promote local program development and leadership; and (c) keeping track of funding levels.

In 1999, 22 states indicated that they have initiatives to build leadership capacity around responsible fatherhood. Strategies include (a) creating coordinating bodies to oversee fatherhood initiatives, (b) keeping better track of fatherhood expenditures, (c) assisting in creating coalitions or networks of leaders, (d) using mini-grants to encourage innovative programs on fatherhood, and (e) using TANF savings to sponsor fatherhood programs.

Despite the widespread changes seen at the state level, there is evidence emerging from fatherhood literature, from among practitioners, and from among fathers that a series of critical issues will become more central in the coming years in response to the popular media, new policy directions, and fatherhood advocates. While a handful of states are addressing one or more of these issues, most do not.

- Helping fathers in families trying to balance family and work responsibilities
- Integrating strategies to encourage fathers as economic providers and as nurturers
- Understanding the gender issues confronting the field (e.g., how has the idea of what is masculine changed in the past 20 years? What is feminine? What is marriage?)
- Connecting fatherhood to the broader child and family agenda (e.g., how is fathering figured into welfare reform?)
- Keeping the momentum of the movement going despite changes in state leadership
- Building the knowledge base about fatherhood through research

---

Perspective: Tipping Point Theory

David Cohen suggests that we apply tipping-point theory, to understand how we can change norms related to fatherhood. This theory—which has been used to explain the spread of epidemics as well as social ideas—suggests that peer pressure, religious leaders, community programs, and corporate culture all play a role in changing norms. In addition, it can be seen how larger social norms and state and federal policies and practices can play a part in this change. How do you see these factors coming to play in changing norms related to fatherhood? How would you attempt to bring about positive changes through use of peer pressure, religious leaders, community programs, corporate culture, and state and federal policies?

Workplace Policies

Beyond the national and state efforts to provide support to fathers' efforts to stay involved with their children, many businesses, corporations, and other places of work have made efforts to change the work environment to be more father-friendly. This is consistent with tipping-point theory, which suggests that changes in corporate culture are needed to help bring about changes in norms related to fatherhood. It should be noted, however, that one misconception that has existed in the workplace is that family-friendly work policies are automatically father-friendly (Levine & Pittinsky, 1997). In reality, it is often the case that family-friendly work policies are typically mother-friendly and not geared toward the specific needs of the working father. In many cases this prevents working fathers from participating in supportive work programs because they may view the programming as being focused more on the needs of working mothers. Levine and Pittinsky (1997) present a list of issues that should be part of creating a father-friendly workplace, which are as follows:

FATHERHOOD AS A GUIDING VALUE AT THE WORKPLACE

Levine and Pittinsky suggest that it is very possible for a company to commit itself to valuing families and to organize its work to preserve that commitment and still remain competitive. This commitment may require companies to reduce billable hours, but the long-term payoffs for fathers, as well as for the company, are virtually immeasurable. However, a sacrifice of income requires a mutual agreement between workers and management. All must commit to the idea that family (and fatherhood and motherhood) is more important than money. One law firm reported that this new emphasis on fatherhood and family actually improved its ability to recruit and retain the best attorneys. Of course, it will always be difficult to balance career and family. As one father stated to Levine and Pittinsky, "Being a dad is more important than having a career, but you have to have a career to pay the bills" (1997, p. 80). This is an internal conflict that most fathers must struggle with as they try to manage multiple roles. In addition, only those fathers who work in companies and in positions that have flexibility in what a "billable" hour is would be affected by these solutions. These options may have little value to the father who works at the factory or in a service job.

Perspective: Role Conflict and Role Confusion

Many fathers report a great deal of conflict and role confusion over the numerous roles they must balance in their life. Stone and McKenry (1998) found that role conflict and role confusion can have a significant impact on nonresidential fathers and whether they stay involved with their children after divorce. Their study found that fathers who were clear about the expectations of their role as nonresidential fathers were more likely to stay involved. The study also found that fathers who placed the role of father above all others were more likely to stay involved with their children after divorce. What would you do to help clarify the role of the nonresidential father? What would you do to assist fathers in seeing the importance of their fathering role?

USING COMMUNICATION TOOLS TO SUPPORT WORKING FATHERS

Levine and Pittinsky (1997) also suggest that advanced forms of communication can be used to help support working fathers, including e-mail, Internet connections, and in-house parenting forums. They report that some companies are using e-mail to encourage fathers to seek advice on parenting issues. They describe the success of a program started at Eastman Kodak called Kodak's Working Parent's League, which started as an e-mail newsletter that had 12 subscribers and grew to more than 400 subscribers. During one 2-week period, 8,000 notices were posted about everything from babysitting to used high chairs. One critical element of success was the special outreach efforts that were made to include fathers, in essence to combat the notion that a family-friendly program did not mean a father-friendly program. Efforts speak for themselves in the success in getting fathers to use the service.

OFFERING WORKPLACE EDUCATION AND SUPPORT FOR FATHERS

It seems obvious that one way to demonstrate support for fathers at work is to provide on-site father-education and training programs. This can be an excellent way to demonstrate that family friendly workplace also means father friendly workplace. The National Center for Fathering has developed workshops specific to the father issues in the corporate and business world and provides seminars for groups of men and women and fathers-only groups. Presentations range in length from a 40–minute overview to in-depth and intensive workshops that run to 8 hours. Topics include the impact of fatherlessness on America, the impact of a father, practical tips, and the life stages of fathering. These are designed to be offered at the workplace and could appeal to fathers who are concerned that family programming at work does not include father programming (see http://www.fathers.com/ for more information).

Employers are also finding that by offering these types of workplace programs they may be able to recruit and retain the best employees (Levine & Pittinsky, 1997). In essence, this sort of innovative approach to the role conflict and role confusion that fathers experience helps set companies apart from others and therefore may help them obtain the best talent. They also may find that they have happier and more productive employees. By helping fathers work out the dilemma of how to be both the manager at work and the manager of their daughter's softball team, companies can reduce the level of stress that the father experiences, and less stress can mean better work.

Reflection

Sam attended a seminar on fathering that was sponsored by his workplace. Afterwards he reported that he had a new appreciation for the importance of his role of father to his two children. He also reported that the seminar gave him helpful suggestions how to balance his career and his role as father. Why aren't there more seminars being offered like the one Sam attended? By sponsoring this type of seminar what message has Sam's workplace sent about the importance of fathering?

ENCOURAGING FATHERS' PARTICIPATION IN THEIR CHILDREN'S
SCHOOLS

Research has consistently shown that a crucial ingredient in a child's performance at school is the level of engagement evidenced by the parents. During the 1990s, I (Glenn Stone) was involved in numerous meetings between corporations and school systems that were looking for ways by which companies could make a meaningful contribution to improving the education of children. We brainstormed creative solutions that included having companies serving as special financial sponsors of individual public schools or sending employees to give motivational talks to help kids see the benefit of a good education. Many of these ideas became reality and were helpful in their own way. Yet somehow we missed one of the most obvious: How could employers provide sufficient flexible scheduling to allow parents to be more involved with their child's schooling? A father-friendly (and mother-friendly) workplace would make it easier for fathers to take time to participate in their child's school activities without feeling it would jeopardize job security and chances for advancement. Levine and Pittinsky (1997) describe an innovative approach to this issue that was employed at Hemmings Motor News in Vermont, where workers are given 2 paid days off per year to be involved in either education participation or community service. In 1995, approximately 25% of Hemmings's workers took advantage of this opportunity.

SUPPORTING FATHERS WHO NEED TO STAY HOME WHEN A CHILD IS ILL

The American Medical Association reports that the average school-age child is sick between 6 and 9 times a year, with the average length of illness ranging from 1 day to a week. It seems logical that many of these times a child will be too sick to attend school. Who will take care of this child when both parents work? What does the single father do if he has limited or no support at work for staying with his child? While some workplaces may look favorably upon the mother's taking the time off, a father may not be afforded the same support.

Serious efforts to change workplace culture in a way that is father-friendly will need to address this issue. Levine and Pittinsky (1997) report an innovative plan at John Hancock Insurance, which provides 3 paid-family leave days so that employees can stay home with a sick child or other family member.

PAID PATERNITY LEAVE

The federal government's legislation for parental leave was a step in the right direction of encouraging fathers to be involved in the early phase of being a new father. Yet there is still little chance that men will pursue family leave because it is unpaid. It will be an uphill battle getting employers to change their internal policies on this issue. When 1,500 CEOs and human-resource directors were asked how much work leave is reasonable for a father after the birth of a child, 63% indicated "none" (Pleck, 1991). As reported earlier, statistics show that very few fathers take paternity leave (approximately 6% in 1994), and this number has been shown to grow dramatically when paid leave is offered. Levine and Pittinsky (1997) report that when Sacramento became the first county in California to offer paid paternity leave, more than 50% of those who used it in the sheriff's department were men (52 total leaves were taken). Interviews with those showed that they viewed paid paternity leave as a significant way for them to be involved in the early childhood experiences.

Reflection

Malcolm works at a social service agency that offers paid paternity leave for fathers. When he approached his supervisor about taking two weeks off after the birth of his daughter, the supervisor hesitated and suggested that the timing was bad. The supervisor also questioned Malcom about the necessity of taking the time off since the mother was not going to be working for the first 6 months after giving birth. What messages is the supervisor sending to Malcolm about the importance of paternity leave and about the importance of father involvement with an infant?

In addition to the suggestions put forth by Levine and Pittinsky (1997), the National Fatherhood Initiative provides similar suggestions, but also a few different ideas that seem noteworthy:

- *Establish flexible spending accounts.* These types of accounts allow employees to "shelter" parts of their income from taxation for specific purposes. Examples of areas that may be tax sheltered include medical expenses and child care expenses. By placing parts of one's income into a flexible spending account, the financial burdens of parenting can be reduced, in effect providing more disposable income to parents to care for their children.

- *Allow flextime and flexible work hours.* Although this suggestion was implied in many of the ideas put forth by Levine and Pittinsky (1997), it seems particularly worth noting. Although federal, state, and local policies may dictate the type of flextime that might be available to workers, it is an option that more employers should explore. In essence, flextime allows employees to exchange overtime hours for days off. Rather than being paid for overtime, the worker could choose to take time with his family without fear of losing income. Employers may also want to consider allowing workers to swap shifts with other employees in order to take children to see the doctor, attend a child's sporting event, or meet other family obligations.

- *Encourage telecommuting.* In the new information age, geographic location becomes less relevant for many types of work (Cleveland, 1985; Huey, 1994), and there is a significant redefinition of what we refer to as the workplace. Work that can be done almost anywhere and sent to a central location via telecommunications is called telecommuting or telework (Nilles, 1991). E-mail, fax, telephone, the Internet, and video conferencing have made it increasingly possible for workers to be highly productive without ever leaving their home to travel to the office. Currently, almost a third of the U.S. labor force does at least some of their work from home. The home workplace could have far-reaching effects on individual and family life. For fathers, telecommuting may permit them to have more contact with their children. Furthermore, this option would allow many fathers the benefit of home care for their children, while relieving the stress and cost of commuting. There seem to be benefits for the employer as well. A recent study by the International Telework Association and Council (1999) found that employees who telework save their employers approximately $10,000 a year in reduced absenteeism and job retention costs. The survey also reported that productivity rates for teleworkers increased by 22%.

SUMMARY AND IMPLICATIONS

For decades, the predominant policy in this society relative to nonresidential fathers has been finding ways to get fathers to pay child support. Within the past decade we have seen some changes that focus on finding ways to include fathers in their children's lives in more meaningful ways. These changes have been slow in coming, but any shift toward positive and inclusive policy development constitutes a minor revolution in comparison with our past history of dealing with this population.

It is important to note that there are still areas in need of change. Practitioners who work with fathers and have an interest in exploring macro changes may want to consider ways to advocate for the continuation of the gains that were made in the last decade (e.g., increased access policies, workplace policies) as well as consider advocating for additional changes. The areas still in need of improvement including the following:

Paid Paternity Leave

Research has consistently demonstrated that fathers are unlikely to take paternity leave if it is not paid. It seems logical that fathers would be reluctant to take unpaid leave at the very moment when financial resources are most needed.

Employment-Related Services for Low-Income Noncustodial Fathers

Research has shown that many noncustodial fathers do not have adequate income to provide financial assistance for their children. A recent study found that nearly one half of low-income noncustodial fathers who do not pay child support have not completed high school, and fewer than one in five have full-time, year-round work. Personal income is barely enough to support themselves, making it nearly impossible to support children living in another household.

At this point there is no funding stream dedicated to providing employment-related services to low-income noncustodial fathers. States have the option but are not required to serve this population. One approach might be to establish a new block grant to states. The Fathers Count Act of 1998 did just that but never made it to a vote. Other options include using parts of existing block grants or using part of the existing funds for child-support enforcement to provide these services (Sorenson, 1999).

Incentives to Pay Child Support

Although we have stressed the view that fathers should be thought of as more than "wallets-in-waiting," the reality of the current situation makes it clear that any support a noncustodial father can give to his child is critical to the quality of life that the child will enjoy. The pass-through policies discussed earlier were supposed to provide additional incentives for fathers to pay support. A more radical approach being used in Wisconsin is to allow the mother to keep all of the child support paid by the father on the child's behalf and to disregard that amount in determining welfare benefits (Sorenson, 1999). Another incentive is to encourage fathers to pay directly for some things like medical insurance, summer camp, or a child's clothing and to count this toward their child support responsibilities. It can help them to become involved in spending for their child's needs and also increases bonding with their child, for instance, by taking their child on a shopping trip for a new winter coat (Dudley, 1991b).

Revamp Child Support Enforcement Policies

It is time to reconsider whether current child-support enforcement policies treat noncustodial fathers fairly, particularly low-income fathers. Child-support orders are very regressive because of current state guidelines, combined with practices regarding default and retroactive orders. These require low-income fathers to pay a considerably higher percentage of their income in child support than do fathers with higher income. Obviously, new support guidelines need to be formulated for these low-income fathers.

Given this unfair setup, many low-income fathers fall behind in child support quite quickly. It might be helpful if states were to establish amnesty programs that forgives this debt as long a noncustodial father keeps up with his current child support. Of course the current payments would need to be based on a new set of guidelines that would be fairer to low-income fathers and less regressive (Sorenson, 1999).

Support Programs

The support programs mentioned in the state initiatives section represent creative ways to assist noncustodial fathers in remaining actively involved in the lives of their children. It seems vitally important that these efforts continue and that they be expanded. A reduction in the number of states that implement programs to promote fathers as nurturers was noted earlier (down from 40 states in 1997 to 36 states in 1999), and it seems critical that advocates not allow this downward trend to continue.

Much of the policy aimed at encouraging fatherhood among nonresidential fathers in the past century has focused on ways to make them pay child support. This rather single-minded pursuit of financial support has in many ways created a situation in which other aspects of fathering are devalued. Only recently have policies and programs been developed that focus on ways to increase father and child contact, improve the quality of their relationship, and improve the co-parental relationship between the parents after divorce or separation. There are still fathers who will need negative sanctions in order to motivate them to take responsibility for their role as father; however, there is a significant number of uninvolved nonresidential fathers who would respond better to less punitive, more supportive approaches to assist them in connecting with their children and engaging in responsible fathering.

Questions for Discussion

1. Contact your state representative and ask about father-related legislation currently under consideration in your state. How would you characterize the legislation? Is it primarily punitive or supportive?

2. Consider the various reasons that a father may become an absentee father. What policies and programs would you pursue to address the diverse causes of absentee father?

9

Programs for Preparing Teenagers for Fatherhood

Leon was 17 years old when his girlfriend, Felicity, became pregnant. At first he didn't want to believe it, but when the truth sank in he began to think about what it would mean to have a child. Problems started long before the baby's birth. When Felicity's family found out about the pregnancy they became very angry at Leon. He was told that he was not to come to their apartment anymore and to stay away from Felicity "or else."

By the time his daughter, Tawny, was born, a week after his 18th birthday, Leon had found a job and was able to help out with the support. Felicity was not sure if she wanted to "be with" Leon (as in being married), and he was finding it more and more difficult to get along with her. He would visit and end up arguing with Felicity and her family, even in front of Tawny. He kept saying that his main hope and goal was to "be with his child," but the fighting and arguing was jeopardizing this goal.

This chapter will help the reader gain a clearer understanding of the myths and realities about teenage fathers. The scope of the problem will be explored, explanations for the current trends will be offered, and programs that help prepare teenagers for fatherhood will also be discussed. The purpose of this chapter is to help the reader

- Analyze facts versus "stereotypes" regarding teen fathers
- Describe the current trends in teen fathering
- Identify explanations for the trends in teen fathering
- Describe the important components of teen-father programs
- Identify the pros and cons of teen-father programs

Get a piece of paper and let's play word association. What five adjectives first come to mind when I say, "teen father"? Be honest. If you are like many people in this society you wrote down words like *irresponsible, uncaring, immature, deadbeat,* or *uninvolved.* You even may have had images of various racial or ethnic characteristics that you associate with teen fathers, which are based almost entirely on stereotypes. Very little factual material about teen fathers is found in the popular press or media. Most often these sources continue to propagate myths and stereotypes about this population. Hopefully this chapter can help us gain a better understanding about what we really know about teen fathers like Leon in the case example. In addition, we will explore programs that are designed to prepare teens for fatherhood.

TEEN FATHERS: WHO ARE THEY?

If we were to have asked this question in the early 1980s, the response might have been something like this: "We don't know, and we're not sure that we really care." Teen pregnancy was considered a women's issue and the male partner was virtually ignored. In the absence of facts about teen fathers, there was an abundance of public opinion, most of it negative. For the most part they were viewed as one-night-stand victimizers of young women and were considered to be uncaring, uninvolved, and irresponsible (Adams & Pittman, 1988). It is easy to understand that because of these views about young fathers there was little interest or effort in attempting to strengthen the role of the young father. Why would you want to put a child in contact with a young father who possessed such negative characteristics, an uncaring, impulsive, hit-and-run artist? It is quite likely, however, that these negative views led us to overlook the potential contributions that young fathers like Leon could make to the well-being of the child and young mother (Cutrona, Hessling, Bacon, & Russell, 1998).

It is not uncommon to assume that most of the fathers of children born to teenage mothers are themselves adolescents, yet this is not usually the case. Most of the fathers of children born to adolescent mothers are more than 20 years old (Landry & Forrest, 1995). More than half are in their early 20s, with only 6% younger than 18 (Adams & Pittman, 1988). Most teenage pregnancies involve 18- or 19-year-old females and males in their early 20s, so the age difference between the father and mother is typically only 3 to 4 years. The National Center for Health Statistics indicates that only 29% of babies born to teen mothers had teen fathers. The Children's Defense Fund (1988) estimates that approximately 30% of the children born to adolescent mothers were fathered by teenage males. Thus, although it would appear that there are a substantial number of teenage fathers in this country, the majority of adolescent pregnancies are caused by male adults, not teenage boys.

It is also important to note that while the increasing rate of teenage pregnancies is a cause for concern, teenage pregnancy is not a new phenomenon in this country. National records show that hundreds of thousands of births among teenage girls occurred yearly during this century (Males, 1993). What is a new trend in this society is the growing number of teen girls having children outside of marriage. The number and rate of children born out of wedlock to teen parents has risen steadily over the past three decades, from 12% of all teen births in 1960 to 68% of all births to teens in 1990 (Moore, Snyder, & Hall, 1992). This trend has significant consequences for the children of these young fathers, as well as for the young mothers, which will be discussed later.

Racial and Ethnic Variations

Sonenstein (1986) notes that while fairly accurate information exists about the demographic characteristics of teen mothers, very little precise demographic information on teen fathers is available because the father is often not listed on the birth registration forms of children born to teen mothers. Despite the shortage of information, some research has found that birth rates vary significantly by ethnicity. In a study by Lerman (1992), it was found that the probability of becoming an unwed father ranged from 1% for nonpoor Whites to 11% for Black youths. The Black rates were more than double the rates for Hispanics (5.1%) and poor Whites (4.1%). The probability of becoming an unwed father was only 1.6% for Asian teens and 3.6% for Native American teens. These findings suggest that African American teens are at greatest risk of becoming teen fathers. The likelihood of a young African American man becoming a father before age 20 is 146% greater, even when differences in income, family structure, and attitudes are statistically controlled (Hanson, Morrison, & Ginsburg, 1989).

Educational Attainment

Young fathers have a lower level of educational attainment than their peers who are not fathers. Various studies found that men who become parents while they are teens are much more likely to drop out of high school. However, it is not clear whether the low interest in schooling resulted from the pregnancy or whether this lack of interest was a existing characteristic (Lerman, 1986; Marsiglio, 1988).

Family Background Factors

Various studies have looked at the teen father's family of origin as a possible source of influence on becoming a father. Marsiglio (1988) reports that males not living with two parents at age 14 are overrepresented among teen fathers. Other familial factors that have been shown to increase sexual risk-taking and early parenting among young men include poor parent-child relationships, poor communication, and overly permissive parenting (Chilman, 1980; Miller, McCoy, Olson, & Wallace, 1986; Robbins, Kaplan, & Martin, 1985). It has also been found that teen fathers are more likely to have grown up in families that are poor. As family resources increase, the likelihood of becoming a teen parent decreases (Michael & Tuma, 1985).

Psychological and Behavioral Profile

Clinical studies conducted on young fathers have attempted to provide a rudimentary understanding of the psychological, emotional, and developmental issues related to teen fathering. However, studies which focus on predisposing psychological factors that would lead to teen fathering are marked as much by what isn't found to hold true as elucidating common traits or characteristics. Much early research sought to connect teen fathering with the young male's sense of "locus of control." This psychological term refers to a belief about whether the outcomes of our actions depend on what we do (internal control orientation) or on events outside our personal control (external control orientation) (Zimbardo, 1985, p. 275). It is believed that individuals tend to either internalize or externalize their behaviors according to their level of locus of control. Those with an internal locus of control will likely attribute their behaviors more to internal factors, whereas those with an external locus of control will likely attribute their behaviors more to external factors (Rotter, 1966). According to Rotter, external factors are the forces perceived to be outside one's control, and internal factors are the forces perceived to be within one's control. With regard to teen fathers, it was thought that teens who held to an external locus of control would be more likely to engage in unprotected sex because they felt they had little ability to control what would happen to them, that is, other factors (outside of their actions) determined what occurred in their life (good luck, bad luck, fate). There is some research indicating that this theory may hold some validity for African American teen fathers but not for other racial and ethnic groups.

Reflection
What might the reasons be for the difference between the levels of locus of control that exist between African American teen fathers and other racial and ethnic groups? Why might African American teens feel lower levels of internal locus of control than others?

Elster and Lamb's (1986) research found that teen fathers fall into two categories: those with relatively severe conduct problems (e.g., school truancy, school expulsion, substance abuse); and those who appear developmentally appropriate. Pirog-Good (1988) found teenage paternity and criminal behavior related, but not in a causal manner. She proposes that both behaviors are due to similar overarching life situations: (a) the lack of appropriate role models, (b) the need to confirm one's social identity, (c) low self-esteem, and (d) misguided public policy.

Summary

Much of the research paints contradictory pictures of what teen fathers look like. In general, the father of the child born to a teen mother tends not to be a teen himself. On average, he is around 22 years old and has not finished high school. He may be employed but he is probably not earning enough to support a family. Psychologically he does not differ dramatically from his nonfather peers, although he is more likely to have a criminal background or a history of other behavioral problems. However, the broad negative stereotypes of these fathers do not seem to fit everyone. Teen fathers, while at times clustered in higher rates within certain demographic groups, exist across all socioeconomic, behavioral, and racial and ethnic segments in this society.

THE DEFICIT PERSPECTIVE

Rhoden and Robinson (1997) suggest that the cumulative effect of years of negative stereotypes of teen fathers has led society to take a "deficit perspective" in regard to teen fathers. According to Rhoden and Robinson, a deficit perspective "involves comparing two groups, emphasizing the ways in which one group differs from the other, and framing those differences as deficits" (p. 107).

When we apply this perspective to teen fathers we find ourselves comparing their efforts at parenting with the efforts of the teen mother or adult males. Either of these comparisons is actually unfair to the teen father, and neither allows for a strength perspective to emerge in evaluating the teen father's contributions to his child. For example, a study by McGovern (1990) compared teen fathers and teen mothers on their responsiveness to infant communications. This study found teen fathers to be less responsive than teen mothers in this area. While this is useful information, the study made no effort to discover what positive behaviors these young fathers may have possessed in the area of caring for young infants. The original design of the research did not allow for such discoveries; it was designed to confirm deficits rather than to discover strengths. Rhoden and Robinson point out that the deficit perspective is consistently used in the literature on adolescent fathering. It is their contention that holding a deficit perspective on teen fathering will exclude teen fathers from involvement in parenting.

Debunking the Myth of Deficit Perspective

Robinson (1988b) has observed that there are several commonly held myths that have emerged related to teen fathers. These myths perhaps began as isolated stories that later were popularized by the media, which led to an inaccurate portrayal of teen fathers. Let's explore the factual elements related to some of these myths.

THE SUPER-STUD MYTH

This myth holds that the teen dad is worldly, wise, villainous, and a stud who knows a lot about sex. While this may have had some validity in the past, there is substantial evidence suggesting that the teen father of today knows little more than other teens about sexuality and reproduction (Barret & Robinson, 1982). Although it may be common for adolescent males to say they know a lot about sex, the reality is often that they lack basic knowledge that could help in prevent unwanted pregnancy and sexually transmitted diseases. When service providers buy into this particular myth, they may miss out on an opportunity to provide prevention services to a population at risk.

THE DON JUAN MYTH

The key belief in this myth is that the teen father exploits unsuspecting and helpless teenage females who are significantly younger than himself. The reality is that teen partners are usually within 3 to 4 years of each other in age, come from similar socioeconomic backgrounds, have equivalent schooling, and are involved in a meaningful relationship. The "love 'em and leave 'em" notion that goes with the Don Juan myth doesn't seem to match research findings either, as many teen fathers remain involved throughout the pregnancy and childbirth experience (Achatz & MacAllum, 1994).

THE MACHO MYTH

This myth proposes that the teen father has no self-control and has a psychological need to prove himself. In fact, research would seem to indicate that teen fathers do not differ significantly from their nonfather peers in psychological and cognitive makeup (Earls & Siegal, 1980). The primary difference would seem to be that their sexual activities resulted in the birth of a child.

THE PHANTOM FATHER MYTH

It is a commonly held belief that the teen father is absent and rarely involved in rearing and supporting his children. Once again, research would seem to indicate otherwise. The research of Achatz and MacAllum (1994) indicates that teen fathers often remain involved throughout the pregnancy and birthing process. They also found that many fathers maintain intimate feelings toward the teen mother and their babies and contribute financial support. Pirog-Good (1993) points out that even if teen fathers are not in the position to contribute financially, many contribute in-kind contributions as a form of child support.

Reflection
Why do you think these myths about teen fathers persist? What can be done to debunk them?

Although there will always be subgroups of teen fathers that may bear a resemblance to one or more of these myths, the facts indicate that many more teen fathers do not behave in these ways toward the teen mother and child. These myths are the epitome of the deficit perspective of teen father as they indicate that he has little interest, skills, or desire to contribute positively to the lives of the teen mother and baby. Dispelling such myths is an important step toward building a realistic view of the possible special contributions that the teen father can make to the mother and child. However, there are still challenges that will inhibit teen fathers from fulfilling their potential contributions.

SPECIAL CHALLENGES FACED BY TEEN FATHERS

There are special challenges that could easily interfere with a teen father's ability to enact his role of father with his child. In this section we will identify these challenges and discuss the ramifications for teen fathers' involvement with their children.

Poverty and Unemployment

Although teen fathers can be found across the broad socioeconomic spectrum, there is a clustering of teen fathers at the lower end of the socioeconomic continuum. Lack of resources and unemployment or underemployment can play an important role in the opportunities the father has to enact the role of father and in what resources he can bring into the situation.

Lack of Education and Job Skills

Many fathers are able to finish school and receive their diploma, yet a significant number do not finish high school. Lack of education then interplays with poverty, unemployment, and lack of job skills in a way that undermines the young father's efforts to contribute financially to the well-being of his child.

Low Self-Esteem

There is some data that indicates that teen fathers may experience lower levels of self-esteem than their nonfather peers. If a teen father is lacking in self-esteem, he may come to believe that he has little to offer both the teen mother and child.

Alienation From Peers

Other researchers have indicated that teen fathers experience a degree of alienation and separation from their peers. This can lead to feelings of depression that can further limit the functioning of the teen father. It is also possible that the teen father may pull away from the child and teen mother and reconnect with peers in an effort to combat his feelings of alienation. It is easy to see how these types of feelings can serve as a significant challenge to a young father as he attempts to escape the uncomfortable feelings associated with being different from his friends. He may also experience a lack of support from his friends that can serve to heighten his sense of isolation and depression, and at times, anger.

Gender Bias From Service Providers

Weinstein and Rosen (1994) suggest that stereotypes exist that label young males as "not mature enough, capable enough, or interested enough in providing responsible care for very young children" (p. 724). It is quite possible that this negative stereotype about young males has led to a situation in which only the needs of teen females have been consistently served by pregnancy-prevention programs and teen parenting programs (Foster & Miller, 1980). Other writers have noted that societal responses to teenage fathers have typically been limited to punitive measures, such as denying them access to their child unless they provide monetary support (Allen-Meares, 1984; Robinson, 1988). After reviewing several national reports, Kiselica and Sturmer (1993) suggest that "biases against teenage fathers are manifested in programs for teenage parents that tend to provide medical, educational, and psychological services to teenage mothers but fail to offer such services to teenage fathers" (p. 488).

Kiselica and Sturmer (1993) suggest that our current approach to teen fathers is sending them a mixed message: "We expect you to be a responsible parent but we won't provide you with the guidance on how to become one" (p. 489).

Reflection
Are you aware of any biases you might hold toward teen fathers? How would you avoid engaging in the worker bias discussed above? Why do you think these biases persist?

Decisions About Abortion or Adoption

Very little attention has been given to the teen father's participation in the decision-making process following conception. Redmond (1985) studied adolescent males' willingness to take part in the decision-making process should a pregnancy occur. One third of the 74 males who took part in the study had been involved in a teen pregnancy, and the respondents were almost unanimous in their desire and willingness to be involved in any decisions related to the pregnancy. Yet research has shown that young fathers often are not told when the baby is born and have little say about adoption or abortion decisions (Robinson, 1988b; Robinson & Barrett, 1985) Redmond suggests that those fathers who are left out of these decision-making processes feel a sense of isolation and confusion. It is also possible that this situation can serve as an avenue of escape from responsibility for the teen father.

Inadequate Parenting Skills

Very little research exists regarding the parenting skills of teen fathers. Some studies have noted the positive influence that teen fathers can have on the cognitive and social development of their children (Parke, Power, & Fisher, 1980). However, a recent study suggested that teen fathers were limited in their ability to respond to small infants' communications (McGovern, 1990). It would seem that although teen fathers can have a positive effect on their children's development, at least some of them may not know how to respond to their infants' communications in a consistently sensitive manner. These findings should not be seen as evidence for limiting contact with their young children, but rather as Kiselica (1995) suggests "teenage fathers might benefit from parenting programs through which they are given information on child development, child care skills, and parent-child relationships" (p. 24).

Relationship Problems With Child's Mother

It is quite likely that teen parents may have mixed feelings toward one another and experience ambivalence about maintaining their relationship. There are a number of possible flashpoints that are virtually inherent in the development of a relationship between young parents, including a desire to date others, financial difficulties, disagreements over child-rearing practices, conflict over friends, feelings of loss related to their own youth, tensions with their own parents and their partner's parents, and other stressors common to adolescence. In view of these demands on the young couple's relationship, it is easy to see why the majority of teen parents do not marry and why most who do marry eventually divorce (Children's Defense Fund, 1988).

Maternal resistance to father's visits can also be a critical factor in determining teen father involvement. Teen fathers in a recent study (Rhein et al., 1997) stated that the teen mother's resistance to their participation was a major reason for their lack of involvement in child rearing.

Relationship Problems With Family of Child's Mother

Other studies indicate that the family of the child's mother may pose a challenge for ongoing involvement by the teen father with the child and teen mother. For example, one teen father shared how frustrating it was to be confronted by the mother of his partner about child support. He reported a sense of humiliation as she would yell out of the window at him, "When are you going to bring some money?" For the teen father, this type of public humiliation can be very difficult and lead to decreased contact with his child and partner.

SPECIAL PROGRAMS FOR TEEN FATHERS

Programs that aim to serve teen fathers need to take into consideration the special challenges faced by this group. In this section we will explore some of the exemplary programs that have been developed to successfully serve teen fathers.

Mentoring Programs

One important method of assisting young fathers gain a better understanding and appreciation of their fathering role is through a mentorship relationship. Researchers have noted the importance of mentoring for male identity in general. As noted by researchers, "the mentor relationship is one of the most complex and developmentally important a man can have in early adulthood" (Levinson, Darrow, Klein, Levinson, & McKee, 1978, pp. 99–100). Mentors are typically older males who provide guidance, counsel, and support to younger males. This relationship can be very intense and can serve as a transitional function for the young person by helping him mature into adulthood. In the special case of father mentors, the goal is to help the young father develop a mature father-identity that will enable him to learn the skills necessary for successful fathering.

Former Vice President Al Gore has been given at least partial credit for increasing the national interest in mentoring programs for men. In July 1994, Vice President Gore issued a challenge to 1,000 community leaders who were gathered in Nashville to participate in Family Reunion III: The Role of Men in Children's Lives. He stated:

> [B]eginning here today, I am asking you to join me in launching a nationwide Father-to-Father movement. There are new young fathers struggling with every facet of their role, from changing diapers to finding the job that can support their sons and daughters. There are mature, experienced fathers who would love to volunteer to help them. Let's bring them together.

This speech served as a catalyst for a group of national organizations to join forces to create a plan for designing and implementing a Father-to-Father program. This effort was intended to be a nonpartisan, nonpolitical, nongovernmental means of promoting effective fatherhood. It is the mission of this group to help establish local mentoring programs across the nation. Their stated beliefs are that

- All men need support in the difficult task of being a good father.
- Both children and fathers benefit in a reciprocal way from good fathering.
- All fathers involved in *Father-to-Father* will benefit from each other in a reciprocal relationship.
- Men must help each other to support a child's mother in her mothering role and to be active partners in parenting regardless of the status of their personal relationship with the mother.
- Connecting fathers with their children connects them in a productive way with their communities.

Reflection
Why do you think mentoring programs might be effective. What value might Leon (from the case study) receive from linking up with a father-mentor?

An example of such a mentoring program can be found in the Dad 2 Dad program in Indianapolis, Indiana (Innovative Program), designed to serve low-income African American teens. Many of the participants come from homes in which there was no significant positive male influence as they were growing up. It is the goal of this program to increase the frequency and quality of the involvement of young fathers with their children by teaching and modeling parenting skills and encouraging emotional bonding. Young fathers in this program attend weekly parenting-education programs. Upon successful completion of the classes they are paired with successful, experienced fathers from the community for a yearlong mentoring experience. The mentor is called a father-friend and both mentor and teen commit to weekly one-on-one contact for the next 12 months. Once a month, they participate in an informal support group, and a father and child social event is also scheduled three times per year. Preliminary evaluation results suggest that this is an effective program.

Sex Education Programs

Another approach taken by some communities to address the problem of young fatherhood is to provide pregnancy prevention programs. Historically, these types of programs have been directed primarily to young woman. Unfortunately, this can send some very unhealthy messages to the youths. First, providing services only to young women suggests that they alone should be responsible for making sexual decisions, that it is up to them to set the limits and to be knowledgeable about safe-sex practices. This leads to message number two, which is that young males are not expected to take on the responsibility of making safe sexual decisions. Finally, offering services to only young woman keeps young males in ignorant about safe sex. They are not informed about the numerous risks involved in early sex, particularly early unprotected sex. In essence, this lack of information is hazardous to the young male's life as he is less informed about the dangers of HIV and STDs.

THE MALE PREGNANCY PREVENTION PROGRAM OF PHILADELPHIA

Fortunately, we have seen an increase in prevention programming for young males in the past decade. One exemplary program is the Male Pregnancy Prevention Program (MPP) located in Philadelphia and supported by Workforce 2000 (Innovative Program). One of the unique features of this particular program is that it has a Web site that serves as a resource for adolescent males throughout the country (http://www.mpp-online.org/home.html). Given the large number of teens using the Internet, the presence of pregnancy-prevention materials aimed at young men seems highly appropriate. The actual program is designed to help adolescent males understand their roles and responsibilities in pregnancy prevention and parenting. The program includes various intervention activities: workshops, peer-counseling forums, and community outreach. Activities are structured to help participants develop greater self-esteem and a sense of empowerment and ownership of their responsibility in pregnancy prevention and parenting. The MPP Program focuses on the sexually active adolescent male, acknowledges the physiological changes he is experiencing, the conflict it imposes, and the impact it has on his personal growth, development, and economic security. The goals of the MPP program to help young African American males are as follows:

Goal 1: Increase awareness and sensitivity to the importance of their role in birth control and parenting

Goal 2: Develop greater self-esteem and ownership of pregnancy prevention and parenting

Goal 3: Develop mechanisms to cope with or reverse peer pressure as it relates to the demonstration of their sexuality or manhood.

Goal 4: Connect clients with needed services through appropriate referrals to health care and related services

Participants in the program are introduced to a wide range of issues about growing up male. Five main topics are covered in the program: (1) personal growth and development; (2) personal health and hygiene; (3) job readiness; (4) family planning; and (5) communication and interpersonal relationships. Several primary topics are diffused throughout the curriculum. For example, participants are able to see how issues like STDs and abstinence impact every facet of their lives. Extensive time is also allocated to talk about the degree of peer pressure on sexual decisions and how to stand up to such pressure.

Reflection
In our society it is often assumed that females will be responsible for sexual decision-making, that it is up to them to make informed decisions (when to say no) about having sex. How is this unfair to females? How is this unfair to males?

POSITIVE SEXUAL DEVELOPMENT PROGRAM WITH INCARCERATED YOUTHS

The Positive Sexual Development Program (Innovative Program) was created with the primary goal of decreasing high-risk sexual behaviors in youths confined at a juvenile treatment facility in Indiana. It was hoped that youths who completed the program would be less likely to contract HIV or STDs in the future. It became evident that any effort to decrease risky sexual behaviors would involve addressing the wider range of consequences from engaging in unprotected, unsafe sex, including early fatherhood. Research conducted within the treatment center indicated that approximately 90% of the youths readily admitted to engaging in unprotected sex, behavior that could easily lead to disease or early fatherhood. National statistics regarding confined youths yield similar results. The ironic aspect of this situation is that despite evidence of these risky behaviors among this population, very little formal programming has been offered to confined youths, particularly teen males.

The program development phase called for extensive cooperation between the staff and administration at the treatment center, local youth-service providers, Planned Parenthood, and faculty from the social work program at a local university. One of the first issues that was discussed involved the barriers to services that might exist. Foremost among the concerns was how the current facility staff would respond to sexual education classes within the facility. Members of the planning committee felt that a more favorable and supportive milieu must be created within the facility before teens were served. It was decided, therefore, that the program implementation would be conducted in two phases: During phase 1, facility staff would receive rudimentary training in sex education as well as learn appropriate ways to respond to the questions that the youths might start asking once the program for the teens was initiated. Planned Parenthood was asked to train facility staff in these areas. Every staff person attended two half-day seminars presented by Planned Parenthood, and the reactions from staff regarding this training was very positive.

In phase 2 of the program, comprehensive education, risk reduction strategies, and counseling were provided of confined male adolescents. The first strategy used to facilitate long-term behavioral change was the implementation of small interactive groups with trained group leaders. These groups helped foster the acquisition of new social skills such as negotiation and refusal, increased participants' knowledge of HIV/STDs, and improved decision-making skills such as deciding to wear a condom during sexual activity. An important element to the success of these groups was that a collaborative strategy was employed. Participants were actively involved in selecting group activities or related topics. This youth-centered approach helped youths' learn skills such as taking responsibility for their actions, rational thinking, and initiating change efforts.

Role-playing as a learning strategy was employed throughout the group meetings. Role-playing has been demonstrated as an effective way to teach youths alternative problem-solving approaches and social skills, as well as to enhance their ability to empathize with others, particularly their chosen sexual partners.

Group participants were also required to keep a journal while in the group. Journals provide an opportunity for individuals to reflect on past, present, and future life events. Such reflection can improve one's skill in understanding choices and consequences. These groups were held once a week for 1 hour at the treatment facility. The groups were facilitated by two current staff members of the treatment facility, a masters'-level health provider, and masters'-level counselor. Individual counseling were also provided by the facilitators.

A visit from an HIV-positive guest was another strategy. This activity was extremely helpful as the youths were required to prepare for the visit beforehand by discussing ground rules, preparing questions, and discussing empathy and sensitivity to individuals with HIV. In essence, the youths owned the session. This strategy encouraged skills such as empathy, planning and preparation, and appropriate social skills.

Another strategy that was part of this program is one-on-one counseling. This provided youths an opportunity to learn skills necessary to deal with their unique and personal issues related to sexuality and HIV/STDs. In addition, the counseling reinforced what they had learned in the group experience and provided an opportunity for confidential discussions and individual problem-solving.

Reflection
What special challenges would you foresee in leading a discussion of sexual issues with a group of male teens? What personal challenges would this present for you?

Parenting Education

Although programs designed to prevent early pregnancies may be considered the best approach by many communities, the reality is that many male teens will still become fathers. The question then becomes, How can we prevent these young fathers from becoming absent, unsupportive parents? and the goal becomes finding ways to help teen fathers become caring, committed, and effective parents. This is certainly a challenge given what we know about the obstacles that confront teen fathers discussed earlier in this chapter.

The Teen Father Collaboration

In the 1980s, the Teen Father Collaboration project was started in order to address the special challenges involved in providing services to teen fathers (Innovative Program). This project was designed to assist teen fathers in contributing to their children's social, emotional, and financial well-being. It included eight social service agencies from around the country. More than 400 young fathers and prospective fathers (mostly 17 to 19 years of age) were provided a variety of services, including counseling, educational assistance, and job training (Sander & Rosen, 1987). The researchers found these young fathers often quite willing to participate in parent-education programs. Many hoped that such programming would help them become the "good" father that they themselves had never had. As one participant stated, "I want to be a better father than my father was to me. I want something different for my child than what I have" (Sander & Rosen, 1987, p. 108). The agencies provided workshops on child development in which information was given about normative child development. Parenting classes were also offered in which facilitators gave lessons in diapering, feeding, and bathing infants. Workers also addressed some of the young men's masculinity issues such as their fear that they might be seen as "sissies" for engaging in childcare.

In addition to the hands-on aspects of parenting, many agencies also provided young fathers with information about their rights as parents. Some agencies even helped fathers establish legal paternity. This seems like a critical service as many young fathers misunderstand their rights and responsibilities as fathers. Many believe that they do not have any rights when it comes to their child.

The Teen Father Collaboration project also offered some valuable insights into the challenge of recruiting young fathers into programs. Many programs admitted that they were initially very skeptical about how many young fathers would be willing to become involved in their programs. Perhaps they were holding onto many of the stereotypes we explored earlier in this chapter. However, they found that if they were flexible and creative in their recruitment efforts they could experience a high degree of success in their efforts to involve the teen father. Programs often relied on the young father's female partner as an important resource in recruiting the teen father. These young women were encouraged by program staff to let the father know that there was a program specifically for them, yet only about one third of the young men who participated in programs were recruited by their partners. The remaining two thirds were recruited using a variety of offsite strategies. According to Sander and Rosen (1987), successful off-site strategies "depended on a staff member's ability to go into the community and reach young men on a one-to-one basis" (p. 109). Outreach seems to be a critical ingredient of succeeding with young fathers. Workers visited high schools, GED programs, and recreational center and successfully recruited young fathers from basketball courts, poolrooms, and street corners. In addition, the programs also became known in their communities by word of mouth. As the programs became recognized as true helping centers, many young men approached the agencies on their own or at the suggestion of a friend or family member.

In addition to the personal approach, young fathers were also recruited through the use of the media. Television, radio, and local newspaper coverage were helpful in making the communities aware of the types of services that were available for young fathers. In addition, some program participants became vocal supporters and were willing to speak on radio, TV, and through the print media about their positive experiences in the programs.

It is important to note that the majority of fathers who entered the programs did so as a result of outreach efforts. It has been a common misconception that the only effective way to get young men involved in fathering programs was through their partners. This study would seem to refute that belief and instead suggests that young fathers can become involved in programming based on their own interests and needs.

PSYCHOEDUCATIONAL GROUPS

Various authors have suggested that psychoeducational groups may offer a unique opportunity to assist young teen fathers learn more about effective parenting (Hendricks, 1988; Kiselica, Rotzien, & Doms, 1994; Kiselica, Stroud, Stroud, & Rotzien, 1992). Trad (1991) describes psychoeducation as a form of learning that facilitates the mastery of a major life transition. Certainly becoming a teen father would seem to constitute a major life transition. In general, psychoeducational programs are brief, time-limited efforts that use a directive, didactic approach to teach participants about the impact of their transition on their lives as well as the impact on others (e.g., the children and former partner). Psychoeducational programs typically provide participants with essential skills to cope with the transition. The advantages of this type of psychoeducational approach to separation and divorce adjustment include its ability to affect substantial populations, its avoidance of clinical labels or status, its short-term nature, and its building on strengths rather than concentrating on pathology (Williams, 1979).

Kiselica and colleagues (1994) provide a comprehensive framework for providing psychoeducational groups to teen fathers. This training could be offered within the school or other community settings (behavioral health clinic, child welfare, family planning agencies, etc.). Their course features three phases, each designed to address a concern or issue related to teen fathering. During phase one (usually four to six sessions), workers assist teen fathers in clarifying their feelings and attitudes about masculinity and fatherhood. Establishing a working rapport with members is a critical ingredient of success during this phase and it sets the stage for success throughout the program. Phase two usually last for 5 to 12 sessions and participants are presented with information regarding child development and child care. This can be an excellent point at which to bring in presenters from the community. It is possible that young fathers could use this speakers as resources for future needs that might arise. It is also during the second phase that teen fathers may be surprised to learn about the critical role they can play in healthy child development. This may be a revolutionary concept to them. Kiselica and associates (1994) suggest that workers help the teens process this information. They note that one common response from teen fathers is that they gain a sense of "affirmation about the father's role" (p. 88). During phase three (usually 5 to 10 sessions), the primary focus is to teach teen fathers responsible sexual behavior. Young males may have a hard time believing that they need to change their sexual practices. Kiselica (1996) suggests challenging teen fathers with the following types of questions to encourage teen fathers to rethink their unsafe sexual practices:

- Given your recent experiences as a teen father, are you ready to become a father again?
- Because of the topics covered in phase one, have you thought seriously about your conceptions of fatherhood?
- In light of this thinking, are you acting as a responsible father by engaging in unsafe sex?
- Given your knowledge of child development from phase two,

you should now more fully understand the many needs of young children. Are you capable of responding to the needs of another child (p. 294)?

Employment Training

It seems like common sense to assume that teen fathers who wish to contribute financially to their children will need some sort of assistance in job training. However, employment counseling and training related to teen fathers may not be as simple as it first appears. For example, Kiselica, Stroud, Stroud, and Rotzien (1992) suggested that career counseling with teen fathers varies according to the particular phase of pregnancy. During the prenatal phase, counseling may more closely resemble crisis-oriented decision-making. The worker should help the teen father-to-be avoid making decisions based on panic or external pressures. The teen may be tempted to toss aside his original career and educational plans in favor of one that will meet immediate needs for income but not necessarily meet long-term financial security needs. For example, Leon, the father in our original case example, took a job at a local fast-food restaurant in order to help out with the financial situation. Although the money was helpful, Kiselica and colleagues (1992) warn that young fathers can be lulled into a false sense of security by the money they earn and consequently believe that there is no need to pursue further education or training. This could doom the teen father to a future of lower salaries over the course of their lives. Although there is only limited information about the impact of early fathering on a male's lifelong ability to achieve financial success, there is evidence that teenage fathering is linked with critical factors that would make it difficult for the father to achieve high levels of financial success. Research has shown that men who father a child as a teen are less likely to pursue advanced education (Marsiglio,1986). They are less likely to receive a high school diploma, more likely to receive a GED, and are more likely to receive their diplomas at atypical ages when they do graduate from high school (Marsiglio, 1986). It becomes obvious that it is very important for workers to assist the teen father to make the healthiest decision he can during this period. Once the initial crisis has been weathered, it may be possible to discuss long-term career aspirations with the teen father. It is this exploration of educational and career planning that forms the basis of counseling teen fathers in the postnatal period. During this period, workers can help teen fathers refocus on the long-term goals they wish to pursue. This may involve assisting the teen father in preparing to change jobs, moving from a position that was taken during the prenatal (perhaps based on immediate needs) to ready themselves for a job that can really offer financial security for themselves and their child.

Reflection
Why do you think it is important that teen fathers receive employment training? Beyond increasing their ability to provide financial support to their child, how would this training be helpful?

There are numerous examples of successful employment training programs for teen fathers. An excellent holistic program is offered by the Broward Regional Health Planning Council located in Ft. Lauderdale, Florida, entitled the Culturally Competent Teen Pregnancy Prevention Model (Innovative Program). This is a holistic pregnancy-prevention program that incorporates employment training as one of its many components. The program emphasizes the need for youths to increase the numbers and types of choices in their lives. According to the program, Life Options Training first must create a viable vision of future prospects for each teen at risk, based on creating and reinforcing the perceived value of formal and informal education and creating a framework for innovative educational opportunity for teens, including those who cannot attend regularly scheduled sessions. Their model proposes a learning process in a multisetting environment to enable out-of-school youth participation and also to allow the effective use of out-of-school hours. Teens at risk must learn to examine and visualize beyond the perception of being passive victims in life. They must become used to assuming responsibility for their present and future by acquiring skills in goal setting, problem solving, and conflict resolution, all directed toward their future vision. These are three fundamental life skills, and the lack of them are associated with increased at-risk behaviors. To achieve these ends, the following services are offered.

EMPLOYMENT ASSESSMENT

Creating improved life options for teens who are at risk and setting realistic goals involves opening opportunities in the everyday world of employment. Adolescents who lack or have limited marketable skills and are not candidates for education beyond high school must be trained for jobs they can reasonably be expected to take and retain. This aspect of preventing adolescent pregnancy involves assessing the skill level of the at risk teen, matching those skills with available opportunities, and developing training opportunities that will allow the adolescent to enter the workforce in a satisfactory and lasting manner.

JOB TRAINING

Job training must reflect realistic goals, in terms of the skills that can be acquired and the jobs that are available, coupled with strategies to allow the adolescent to accept the daily routine of work in a reliable and consistent fashion. Job training for teens should not be in opposition to high school completion, but should supplement their needs, particularly for those teens at risk who are already pregnant, have already given birth, or have parental responsibilities. Successful job training will be consumer-oriented, based on a real appreciation of the skills, interests, and potential of the teens and of the real market needs in the community. Adequate planning and provision of these resources depends on interagency coordination between various providers and existing job training and placement programs in Broward County.

JOB PLACEMENT AND RETENTION

Simple needs such as transportation to and from work should not be taken for granted, but must be assessed and community resources need to collaborate and be adequately funded to meet this need. Resources must be found for adequate and reliable child care to facilitate continued education and workforce entry and job retention for parenting teens.

Cultural and Religious Socialization Efforts

It is important that workers be able to work with clients from diverse ethnic and cultural backgrounds. Although culture and ethnicity are related, they are not interchangeable concepts: "Culture refers to the culmination of values, beliefs, customs, and norms that people have learned, usually in the context of their family and community. Ethnicity relates to a client's identity, commitment, and loyalty to an ethnic group" (Jordan & Franklin, 1995, p. 169). There are certainly times when an entire program should be constructed and operated using a specific cultural or ethnic approach. For young fathers, the facilitation of ethnic or cultural identity may increase their sense of self-sufficiency, particularly in the area of developing and maintaining a positive self-concept. This could assist them in their efforts to be a responsible and caring father. For example, Gavazzi, Alford, and McKenry (1996) found that an Africentric approach with young African American males in foster placement had a positive effect on participants.

Reflection
Consider your own spiritual or religious beliefs and cultural values. How might these impact your work with teen fathers?

One example of a culture-sensitive program is From Studs to Fathers, which is run by the African American Achievers Youth Corps (AAAYC) located in Highland, Indiana (Innovative Program). AAAYC was founded to empower young African American males to take control of their lives in a positive way. The primary purposes of the organization are

- Promoting self-esteem among African American males
- Providing educational opportunities and motivation for African American males
- Seeking and/or providing employment opportunities for African American males
- Providing counseling and guidance to African American male youths
- Providing mentors for selected African American male youths
- Providing programs that foster male responsibility

The specific goals of the From Studs to Fathers program are

- To increase the level of involvement of African American teen fathers with their children
- To decrease the number of out-of-wedlock pregnancies among African American teen males
- To improve the high school graduate rate of African American teen fathers

Goal 1 is achieved through counseling with the young teen father. Counseling efforts are also designed to involve the mother of the child. It is hoped that the overall experience the African American youth will receive while in counseling will stimulate an attitude that leads to self-confidence, trust, and a sense of responsibility necessary to survive in a complex society. The specific aims of the counseling interventions are to help young African American fathers overcome self-defeating behaviors, identify their needs, express and cope with their feelings appropriately, improve interpersonal and intrapersonal relationships, and lead a healthy, chemical-free lifestyle. Additional areas of counseling focus include defiant behavior, peer pressure, gang involvement, depression, coping skills, conflict resolution, male responsibility, and anger management.

The second goal is achieved through offering a teenage-pregnancy prevention program that consists of weekly 1-hour sessions for a 4-week period. In these groups, members receive sex education information, skills for coping with sexual pressures, information about the wide-ranging consequences of unsafe sex, and other relevant materials. There is also a mentoring program that provides positive adult role models to assist in the many areas of intervention. Mentors are available to speak to the need to respect women as a topic relevant to sex education.

Goal 3 is achieved through educational and career counseling services, as well as GED preparation classes if needed. Tutors are provided to youths 2 days a week for 3 hours after regular school hours. This tutoring focuses in traditional academic subject areas, and a Summer Academic Camp is held each summer for interested youths. Former teachers and current college students with exceptional skills in subject areas provide one-on-one instructional assistance in a small group setting.

In addition to the program components mentioned, there is also a recreational program for youths that provides a healthy alternative to self-destructive behaviors. Youths in the program are able to use local university facilities to play basketball on Saturdays. Twice a year AAAYC sponsors Sports Night Sleepovers, when participating youths can take part in sports activities from Friday evening until Sunday noon. Once a month participants and guests can take part in cultural and recreational outings.

There are several common themes that permeate the program to increase the cultural appropriateness of the interventions. Empowerment is stressed throughout and young fathers are encouraged to believe that they are in control of themselves and that they must play a significant role in the life of their child. Efforts are also made to develop a sense of "chainism"—that is, "Each one save one." This means that once the young father is on the right track it is his responsibility to find another male and help him. This is consistent with research which suggests the importance of inclusivity and interdependence within the African American community (Gavazzi et al., 1996).

Reflection

There is an African American proverb that states, "I am, because We are, and because We are, therefore I am" (Warfield-Coppock, 1990, p. 124). Discuss what this means to you personally. After that discussion, explore the meaning of this proverb for your work with African Americans.

SUMMARY

Despite the numerous negative images we might hold about teen fathers, it would seem that a number of innovative programs are able to get past these preconceptions and work with young fathers in meaningful and supportive ways. Although workers who chose to help this special population will face a myriad of challenges, it would seem that the potential benefits for the teen father and his children would make the effort worthwhile.

Questions for Discussion

1. Consider some of the myths you held about teen father before you read this chapter. Have you reconsidered some of your preconceptions? If so, which ones?

2. Consider the various special challenges that teen fathers face. What would be the elements of the "perfect" program to address the majority of these issues? What barriers exist to creating the "perfect" program?

3. If Leon (in the case example) shared his story with you what would you say to him that might help to instill hope? What challenges would you face in working with Leon?

10

Programs for Adult Unmarried Nonresidential Fathers

To me, that's the easy way out: give [the kids] some money and then run off. The money doesn't comfort them at night. They can't say, "Hey, dollar bill, I had a nightmare last night" and expect dollar bill to rock them and hold them. Money is there because it is a necessity. But if you give a child love and attention, money is the last thing they are going to look for. (Isaiah, unmarried father in Roy, 1999)

In this chapter, we explore the special issues of older unmarried fathers and explore programs designed to meet their special needs. The chapter highlights several topics describing their circumstances:

- The problems and challenges for unmarried fathers
- Factors to consider when intervening with unmarried fathers
- Innovative intervention efforts with unmarried nonresidential fathers

As we indicated in chapter 2, unmarried fathers are at risk for losing touch with their children. Stop for a moment and consider your preconceptions when it comes to unmarried nonresidential fathers. What images appear to you? Who are these fathers? What do they look like? What are their stories? How would you try to involve them with their children? Would you want to involve them with their children? This chapter will attempt to address these questions and provide program suggestions for working with this very diverse population.

UNMARRIED FATHERS: WHAT ARE THEIR CIRCUMSTANCES?

Historically we have not collected reliable data on unmarried nonresidential fathers. We know that a great deal of diversity exists within the category of unmarried nonresidential fathers and that it includes fathers who were part of a short-term relationship but with no sense of commitment between the sexual partners. In chapter 2 we discussed how Blankenhorn (1995) referred to a special subgroup of these fathers as sperm fathers, and these fathers certainly present themselves as the least likely candidates to take an interest in maintaining a long-term, supportive, meaningful relationship with their children.

At the other end of the continuum we discussed unmarried fathers who actually lived with the child's mother for a period of time in a marriagelike situation. The sense of love, commitment, and parental responsibility was similar to what might exist in a successful marriage, with the only thing missing being a marriage license. This group of fathers would appear to be more likely to respond to efforts to involve them with their children after the breakup with their partner. Of course, a wide range of variations occur between these two extreme types of unmarried nonresidential fathers. The challenge for those working with these fathers is to complete a thorough assessment of the father's situation (as discussed in chapter 5) and develop appropriate interventions.

Unfortunately, we still lack specific and reliable data about unmarried fathers. There is a degree of irony in this dearth of information about these fathers. Although a high degree of interest and research has been directed toward teen childbearing and teen fathering, the majority of nonmarital births in the U.S. are actually to adult women with adult males. For example, the National Center for Health Statistics (1999) reported that 70% of births to unmarried mothers in 1998 were to women 20 years of age or older (compared to 51% in 1970). Therefore, births to unmarried teens accounts for approximately 30% of all births to unmarried females. As we discussed in chapter 9, a large portion of the pregnancies to teen mothers are the result of a relationship with an adult male. It becomes somewhat clear from these statistics that the majority of the fathers of children born outside of marriage are adults rather than teens. Although programs directed toward unwed teen fathers are necessary, there seems an even greater need to direct programming efforts toward unwed adult fathers. Program developers and policy makers consistently make the mistake of assuming that unmarried fathers are predominately teen fathers. This is just not accurate, yet many continue to cluster these two very distinct groups of fathers together.

So what do we know about unmarried fathers and the children who are born to them? Although research is lacking, there is a developing knowledge base that might prove useful for those wishing to work with this population.

Father Characteristics

There has been increased interest in adult unmarried fathers in recent years (Vosler & Robertson, 1996). In a study of teen mothers in Wisconsin, it was found that the fathers of these children were more involved than commonly thought by researchers (Danziger & Radin, 1990). In a study in Baltimore, it was found that approximately 90% of the unmarried fathers had spent some time with their children during the first 15 months of the child's life; however, the frequency of contact diminished over time (Hardy, Duggan, Masnyk, & Pearson, 1989). In a representative sample of unmarried parents in Minnesota, it was found that while less than one third of the fathers lived with the mother and child following birth, nearly two thirds were in attendance at the child's birth (Resnick, Wattenberg, & Brewer, 1994). The same study found that "the majority of fathers indicated ongoing attachment to the child" (p. 292).

Much of the research completed on adult unmarried fathers has indicated that they are disadvantaged both educationally and in terms of work experience. It is quite common that these fathers have not completed high school at the time of the child's birth. While many are employed, the jobs are often only part-time (Danziger & Radin, 1990). These disadvantages are even more evident for minority fathers. Although smaller as a total group, greater percentages of young African American men are low-income single fathers, compared to Latino and European American fathers (Lerman, 1993). Roy (1999) notes that the "new degrees of economic marginalization brought on by the postindustrial economy threaten the regular involvement of African American men with their children" (p. 6). Many African American fathers express simply that "being there" as an involved father is their greatest priority (Allen & Connor, 1997; Allen & Doherty, 1996). Their desire may be complicated by local, state, and federal mandates that make child support a prerequisite for child contact.

Given the disadvantaged state of many of these unmarried fathers, it may come as no surprise that some research indicates that these fathers are at risk for higher rates of depression and social isolation (Vaz, Smolen, & Miller, 1983). In general, survey data indicates that young, unwed nonresident fathers are less well educated, have lower academic abilities, commit more crimes, and are more likely to have been raised in a family that was poor compared to other young men (Marsiglio, 1995). Vosler and Robertson (1996) found that never-married noncustodial fathers were less likely to hold a job than other men. The researchers attributed this difference in work effort to the poor health status of these men as well as their involvement in high-risk behaviors (such as drug use and criminal activity).

Reflection

Given the fact that so many of the unmarried fathers are actually adults, why do you think programs have primarily focused on unmarried teen fathers?

The Father-Child Relationship

In terms of the characteristics of the father-child relationship, it was noted earlier and research indicates that many of these fathers are more involved than previously thought (Danziger & Radin, 1990). Analysis of the National Longitudinal Survey of Youth – Child Supplement (NLSY–CS) data suggests that half of unwed nonresident fathers see their child at least once a week and that most of these relationships are quite stable (McLanahan, 1997). In addition many more unmarried fathers might be involved but they report feeling unsure of their ability to do so, particularly because of unemployment and their financial limitations (Allen-Meares, 1984; Roy, 1999).

Some have suggested that the relationship between unwed fathers and their children is similar to that of divorced fathers and their children. Research on divorced fathers indicates that financial support and visitation often decrease rapidly over time. However, there are distinct differences between these relationships. First, whereas formal child support agreements are much less common among never-married fathers compared to formerly married fathers, informal support—especially the purchase of goods and services for the child—appear to be very common (Edin & Lein, 1997). Therefore, children of never-married fathers are less likely to receive regular financial child support. This may be partly a result of the unmarried father's low level of income (Mincy & Sorenson, 1998). Second, although the initial rate of contact between never-married fathers and their children may be similar to divorced fathers and their children, this may not hold up over time. Some speculate that the high level of involvement of new never-married fathers is because many of these men are still romantically involved with the child's mother. If the relationship with the mother ends, the unwed fathers' involvement may drop off rapidly. Other studies have suggested that contact between never-married fathers and their children is vastly lower than that between divorced fathers and their children. Seltzer (1991) found that 40% of never-married fathers had no contact with their children in the past year, while only 18% of divorced fathers had no contact.

It seems that in some ways the relationship between never-married fathers and their children is similar to that between divorced fathers and their children. However, it is important to note that there are significant differences between these two groups of nonresidential fathers. Never-married fathers are much less likely to provide consistent financial support to their children, and they are much less likely to maintain consistent contact with their children. These differences are critical to consider when developing effective intervention programs for unmarried fathers.

What About the Kids?

There is fairly consistent data indicating that infants born to unmarried mothers are at greater risk for neonatal morality (Public Health Reports, 1998) and for prematurity and low birth weight (Public Health Reports, 1998; Zuckerman, Walker, Frank & Chase, 1986). These problems are most likely a result of the conditions that are related to poverty and adolescence or in some instances older-age pregnancy (Vosler & Robertson, 1998). Other factors that may increase the health risks associated with unmarried mothers are depression, infection, and cigarette, alcohol, and other drug use or addiction (Ahmed, 1990, Shiono & Behrman, 1995; Zuckerman et al., 1986). There is even evidence that unmarried mothers are at greater risk for pregnancy complications that could lead to maternal death (Berg, Atrash, Koon-

in, & Tucker, 1996). After decreasing annually since 1979, the reported pregnancy-related mortality ratio (the ratio of pregnancy-related
deaths per 100,000 live births) increased from 7.2 in 1987 to 10.0 in
1990 among women of all races. A higher risk of pregnancy-related
death was found with advancing maternal age, increasing live-birth
order, the absence of prenatal care, and among unmarried women
(Berg et al., 1996).

Vosler and Robertson (1996) point out that beyond infancy, children growing up in a single-parent household are at greater risk for
poverty. Toomey and Christie (1990) note that family poverty is associated with higher rates of "child placements, school truancy and dis-
placement, and homelessness" (p. 425). Higher rates of poverty have
also been associated with children's lower levels of cognitive and verbal abilities in school (Smith, Brooks-Gunn, & Klebanov, 1997). In
general, single, unwed mothers also report higher rates of physical
health problems for their children (Angel & Worobey, 1988).

Reflection
Do you think there is any value in making unmarried parents more aware of the important role that fathers could play in the develop- ment of their children? Why or why not?

McLanahan and Sandefur (1994) explored the long-term consequences for children who grow up in a single-parent household. They
found that children in mother-only families were more likely to drop
out of high school, that young men from these households were less
attached to the labor force, and that young women were more likely
to become pregnant and give birth while still teenagers. They reported
that these negative outcomes were associated with family disruption,
loss or lack of economic resources, reduced parental involvement, and
loss or lack of community resources and connections. However,
McLanahan (1997) noted the importance of remembering that the
cause of the parent's absence is less important than the absence itself.
In essence, these negative outcomes could occur as a result of a divorce
or in a situation in which the parents never married. As McLanahan
(1997) states: "Children raised by never-married mothers do nearly as
well as children raised by divorced and separated mothers (once mothers' education and race are taken into account), and both do worse
than children raised by both biological parents" (p. 37). Therefore,

when it comes to specifying the exact outcomes for children raised by unmarried mothers, there is scant research to differentiate between children raised by mothers who are single and those who are divorced. The key issue is the absence of the father and the resources and strengths he can bring to his children when he is present.

Father-Mother Relationship

It is not uncommon for the relationship between the nonresidential unmarried father and the mother to be strained. Some have suggested that stress from poverty might harm the mother-father relationship (Hendricks & Solomon, 1987). Much of the research in this area has focused on young fathers, so we are limited in our knowledge of issues that unmarried fathers are dealing with across the life span. Demographers estimate that almost 40% of adult unwed parents are living together when their child is born (Bumpass & Lu, 2000). Another 30% of unwed fathers report seeing their child at least once a week (McLanahan, 1997). It is important to note that the quality of the mother-father relationship may at times be less than satisfactory for all involved. For example, Vosler and Robertson (1998) point out that the relationship between unmarried parents may be at risk of instability, problems in communication, and conflict, all of which "put children at risk for negative outcomes" (p. 153).

Other research presents some starkly contrasting images of the mother-father relationship. At one extreme, Anderson (1989) describes how young inner-city men exploit young women in order to satisfy their sexual needs and gain status with their friends. This type of behavior embodies the myths about teen fathers discussed in chapter 9, and unfortunately describes adequately the true nature of some unmarried fathers: adults who can be seen as predators who seem to have little interest in becoming responsible fathers, who are more interested in conquests. They are perhaps the sperm fathers to which Blankenhorn (1995) refers. Yet these are not representative of the teen fathers we discussed in chapter 9. In an alternative view, Edin (1997) suggests that in many instances it is the mothers who refuse to marry. They may opt not to marry the fathers either because the men are seen as unreliable breadwinners or because they have serious problems with drugs.

Other researchers present a more cooperative picture of unmarried parents, suggesting that many unwed couples start out with high hopes for sustaining an enduring relationship only to find out that they (or their partners) cannot meet earlier expectations (Edin & Lein, 1997). Their views on the nature of the mother-father relationship may be different; however, they are quite similar with respect to the fact that marriage is not a part of their future.

SPECIAL CHALLENGES FACED BY UNMARRIED NONRESIDENTIAL ADULT FATHERS

In chapter 9 we examined the special challenges faced by nonresidential teen fathers. Although unmarried nonresidential adult fathers face many of the same issues, there are a few that should be highlighted before discussing specific intervention strategies. As we have stressed throughout the book, it is important to assess the special needs of the specific population of fathers before planning and developing interventions.

Disadvantaged Social Position

Many unmarried nonresidential fathers are poor, have few job skills, and limited education. These challenges are true for both teen and adult unmarried fathers, but these disadvantages may have different consequences for these two groups of nonresidential fathers. A low paying job and little economic power may lead to an even greater sense of failure and hopelessness among unmarried nonresidential adult fathers than among teen fathers in the same circumstance. In essence, society may hold a different view of an adult who cannot support his child than a teen who is unable to provide assistance because the expectations may be very different. In some instances, the teen father may be permitted some degree of contact despite his inability to pay support whereas the adult father may not be given such consideration. More research needs to be directed into this area to increase our understanding of the special plight of the disadvantage nonresidential adult father.

"Deadbeat Dad" Stereotype

We have discussed in other parts of this book the widespread stereotype of deadbeat dads with regard to absent nonresidential fathers.

Though all groups of nonresidential fathers fall victim to the stereotype, unmarried nonresidential adult fathers may be the group most clearly identified with it. Unfortunately, at first look this label may seem deserved. When we compared visitation and child-support rates between divorced fathers and unmarried fathers in chapter 2, we discovered that unmarried fathers often do not stay as involved as divorced fathers. There is little research to provide a better understanding of the reasons for this difference, an understanding that might help us appreciate the special issues that the unmarried father encounters that contribute to his being absent.

In addition, there are a significant number of unmarried fathers who strongly desire to stay involved with their child, yet are barred from doing so by the mother. However these fathers may still be lumped into the category of deadbeat dads by society. This stereotype also overlooks the unmarried fathers who contribute to the welfare of their child in nonfinancial ways such as providing child care, love, and attention to the child, or forms of in-kind contributions to the mother (clothes for the child, transportation to and from appointments, etc.). Finally, there are a significant number of unmarried fathers who do contribute financially to their children and stay involved as fathers. The stereotype of the deadbeat dad definitely does not apply to this group.

Establishing Paternity

If a couple is married, establishing paternity is not an issue. However, the unmarried father must establish paternity in order for his rights to be legalized. There are benefits for both the mother and father by establishing paternity; for the mother, a child support enforcement order can be issued to assure financial support from the father, and the father can legally assert for social involvement with his child. Paternity can be established without much difficulty if both the mother and father are willing. If the process is so simple, why are there so many instances in which paternity is not established? Following are some of the reasons for this phenomenon.

BARRIERS CREATED BY MOTHER AND HER FAMILY

Wattenberg (1990) notes that the mother wields a great deal of power over the father's legal ties to his child and his continued involvement with this child. For some mothers, establishing paternity may not be desirable because it would afford the father the right to maintain ties with their children even after the relationship with the mother dissolves. Some mothers may not want to be tied down by this type of relationship (Danziger, 1987), or the mother's family may reinforce breaking the ties with the child's father (Wattenberg, 1987). A survey by Sonenstein, Holcomb, and Seefeldt (1990), found that an uncooperative mother was one of the most significant barriers to establishing paternity and that mothers were resistant to giving fathers legal access to their children. If this legal access was granted they would lose their ability to legally deny the father access to their child.

FINANCIAL DISINCENTIVES

Mothers receiving TANF assistance gain little financial benefit when the father legally establishes paternity and pays formal child support. Typically the first $50 per month of collected support is allowed to "pass through" to the mother to supplement TANF benefits, which may be considered a poor trade-off for both the unwed mother and the father. If the father is not identified legally, he could provide informal assistance directly to the mother, perhaps increasing TANF benefits by more than the $50 allowed. This informal support is likely to stop once paternity is established and he is required to pay child support to the state to offset the cost of TANF provided for his child. In a study by Wattenberg (1990) she found that most unwed parents hated the idea of diverting the father's child support payments to the state to offset it costs.

Reflection

Consider the various reasons for a mother refusing to identify the father in order to receive benefits through TANF (Temporary Assistance for Needy Families). How would you deal with this in a practice situation? In your opinion, are there times when it is OK to refuse to identify the father? Why or why not?

PROTECTING THE PARTNER

Some mothers simply fail to push for establishing paternity in order to protect the father from the financial obligations and the hassle of the child-support system. There is often a mistrust of the social service agencies and therefore a strong motivation to avoid cooperating with them, which is evidenced by the mother's unwillingness to divulge personal information.

LACK OF AWARENESS OF THE BENEFITS

Unwed parents are often uninformed of the potential benefits of establishing legal paternity apart from child-support obligations. Research has consistently shown that social service workers often fail to inform mothers and fathers about the advantages of establishing paternity (Brown, 1990; Wattenberg, 1987). This omission may be due to the worker's own ignorance of the benefits of paternity, or it may be due to gender bias a discussed in chapters 5 and 9. Regardless of the reason, many mothers and fathers remain uninformed of the benefits of establishing paternity.

In summary, there are several special challenges that are presented when trying to involve unmarried nonresidential fathers with their children. These challenges—as well as those mentioned in previous chapters pertinent to nonresidential fathers generally—will need to be taken into consideration when designing an appropriate intervention plan. The next section presents two innovative approaches to dealing with unmarried fathers in a way that incorporates the challenges already discussed.

INTERVENTION PROGRAMS FOR UNMARRIED NONRESIDENTIAL FATHERS

In this section, we will discuss two programs that provide services to unmarried nonresidential fathers. These programs share some important commonalities but differ in other ways. The first program focuses exclusively on unmarried fathers, while the second serves both divorced and unmarried fathers through the same format. However, the programs share a common view that unmarried nonresidential fathers can play an integral role in the healthy development of their children.

The Parents and Kids in Partnership Program

The Parents and Kids in Partnership Program (PAK) in DuPage County, Illinois (Innovative Program), resulted from a grant from the Illinois

Department of Public Aid. The program is designed to help never-married parents engage in cooperative co-parenting with a focus on the needs of the children (Dudgeon, 1999). The PAK program believes that all children have a need and right to share a relationship with both their parents. Once paternity is established, all families are mandated to participate in an educational seminar and any other PAK services that the court deems appropriate. It is PAK's goal to reach out to the nontraditional family by providing three distinct services:

1) PAK Educational Seminar

This is a one-time, 3-hour seminar that mothers and fathers are mandated to attend, with no cost to the participants. The seminar is designed to help parents put aside their differences and learn how to focus on the best interests of their children.

The seminar specifically addresses (a) appropriate communication between parents and with their child, (b) the need to establish age-appropriate visitation schedules, and (c) how the needs of a child change as the child develops. The parents do not attend the sessions together. Parents engage in group discussions concerning the challenges they face in their efforts to maintain a co-parenting relationship. Participants also view a segment from ABC's "20/20" that features interviews with children discussing the impact of fathers on their lives. At the conclusion of the seminar, parents are asked to complete a community resources referral questionnaire to identify any pressing needs they might have. PAK staff members later contact those parents to assess further the identified needs and to provide referrals to available resources.

Reflection
The PAK program deliberately avoids putting parents together. What are your thoughts on putting conflicting parents into a meeting at the same time? What would be the risks and what might be the benefits?

2) Mediation of Never-Married Parents

In addition to the PAK educational seminar, special mediation services are provided for parents in need of such services. The mediation services are offered by the court to eligible participants at no cost for those who cannot afford the for-cost mediation services. Once a parent is deemed eligible for the free service they can begin the mediation process immediately to attempt to reach a parenting agreement on all pertinent issues. Each parent is given a brief questionnaire to screen for issues that may make them poor candidates for mediation, such as a history of domestic violence. If the couple is deemed inappropriate for mediation, the parents are returned to court for referral to psychological services or for other action deemed appropriate by the court. In general, no more than three mediation sessions are held unless everyone agrees that additional sessions might be helpful.

3) SUPERVISED VISITATION PROGRAM

The designers of the program recognized that often there is little or no relationship between the noncustodial parent and the child. This represents one of the major differences between noncustodial divorced fathers and noncustodial never-married fathers. As a result, the never-married noncustodial father may have very limited parenting skills or is a stranger to the child. It would seem unfair to both the father and the child to place them into a relationship that might be destined to fail. In an effort to improve the likelihood of success and to ensure the child's safety, a supervised visitation program is initiated. This program provides a bridge to normal visitation for these fathers. The presence of a professional who can both monitor and teach parenting skills in a safe environment meets the needs of both parents. The noncustodial father is given the opportunity to begin building a relationship with his child, and the custodial mother is assured that her child is safe and protected. Supervised visitation is not seen as a long-term solution, so the service is limited to 6 weeks.

Parents and Kids in Partnership is an innovative program designed to reach unmarried nonresidential fathers. (It should also be noted that the same services are available to unmarried nonresidential mothers.) Because this program was only started in 1998, it is still too early to determine the effectiveness of this approach. However, the initial indications from those working in the program is that it provides a much-needed service to these families (Dudgeon, 1999).

Dads Make a Difference

In 1996, Family Services Inc. of Lafayette, Indiana, developed a program called Dads Make a Difference (Innovative Program) with money from United Way. The program was designed to work with noncustodial fathers (divorced and never-married) who had not been physically or emotionally involved in their children's lives and had not been paying child support. The first group began in January 1997 and has continued through the present. In 1997, the program was able to secure additional funding through the Indiana Restoring Fatherhood Initiative (see chapter 8 for a discussion of this initiative). Viewed as an alternative to incarcerating fathers for charges of nonsupport, the program believes that incarceration "prevents fathers from establishing and maintaining regular involvement with their children's lives and inhibits their ability to work and make regular child support payments" (S. Sinha, personal communication, August 10, 2000).

The Dads Make a Difference program is a court-mandated 10-week program for non-custodial fathers who are failing to comply with child-support awards. These fathers meet once a week during this period and cover a variety of topics related to noncustodial parenting. There are several unique aspects of this program. First, the program takes an educational and supportive approach to working with these fathers. Historically (as discussed in chapter 8), efforts to involve absent fathers have used punitive tactics aimed strictly at collecting child-support payments. Dads Make a Difference uses the power of the court to teach fathers about their roles and to support their efforts to become more involved in all aspects of their children's lives, not just the financial. Second, the program includes never-married fathers. Although quite a few programs exist that deal with the noncompliant divorced father, there are few that serve never-married fathers in the supportive way that is incorporated in this program. Third, the program also serves the custodial mothers. They are required to attend five group sessions as well in which they learn about the potential positive impact that fathers can have on child development as well as ways they can learn to be a co-parent with the child's father. Finally, there are two conjoint group meetings with fathers and mothers to help facilitate open co-parental communications. Once again, this is a somewhat innovative tactic as many programs that serve this population avoid putting the parents in the same room at the same time. The facilitators of this program believe that these two conjoint sessions are a vital ingredient to establishing an effective co-parental relationship between the mother and the father.

Reflection

What are your thoughts on the courts mandating that people attend programs like Dads Make a Difference? Does this violate their right to self-determination? Why or why not?

OUTLINE OF THE PROGRAM

Prior to attending groups, each father must attend an individual pre-screening interview with the group facilitator. This is intended to detect those individuals who may not be appropriate for the program, particularly fathers who might pose a threat to the mother. The physical safety of all is the first priority for program staff. Upon completion of the interview the father will be informed of when the next 10-week group sequence will start and of the court order mandating attendance. Fathers are also given a general overview of what to expect in the ten sessions. A similar prescreening interview takes place for the mother as well.

SESSIONS ONE TO THREE

During the first three sessions of the father's group they learn about the important role that they can play in the healthy development of their children. They also learn about the importance of developing a co-parenting relationship with the mothers and are encouraged to begin referring to her as co-parent. Mothers are instructed in similar areas and are also encouraged to begin referring to the father as co-parent. They are urged to stop referring to each other as "ex", and for many this is initially looked on with a degree of humor. As one father said, "What am I supposed to do? Call her tonight and say, 'How's it going, co-parent?' I'm sure that will work!" With time, most participants are able to see the sense in referring to each other as co-parents and actually begin to use the term when talking to each other. Role-play is also an important aspect of the initial sessions. Parents have the opportunity to see how to implement a businesslike relationship with each other when it comes to co-parenting their child.

The first three sessions help prepare the parents for the conjoint meetings of sessions four and five. This is accomplished by talking about the importance of father involvement to children as well as the harm that can result from a highly conflictual co-parent relationship. By session four, parents are generally in agreement that it is important to find a way to involve the father. In addition, they are beginning to understand that it is possible to put aside their relationship differences in order to act in a way that is in the best interests of the child.

SESSIONS FOUR AND FIVE

These two sessions place the parents in the same room at the same time. During session four, parents are asked to look at their co-parental relationship and explore ways to improve their communication. The primary goal of this session is to help parents develop and improve their anger management and conflict resolution skills. During these two sessions parents learn more about the ways they have put their children in the middle of their personal relationship problems. Parents are taught how to communicate directly with each other in a way that avoids this pitfall. Parents also learn about constructive ways in which to deal with their anger and how to communicate in a business-like manner about issues dealing with the children. Once again, parents see the sense in these changes because they are making an effort to do what is in the best interests of their child.

During session five, parents learn negotiating skills and how to establish a parenting agreement. The facilitators demonstrate good and bad ways to negotiate conflicts through role-plays. Parents then have the opportunity to practice the necessary steps in negotiating conflicts. In the last half of this session, parents are presented with the various issues related to their children that will require mutual decision-making (visitation times, child care, school issues, recreational choices, etc.). Following the group discussion, each parent meets with the co-parent and attempts to construct a parenting agreement. The group facilitators supervise these efforts and can provide on-the-spot suggestions for constructive ways of getting past parents' conflicts and sticking points. This is also the last session for the custodial mothers. The facilitators meet with the mothers after the session to process their experiences and allow the mothers to voice any concerns they might have as a result of the session. Referrals can be made if additional resources seem necessary.

Reflection

What are your thoughts on the mothers being mandated to attend the program sessions? How would you handle their angry feelings? What benefits would there be in their participation?

SESSIONS SIX TO TEN

The final five sessions involve the noncustodial fathers only. This is a time for fathers to increase their understanding of their important role in child development, to learn parenting techniques, and to learn their rights and responsibilities as fathers. During session six, fathers focus on learning more about the important role that they can play in healthy child development. They hear the various statistics that indicate the possible negative outcomes for children who have absent fathers and learn what behaviors constitute "good" fathering (for example, "provide, protect, and be present").

Session seven is designed to increase fathers' understanding about child development. The fathers are asked to participate in an experiential exercise that allows them the opportunity to better empathize with their children. In this exercise they are blindfolded and then led through a maze by a "parent." They begin to understand the dependent nature of children and to better appreciate the importance of their parenting role. Fathers are also presented with various child-behavior scenarios and asked to think about the reasons for the behaviors and how they might respond. Participants then discuss the most appropriate ways to deal with the child's behavior.

Session eight focuses on appropriate child-management techniques. The fathers continue to talk about why children misbehave as they explore some of the myths about child misbehavior such as "He's just a bad kid" or "She just doesn't care." The facilitator helps the fathers understand that there is a difference between punishment and discipline, and participants then attempt to apply this knowledge to child-behavior scenarios. Session nine helps fathers better understand their legal rights and responsibilities and how to enforce their legal rights. Since all the fathers have already established paternity, the session usually focuses on child support and visitation.

The final session deals with visitation. Fathers are presented with the cardinal rule of visitation: You have to show up. They talk about ways to arrange visitations and how to deal with resistance from the mother.

Fathers also learn about the range of possible reactions to expect from their children and appropriate ways to respond to these reactions. They are encouraged to be patient and allow time for trust to grow and develop in their relationship. The group also discusses some of the ways to spend quality time with their children while visiting with the child. A list of do's and don'ts for visitation is formulated by the group. Finally, fathers receive some advice on how to maintain a long-distance relationship with their children. At the end of the session, they are given an opportunity to reflect on what they have learned from the 10 sessions and discuss what they will change as a result of attending the group.

EVALUATION OF THE PROGRAM

Bailey (1998) explored the effectiveness of the Dads Make a Difference program. He compared various outcome measures for fathers who attended with the behaviors of a comparison group of fathers who did not. Fathers who attended achieved many more positive outcomes on several measures such as paying the full amount of the child support award and maintaining contact with their children. They also reported higher levels of confidence in the parenting abilities and in taking care of the emotional needs of their children than fathers in the comparison group. They were also more likely to use assertive parenting techniques than fathers in the comparison group, and they were less likely to be overly permissive or overly authoritative in their approaches to parenting. Finally, fathers who completed the program reported much better co-parental relationships, seemed to get along better with the child's mother, and expressed less hostility than fathers who did not complete the program. They also increased the amount of contact they had with their children and the amount of child support they paid. This matches findings from other studies that connect child support with child contact (e.g., Seltzer, 1991).

SUMMARY

Although fathering programs that provide services to unmarried or never-married fathers are in the initial stages of development, evidence seems to be emerging that suggests they can be quite helpful in teaching these fathers the value of their influence in child development and the importance of their assuming parental rights and responsibilities.

Perspective

Sam had been ordered to attend the Dads Make a Difference program due to his failure to pay child support. The severity of his situation was highlighted by the fact that he was in jail at the time of the referral and arrived at his prescreening interview wearing a prison uniform and ankle cuffs. He was angry about the situation and angry about the forced attendance. However, his anger still did not match that of Beth, the mother of his children. Beth was enraged that she needed to attend sessions when Sam was the one with the problem.

During the first three sessions, Sam and Beth softened in their anger about the program. They began to see the value in what the groups were offering. It became clearer to both that part of Sam's problem was his drug addiction. It affected his behaviors, even his memory. Beth began to understand that her children wanted Sam to be a part of their lives. She decided to let go of some of anger and work toward becoming a cooperative co-parent. One example of her change in behaviors was her offer to place reminder calls to Sam to prompt him to call the children and keep his scheduled visits. Sam showed his appreciation for her efforts by following through with his promises to the children. It seemed that this was a success story in the making.

Around week eight, Sam began to call the facilitators to task for "never really being there." As he told one facilitator, "What do you really know about this? You've never been separated from your kids. When you leave group tonight you will go home to your cozy home and be with your family." Rather than becoming defensive, the worker issued a challenge to Sam. The worker agreed that Sam was right and asked Sam to come back to future groups to provide the "inside story." Sam agreed to the challenge and has kept his promise to visit groups and talk about his story.

Whether it is a program that has components geared specifically to never-married fathers, such as the PAK program, or a program that serves divorced and never-married fathers both, evidence suggests that working with the unmarried father a valuable endeavor. Unfortunately there continues to be a consistent shortage of these programs. Perhaps recent advocacy efforts on behalf of this population will help to alleviate some of the disparity in services to these fathers.

Questions for Discussion

1. Create a campaign ad to get the public to pay more attention to parenting by unmarried fathers. What could you communicate in this campaign ad that would convince the public of its importance?

2. How would convince a sperm father that he could still play a significant role with his child? Would you want to convince him to become more involved?

3. How would you help an unmarried father to consider the advantages of marriage if such advantages are evident and the marriage could benefit his children?

11

Postdivorce Educational Strategies

Dave and Mary had been married for more than 8 years when they decided to separate and divorce. The final year of their relationship had been filled with conflict over money, household responsibilities, sex, child care, and trust. Neither felt understood in the relationship and neither thought the other made any effort to change in a positive direction. One night after a big argument, Dave packed his belongings and moved in with his parents.

The two children (Jennifer, 7, and Chris, 5) stayed with their mother. Dave saw his children every weekend and paid child support according to a separation agreement. The separation did not improve the angry and hurt feelings experienced by Dave and Mary. Each began to use the children in subtle ways to get back at the other for past wrongs. Mary would "forget" the time that Dave was to pick up the children and instead be out with Jennifer and Chris when Dave came to get them. Dave would "forget" to put the child support in the mail, thus delaying much-needed resources for several days.

To worsen matters, Dave and Mary began complaining about each other in front of the children. Mary would say things like, "We could afford to go to the movies tonight if only that worthless dad of yours would pay his support." Dave would say things like, "I could spend more time with you kids if only that worthless mother of yours would be there when I came to pick you up."

Dave and Mary started using the children as messengers. Mary would instruct Jennifer and Chris to tell their father to put the support check in the mail or she would not let him see the children. Dave would tell the children to let their mother know that he would not pay support if she did not have them ready when it was time to pick them up for visitation. Jennifer and Chris were powerless and caught in the middle of the anger and hostility that had been part of their parents' marriage and now was becoming part of their parents' divorce. What can be done to help Dave, Mary, Jennifer, and Chris?

This chapter will help the reader understand the importance of ongoing father contact to the adjustment of children after divorce. Issues that affect the entire family's adjustment to the divorce will also be explored. Programs designed to reduce the problems experienced by family members after divorce will be discussed. The purpose of this chapter is to help the reader

- Describe the effects of divorce on all family members
- Identify the factors that can lessen the negative effects of divorce on families
- Describe the important components of educational programs to aid in the divorce process
- Identify the pros and cons of a divorce-education approach
- Compare divorce-education and divorce-mediation programs

DIVORCE: HISTORICAL AND STATISTICAL INFORMATION

Does the story about Dave and Mary sound familiar to you? Unfortunately, it is a story that is played out every day in this society. Dave and Mary and their two children represent the growing number of individuals in the United States who have either gone through divorce themselves or have been part of their parents' divorce. It is currently estimated that one in two marriages will end in divorce and that 40% of children born in the 1990s will experience their parents' divorce (Peterson & Steinman, 1994). Castro-Martin and Bumpass (1989) estimate an even higher rate of divorce among first marriages as they state that almost two thirds of current first marriages will end in divorce if prevailing trends continue.

The story of Dave and Mary also represents an area of special concern related to the changing trends in divorce: a substantial increase in the number of divorces involving families with dependent children. In the past, the presence of children in a marriage has served as an impediment to divorce. Couples once stayed married for the children's sake, but this has changed. In 1956, the number of children involved in divorces was 361,000. By 1995, the number had increased nearly fourfold, with more than 1.5 million children involved in divorce that year (U.S. Census, 1995).

Reflection
Staying married for the children's sake was a common statement heard in the past. What is your view on this reasoning? What are the pros and cons of holding this belief?

Impact of Divorce on Children

As you read the story about the family you were probably thinking, "How will the children be affected by this situation?" Researchers who study the family have turned their attention to examining the effects of divorce on children. Although there is still some disagreement about the extent and duration of the negative effect of divorce on children, a consensus seems to be emerging. Numerous investigators agree that most children initially experience their parents' divorce as stressful and exhibit disruptions in social, emotional, academic, and cognitive development (Amato, 1996; Hetherington, Cox, & Cox, 1979; Wallerstein & Blakeslee, 1989). There is general agreement that this initial period of turmoil constitutes a crisis period for the child in which they are susceptible to various stress-related effects. This period may last for a couple of years after which most children seem to adapt fairly well (Hetherington, 1989).

However, not all children will recover and a significant minority will experience enduring negative effects (Guidibaldi & Cleminshaw, 1985; Hetherington, Cox, & Cox, 1978; Lamb, Sternberg, & Thompson, 1997). Johnston (1994) reports that the rate of clinically significant mental health problems is as much as 300% higher in children from divorced families than in children from intact families. Observed examples of adjustment problems in children of divorce include frequent crying, depression, excessive worrying, refusing to talk, feeling worthless, psychosomatic complaints (headaches,, aches and pains), physical aggressiveness, and anger. Undoubtedly, children like Jennifer and Chris whose parents are engaged in high levels of conflict may be most at risk for mental health problems such as these. When questioned directly, many children state that they would prefer to be left out of their parents' conflicts and that they desire to have equal access to both parents, access that doesn't lead to feeling guilty about still loving both parents, access that doesn't require them to choose one parent over the other.

Reflection

One child caught in the middle of his parent's ongoing conflicts after divorce was made to wear a T-shirt with "My father doesn't pay child support" printed on it. He had to wear this T-shirt on one of his visits with his father. How might such conflicts affect this child? How would this child be affected by being put in the middle in such a way? What would you do if you were working with this child?

How Can We Lessen the Impact of Divorce on Children?

Fortunately for children like Jennifer and Chris, investigators are beginning to identify some of the protective factors associated with successful adjustment. Areas that seem to affect child adjustment include economic factors (Emery, Hetherington, & Dalaila 1985), father contact (Kline, Johnston, & Tschann, 1991), postdivorce custody arrangement (Steinman, Zemmelman & Knoblach, 1985), and a harmonious relationship between separated partners (Amato & Keith, 1991; Camara & Resnick, 1988; Johnston & Roseby, 1997).

In reviewing this list of factors that assist children to adjust to divorce, it is significant to note that the role of the father is critical in each of the areas listed. Positive father involvement has consistently been associated with improved adjustment in children after divorce (Hetherington, Cox, & Cox, 1979; Furstenberg & Cherlin, 1991; Kline, Johnston, & Tschann, 1991). These positive effects are not limited to White middle-class families. Jackson (1999) recently demonstrated that involvement by nonresidential Black fathers had positive effects on child problem behaviors. It would seem that fathers who interact in a positive way with their children after divorce help to lessen some of the experiences of loss and grief that many children undergo as the result of their parents' divorcing. Positive father involvement seems to help children with their overall ability to adapt to the changes brought on by divorce. Ongoing access to the nonresidential father may serve to lessen the anxieties of the child and reduce fears that they are going to lose their father.

Reflection

Some writers have characterized our children as "father hungry"; that is, they are growing up in a society in which fathers are disappearing. What are your views on this? Does this term describe what you have seen in children without father contact?

Other studies have suggested that positive father involvement can also be helpful to the children's mother (Bursik, 1991; Kurdek, 1986) and that these positive influences hold true for various racially and ethnically diverse groups. For example, Jackson (1999) reports that involvement by African American nonresidential fathers actually lowered the levels of depression experienced by mothers. This positive influence may be partially due to the fact that fathers can still share in the responsibility of raising the children, which in turn can give mothers a much needed break from direct parenting. In essence, positive father involvement can serve as a positive resource for mothers to rely on. It has also been shown that involved fathers are also more likely to pay child support (Dudley, 1991b; Seltzer, 1991; Teachman, 1991). The importance of ongoing financial assistance to children and their mothers has consistently been linked to better adjustment after divorce. Although the father role has moved beyond strictly that of breadwinner, the reality is that the financial earning power of the father is still a critical element to postdivorce adjustment for children.

It is also important to note the evidence that fathers who maintain contact with their children after divorce experience higher levels of well-being themselves (D'Andrea, 1983; Dominic & Schlesinger, 1980; Rosenthal & Keshet, 1981). Researchers and family practitioners often focus on how children and their mothers are doing after the divorce. Very little research has actually looked at the special adjustment issues of fathers after divorce, but it has been found that maintaining positive parenting after divorce is also healthy for the father. Fathers who are able to maintain a positive relationship with their children after divorce have been found to report lower levels of depression, anxiety, and stress.

The period after separation and divorce can lead to role confusion for the nonresidential father as the norms and guidelines for how one is to father after divorce are not clear (Stone & McKenry, 1998). Ongoing positive contact with one's children is one way to help reduce this sense of role ambiguity and to reinforce the importance of the fathering role after divorce. This type of validation perhaps can improve the psychological adjustment of fathers after divorce.

Reflection

Role confusion suggests that parents may be unclear about their parenting roles and that of their former spouses after a divorce. It is possible that children also are unclear about the role of their non-residential parent after divorce. This suggests that there aren't many clear guidelines on how divorced parents are supposed to relate to each other after divorce. What are your thoughts about role confusion as an issue for divorcing parents? Where do parents get information on how relate to each other after divorce? Is this an important area to explore?

It should be pointed out that positive father involvement after divorce is not merely limited to the traditional visiting-parent role. Changes in custody laws have increased the number of children being raised in joint custody arrangements. For example, nearly 80% of families in a recent California study reported joint custody (Maccoby & Mnookin, 1992). Similar rates were reported in a study of Washington State families, where 69% of parents had joint legal custody (Ellis, 1990). Many states have gone from merely allowing joint custody to making it the preferred custody arrangement (Robinson, 1985). In addition, approximately 10% of fathers actually have sole custody of their children after the divorce.

So it is possible that we may be entering a new era of divorce arrangements in this society. In the past the story of Dave and Mary might have ended with Dave's gradually reducing visits with the children and eventually discontinuing paying child support; it now possible for Dave to remain actively involved with his children through joint custody arrangements. Recent research (Braver & O'Connell, 1998) even casts doubt upon the accuracy of the traditional view that fathers drop out of the picture altogether. In fact, Braver and O'Connell found that more divorced fathers than we think do maintain significant contact with their children. When they do reduce contact, it often has more to do with the custodial parent's interfering with visitation. Braver and O'Connell found that a third of the noncustodial fathers in their study claimed they had been denied visitation privileges at least once, and a quarter of custodial parents *admit* the denial (italics in original). This study focused entirely on residents of Arizona, but the findings still resonate with beliefs held by many who work in the area of divorce.

What these data indicate is that postdivorce parental conflict continues to be a major factor affecting father contact with their children after divorce. Goldsmith (1982) suggests that general systems theory can provide an excellent vantage point from which to view and understand the family that is undergoing divorce. She points out that although divorce alters the family system, it does not terminate it. What Dave and Mary (and many family practitioners and researchers) fail to understand is that the preexisting conflicts that led to the divorce do not disappear magically once the final divorce papers are signed. As with the married family, symptomatic behavior of individual family members is often related to dysfunction within the family system. It is even possible that children may be "selected" as symptom bearers (Wood & Lewis, 1990). Thus the family system survives past the point of divorce, but in an altered and perhaps increasingly dysfunctional state.

HELPING FAMILIES GOING THROUGH DIVORCE

The challenge for service providers is to develop programs that encourage fathers to continue positive involvement with their children both in terms of personal contact and financial support; and help fathers develop strategies for working with the children's mother after divorce in a way that doesn't lead to high levels of conflict. Efforts also must be put forth to educate the children's mother about the importance of ongoing father involvement and help her to co-parent with the children's father after divorce. Effective intervention strategies must assist the family system transition from marriage to divorce.

Concern about the effect of postdivorce conflict between parents has led many researchers and program developers to search for ways to lessen the degree of hostility that can exist in the postdivorce family system. Kelly (1988) stresses that "it is important to provide parents with the forum and the tools they need to separate the unsatisfactory marital relationship from their continuing role as parents after divorce" (p. 135). Camara and Resnick (1989) suggest that efforts should be made to help parents develop negotiation skills. They suggest that improving parental abilities in negotiating may also help improve the long-term adjustment of the children.

Reflection
Interview a parent who has recently been divorced. How do they negotiate their conflicts over the children? Are they confident with their ability to handle these types of disagreements?

Family mediation involves one or two professional mediators (typically a mental health worker or a lawyer or both) who meet with both parents to help them resolve conflicts, reach decisions, and negotiate agreements about the dissolution of their marriage or shared residential arrangement. Chapter 12 provides an extensive discussion of this option.

Educational Divorce Workshops and Programs

Educational divorce workshops operate under the assumption that the participants can benefit from a time-limited educational approach for transmitting information to parents about how to lessen the effect of divorce on children. Divorce-education programs are a relatively new phenomenon. Arbuthnot and Gordon (1996) report that 20 years ago there was perhaps one such program, and as recently as 10 years ago they numbered in the dozens. Blaisure and Geasler (2000) reported that more than 500 counties had such programs in place by the mid-1990s.

Hodges (1990) suggests that "mental health professionals often overlook the power of education in helping others" (p. 286). Because of the need to better prepare divorcing parents for the realities of co-parenting after divorce and the limited resources divorcing parents have to pay for intensive services, it is critical to consider the relative merit of educational divorce programs to reduce the destructive consequences of divorce on the family. Though not a panacea, it is possible that educational divorce programs can even be combined with other interventions such as court-sponsored family mediation to help parents learn to co-parent after divorce. These interventions are discussed in chapter 12, and the following are examples of some educational programs.

Parents' Education About Children's Emotions (PEACE) (Innovative Program)

This program in Marion, Ohio is an example of a psychoeducational parents' program that has demonstrated effectiveness in teaching parents to co-parent after divorce in a manner that is respectful of the special needs of their children. The PEACE program was one of the first in Ohio to be legally mandated for divorcing parents. Begun in August 1990 as a collaborative effort with the Marion County Court of Common Pleas and Big Brothers/Big Sisters of Marion County it has served more than 5,000 individuals. The program consists of a 2 1/2-hour seminar after parents have filed for divorce or significant custody or visitation changes. Parents are mandated to attend the program prior to the granting of the final decree. The program is offered twice a month with an average attendance of 40 parents per session, and parents are not required to attend the session with their spouse. They pay a fee of $20, which may be lowered to $5 with proof of need. The sessions are held in the county courthouse courtroom with a uniformed deputy on duty. The seminar is facilitated by a male and female team, each of whom has more than 10 years of experience in children and adult services.

The overarching goal of the PEACE program is to enhance children's postdivorce adjustment. Like other divorce-education programs, PEACE is based on the premise that most children have a difficult time adapting to divorce and that parents are not as effective in their parenting efforts during the postdivorce adjustment period (Arbuthnot & Gordon, 1996; Braver, Salem, Pearson, & Deluse, 1996). Parents are seen as intentionally or unintentionally involving children in ongoing conflicts and unresolved marital issues with their former spouses. You can remember from our example of Dave and Mary that it is easy for parents to develop routines and patterns that use their children in unhealthy ways. PEACE would assist Dave and Mary in understanding how the divorce impacts their children and how they as parents can have a direct effect on their children's adjustment.

PEACE is based somewhat on social learning theory (Norton, 1977) and also draws upon parenting-skills training (Seligman, 1996). Parenting-skills training teaches parents about child development, but focuses on structuring the child's environment and seeing the environment from the child's point of view. Structuring the environment is a way of anticipating difficulties and planning in a manner that will avoid problems. Within this framework, Dave and Mary would learn to look at

---

Perspective: The PEACE Program

I.   Introduction: Facts and Statistics
  A. Role-play of angry scene
  B. Divorce
  C. Remarriage
  D. Impact on children
II.   Dealing with Losses: Stages of the Grief Process
  A. Denial
  B. Anger
  C. Bargaining
  D. Depression
  E. Acceptance
III. Typical Behavioral Reactions to Loss
  A. Developmental stages
  B. Slides to emphasize points
IV.   Tools in Assisting Children
  A. Listening (role-plays)
  B. Avoiding harmful games
     1. Parental games
        ("Messenger," "Spy," "Poison")
     2. Children's games ("Poor Me")
V.   Coparenting After the Divorce
  A. Parental relationships
     1. Custodial
     2. Noncustodial
  B. Video: "Tender Places"
VI.   Empathy-Building: Seeing It from the Child's Perspective
  A. Videotape
  B. Problem-solving
     1. Ineffective ways to deal with video vignettes
     2. Effective ways to deal with video vignettes
  C. Children's bill of rights
     1. Redo opening role-play of angry parents
     2. Advice: Children want both parents
VII. Questions and Answers/Evaluation of Program

problems from the child's view and then choose from various nurturing or structuring responses (Brock, Oertwein, & Coufal, 1993). They would be taught to isolate the interpersonal conflicts that are most harmful to children and would be given instruction through role-plays, slides, videos, and didactic materials to help assist them to replace harmful parenting and co-parenting practices with cooperative techniques. PEACE also attempts to validate the parents' importance, especially that of the nonresidential parent (most often the father), by reinforcing the advantages of successful co-parenting to the child, the mother, and the father. It is also emphasized that all can benefit from the nonresidential parent's sustaining the relationship with the child. The PEACE program also uses the grief-loss perspective to help parents understand divorce as a crisis event. Within this context, Dave and Mary would be encouraged to understand that the reactions of their children and their own reactions are normal responses to a crisis event. Parenting techniques would be demonstrated to help Dave and Mary (and all group members) attend to their child's psychological and emotional needs in each stage of the grief process.

Reflection

Consider the types of interpersonal conflicts that divorcing parents might experience. How might these conflicts affect their children? What makes it hard for divorcing parents to set aside these conflicts?

A detailed outline of the program can be found in the Perspective entitled The Peace Program. What would our fictional couple experience by going through this program? First Dave and Mary would view a highly emotional role-play presented by the female and male facilitators that demonstrates many of the common beliefs and emotions of those going through divorce (anger, betrayal, mistrust, blame). The facilitators then would lead the participants on a journey of exploration that includes a better understanding of how the divorce process affects them and how divorce affects their children. Two videos are used to increase parents' awareness and understanding of what their children are going through. Dave and Mary would likely be able to identify with the hurtful practice of putting their child in the middle of their disputes and of using their child to get back at each other. This awareness may lead them to be more open to alternative ways of handling their own emotions and other ways to communicate as a co-parent with their former partner.

Dave and Mary would also learn more about the grief process itself and would have the opportunity to increase their understanding of their own reactions to the divorce. They would be able to see that their initial denial and anger about the situation were very normal reactions. They would also appreciate that when handled properly grieving is a process that can move through the remaining bargaining and depression stages to the point where each could accept the ending of their marriage and be able to fulfill their new roles as co-parents to their child after the divorce.

Dave and Mary would also be introduced to information on the negative effects of divorce on children, developmental variations in children's reactions to parental divorce, factors that contribute to a more positive postdivorce adjustment, the role of the residential and nonresidential parent, communication skills, how to co-parent in the context of single-parent families and stepfamilies, and the legal aspects of divorce (e.g., definition of terms, types of parenting arrangements, use of mediation). At the end of the session, Dave and Mary would be given a handbook containing detailed information from the session, a complete list of community referral resources, and a reference list of books for adults and children who are experiencing divorce, single-parenting, and stepfamilies. Finally, they would be asked to complete a three-page program evaluation before they leave.

CHILDREN OF SEPARATION AND DIVORCE (COSD) (INNOVATIVE PROGRAM)

This center in Maryland offers a two-session divorce-education program in which parents have the opportunity to increase their understanding of the impact of divorce on their children and on themselves. Their belief is that by becoming aware of children's needs during times of transition, parents can continue to play a vital role in their children's lives and learn strategies for healthy co-parenting. The COSD workshop is an educational program led by trained clinical psychologists and mental health counselors. Workshops are conducted in lecture format with a question and answer period. By offering more than one session, the COSD program is able to cover additional material.

There may also be advantages in seeing participants a few days after session one in order to allow for follow-up questions. Topics included in the COSD workshops include

- what adults and children experience after separation and divorce
- emotional impact of divorce on children
- social impact of divorce
- financial impact of divorce
- work/educational impact of divorce
- how to cope with changes resulting from divorce
- explaining divorce to children
- changes in the parent-child relationships
- children's development at different ages
- how parents can help their children through each phase of development
- making healthy life decisions based on children's needs

The program also includes a panel of parents that discusses issues such as positive coping strategies as a single parent, communication between parents, and support for single parents. It also explores ways to help divorcing couples create parenting arrangements based on children's needs and how to build a constructive co-parenting relationship. One innovative aspect of this program is that it includes panels made up of children of divorce and parents who have been divorced. This allows parents to hear real life experiences from individuals directly affected by divorce. In particular, it can be a very thought-provoking and emotional experience to hear children talk about their feelings and experiences.

PARENTING PROGRAM FOR DIVORCED FATHERS (INNOVATIVE PROGRAM)

This program was described in research conducted by Devlin, Brown, Beebe, and Parulls (1992). One of the unique aspects of this program is that it serves only fathers. The parenting workshops also consists of six sessions rather than one or two that are typically seen in divorce-education programming (Arbuthnot & Gordon, 1996). Participation is voluntary. Each of the sessions is 90 minutes and is held on the same evening for 6 consecutive nights. The group is cofacilitated by two male professionals with a female facilitator added for the session on co-parenting and for the final session.

The program covers six primary areas:

1. *The experience of the divorced father*: This helps participants (a) understand and absorb the shock of divorced fatherhood, (b) explore their own experiences with their fathers and mothers, and (c) explore same- and opposite-sex parent role modeling.

2. *Methods to enhance parent-child communication through listening*: This helps fathers (a) learn to listen so their children will talk to them, (b) better understand how kids tell adults their rules, boundaries, and limits, and (c) gain a better understanding of sibling rivalries and feelings.

3. *Methods for enhancing parent-child communication through talking*: Fathers learn how to (a) talk so their children will listen, (b) establish rules and boundaries, and (c) set limits while minimizing resistance and anger.

4. *Co-parenting strategies*: Fathers also learn how to work more effectively with the child's mother and gain a better sense of how to meet children's needs with help from their former partner, maintain an effective co-parenting relationship, and learn to live with the other parent's set of rules.

5. *What do you do with the kids?* Fathers also receive suggestions about: (a) how to spend time with their children without giving up all their time, (b) how to have fun time, intimate time, and chore time, and (c) different types of indoor and outdoor activities to engage in with their children.

6. *Where do we go from here?* Fathers are assisted in future-planning, and explore such issues as resource identification, networking, and time for questions and answers.

Each of the six sessions concluded with a one-page evaluation of the evening's session. The leaders wanted feedback on the effectiveness of the session and suggestions for improvement. The research findings suggest that fathers gained many new and useful skills from the program (more information related to evaluation will be discussed later in this chapter). Devlin and colleagues (1992) did note that based on their findings they would suggest adding three additional sessions to the programs because the program failed to have a significant impact on co-parenting relationships. They recommended adding one session

---

Reflection

Quite often the adults forget about the basic needs and rights of the children involved in a divorce custody case. The following Bill of Rights for children encourages adults to rethink what children should be entitled to in a divorce situation:

CHILDREN'S BILL OF RIGHTS*

1. The right to be treated as important human beings, with unique feelings, ideas and desires, and not as a source of argument between parents.
2. The right to a continuing relationship with both parents and the freedom to receive love from and express love for both.
3. The right to express love and affection for each parent without having to stifle that love because of fear of disapproval by the other parent.
4. The right to know that their parents' decision to divorce is not their responsibility and that they will continue to be loved by both parents.
5. The right to continuing care and guidance from both parents.
6. The right to honest answers to questions about the changing family relationships.
7. The right to know and appreciate what is good in each parent without one parent degrading the other.
8. The right to have a relaxed, secure relationship with both parents without being placed in a position to manipulate one parent against the other.
9. The right to have both parents not undermine the other parent's time with the children by suggesting tempting alternatives or by threatening to withhold parental contact as a punishment for the children's wrongdoing.
10. The right to experience regular and consistent contact with both parents and to be protected from parental disputes or disagreements.

What are your thoughts on these rights? Are there any that you question? Are there any that you would add?

* From the S.M.I.L.E. Home Page (http://www.co.washtenaw.mi.us/ DEPTS/foc/smile.html#Bill)

to each of the three communication and relationship topics on co-parenting.

Reflection

Do you think it is possible that a "one-time" divorce education program could effect the way divorcing parents interact? Have you had brief experiences in your life that changed your values, attitudes, behaviors? What were those experiences?

EVALUATING EDUCATIONAL DIVORCE WORKSHOPS

The next question that we should ask is, Does this type of program work? Studies by several researchers have demonstrated the positive effects of divorce-education programs in general on postdivorce adjustment. Frieman, Garon, and Mandell (1994) found that a one-time parenting seminar helped parents understand how their children cope with divorce. These researchers also reported that parents going through the studied program felt more confident in helping their children. Arbuthnot and Gordon (1996) found several effects of the program in a 6-month follow-up of participants in a single video-oriented, 2-hour discussion group. This program focused on reducing the frequency with which parents involved children in loyalty conflicts. Compared to those not in the program parents who participated indicated greater improvement in empathizing with their children, more favorable child outcomes, and greater use of skills to protect children from parental conflict. In a 2-year follow-up study of this same program, Arbuthnot, Kramer, and Gordon (1997) found that participating parents relitigated less than half as much as those who had not participated.

Unfortunately, very few evaluations of divorce-education workshops have focused on the nature and extent of the impact these programs may have on fathers. Some program evaluations have even left fathers out of the evaluation process altogether. An exception to this can be found in a qualitative evaluation of the PEACE program by Stone, McKenry, and Clark (1999) in which 20 fathers who had attended the PEACE program were interviewed. These fathers overwhelmingly reported that they felt the program was very helpful. Fathers in this study were also able to relate specific examples of how they implemented what they learned through the PEACE program in their parenting practices and in their interactions with their former spouses. As one father stated: "It [the program] helps you to see things the way children see them. You hurt your children sometimes when you didn't mean to" (p. 106). The fathers also reported that the program was very supportive of their role after the divorce. Workshop attendance apparently helped to clarify their postdivorce fathering role.

In another study of a divorce-education program designed particularly for fathers Devlin and colleagues (1992) found that the divorced fathers' perception of their performance as parents improved as a result of workshop attendance. Fathers who attended the workshop also increased their effectiveness in talking and listening to their children and reported higher levels of overall parental satisfaction. However, the program seemed to have little effect on the co-parenting relationship, and program facilitators saw this as a concern to be addressed in the future. It seems that the co-parental relationship remains one of the more difficult divorce issues to resolve within a short-term intervention.

The problem with co-parental conflicts and hostility continues to be one of the major limitations of divorce-education programs like the PEACE program. Because 30 to 40 participants may attend each session, it is difficult to address the special needs of each one. Maccoby and Mnooken (1992) identified a subpopulation of postdivorce parents who were considered to be engaged in conflicted co-parenting. This group was characterized by low levels of communication and high levels of discord. These characteristics were found in about 24% of the couples even 3 to 4 years after the divorce. Divorce-education workshops may have only minimal impact upon couples with such high levels of conflict. These types of couples may need more intensive interventions such as the mediation programs discussed in chapter 12.

SUMMARY

As we return to our case example from beginning of the chapter, we can start to see how Dave and Mary might benefit from attending divorce education programs. They would begin to better understand the impact that their current behavior is having on their children. They would better appreciate what the children are going through a better understanding of their own grief-loss reactions. Dave and Mary could learn new ways of dealing directly with each other as co-parents, thus reducing the destructive games that can put their children into no-win situations when they are forced to choose or side with one parent. Dave and Mary would also learn more about how important it is for Dave to have an ongoing role after the divorce and they could discover ways to make this involvement more likely. Of course, this type of programming will not work for everyone. If the parents do not live in the same vicinity it may be difficult to get both parents involved. Motivation to attend can also be a challenge. While it may appear that this type of program would only work for the highly motivated parent, research suggests that even those who are not motivated at first can benefit from such an intervention (Arbuthnot & Gordon, 1996; Stone, McKenry, & Clark, 1999). The PEACE Program has dealt with two issues by working with the court system to make program attendance mandatory for divorcing parents. Even parents who do not live in the same area have found a way to meet the court edict. And while many of the attendees are at first resistant and unmotivated to take part in the program, the majority find that the program was helpful and think it should continue to be mandated for other divorcing parents. The PEACE program and other well-designed divorce education programs across the country may offer a degree of hope for those undergoing the divorce process.

Questions for Discussion

1.   How would you deal with Dave and Mary's use of the children as messengers? Why do you think it would be important to deal with this problem?

2.   How would you improve the PEACE program?

12

Mediating Co-Parenting Agreements

*I've heard from people that these poor children [in joint custody ar-
rangements] shouldn't have to get bounced back and forth between households and it's confusing to them. From my experience this is a paradigm
that mainly exists in some adults' heads and is based more on the societal view of the nuclear family than anything. All three of our kids live
in 2 different homes at varying schedules/times. They have come to
accept this and display no confusion at all.* (Anthony, joint-custody father of three children, www.fatherhood.org)

Voluntary co-parenting agreements after separation and divorce are
clearly preferable to involuntary agreements arranged through the
courts. Parents and their children are likely to benefit greatly from
such an arrangement. This chapter will help the reader learn more
about

- The shared-parenting movement that began in the 1970s
- Custody options and the advantages of joint custody
- Principles and goals of family mediation and its advantages
  over alternative approaches
- Relevance to unmarried parents of joint custody and media-
  tion
- Caveats in circumstances in which family mediation and joint
  custody are not advised
- Important components of an effective co-parenting agreement

Braver and O'Connell (1998) found one reason that more than any
other explained why fathers disengaged from their children: feeling
that they were parentally disenfranchised. Whether it was the judge

who decided against them on child custody or their former spouse who opposed their continued involvement or both, they felt that they were not valued as a father and had no real rights of parenthood anymore.

Ways need to be found to enfranchise fathers, particularly those who are likely to disengage. Braver and O'Connell (1998) found that the most important path involved the biological mother—that is, her desire and encouragement for the father's continued connection with his children. When a mother does not see the value of the father's involvement and instead sees only a hassle, she is very likely to communicate this to him. And many fathers respond to this message by withdrawing. In contrast, fathers are more likely to respond favorably by paying child support and remaining active in their children's lives when mothers welcome the fathers' continued involvement.

THE SHARED PARENTING MOVEMENT

Beginning in the 1970s, a shared-parenting movement unfolded, led by human service professionals and some parents' groups. This movement advocated for expanded opportunities for cooperative postdivorce parenting. Proponents became the champions of a custody option that was relatively unknown up to this point—joint or shared custody (these terms are used interchangeably). They hoped that a new generation of parents who were uncoupling would choose this family-centered alternative over sole custody. Seminal writings on joint custody began to be published during this period, and the authors were among the leaders of the shared-parenting movement (e.g., Bowman & Ahron, 1985; Wallerstein & Kelly, 1980).

The shared-parenting movement sought to defuse the combative custody battleground that had prevailed in the courts for decades. They believed that with sole custody, only one parent would be able to win and the other would lose. By contrast, they reasoned, joint custody would open up more choices and there would be greater participation from both parents and less rancor. Joint custody would be a major breakthrough for children as well because it would assure them that both of their parents would remain involved in their lives. And fathers in particular would become the beneficiaries of a special opportunity to parent that was unavailable to countless men of previous generations.

Joint Custody

Joint custody evolved in the 1970s as a result of several factors (Kelly, 1997). Claims by fathers' rights groups of sex discrimination against men in custody decisions, women's groups advocating for women's equality, and increasing numbers of women entering the workforce all played a role. By the mid 1970s many states replaced the *tender years* presumption that heavily favored the mother with the *best interests of the child* standard in determining custody. For the first time in history, custody decisions considered what children needed rather than favoring one parent simply because of gender. This historic shift prepared the way for joint custody.

A joint-custody mother of three children offers further thoughts about the benefits of this option.

> What is the justification of joint custody? Quite simply, a belief that children need TWO parents. Period. It is no more complicated than that. If you can communicate with the other parent (a lot), if you can put the children ahead of your own struggles (because you will have to swallow A LOT of feelings about your ex until tempers cool), and if you think both parents are truly ready to separate and move forward with their individual lives (otherwise the kids become the sticky link), then try it [joint custody]. You don't have to be friends with your ex to make it work (although a friendliness has certainly developed in our case); you just have to be dedicated to communicate about the kids. It can be a rewarding, loving experience for children, giving them a true sense of family instead of feeling fractured or cheated. (www.fatherhood.org)

As joint custody became a reality for a growing number of families, research studies have attempted to evaluate its effectiveness. Some of the essential questions that beg for an answer are: Does joint custody work? What are its advantages? Is it preferred over sole custody? Under what circumstances is it likely to fail? (Bowman & Ahrons, 1985; Buehler, 1989; Folberg, 1984; Luepnitz, 1986; Nelson, 1989; Pearson & Thoennes, 1990; Volgy & Everett, 1985). Overall, families that have voluntarily chosen joint custody have had favorable views and prefer it over a sole custody arrangement. In contrast, joint custody decided in court against the will of one parent does not have such favorable views and may be contraindicated because of its potentially harmful effects for children (Johnston, Kline, & Tschann, 1989).

Family Mediation

It was no coincidence that family mediation gained unusual popularity during the 1970s along with joint custody, particularly mediation that specialized in resolving issues of divorce. The shared-parenting movement envisioned a cooperative approach to settling custody issues and other aspects of divorce that would avert much of the conflict and at the same time optimize the possibility for joint custody to succeed. Mediation became a natural ally of joint custody because of its emphasis on cooperation, which would likely be a critical ingredient in cultivating successful shared-parenting arrangements. Family mediation was also a distinct alternative to the resolution process involving adversarial divorce proceedings that pit two attorneys and their clients against each other.

Along with the emergence of joint custody and divorce mediation came new, more inclusive terminology that emphasized the value and participation of both parents. Terms like the binuclear family, shared parenting, parental partnership, and mom's house/dad's house are prominent examples (Ahrons, 1979; Ricci, 1980). Some authors have gone so far as to suggest that these terms replace others like custody, visitation, and single-parent families in order to further promote and accentuate the roles and responsibilities of both parents.

Reflection
Do you think that it's possible for joint custody to become the preferred custody option for most postdivorce families, or is it only relevant to a relatively small group of divorcing parents? Do you think joint custody could work for unmarried parents as well? Why or why not?

Joint Custody and Other Custodial Options

The Reflection poses an important question: How large a segment of the postdivorce population can realistically benefit from joint or shared custody arrangements? We still have not fully answered it. Yet as shown in Figure 12.1, shared parenting accounted for 22% of all postdivorce living arrangements in 1997. This is a dramatic increase from what shared parenting was in 1970—a largely unknown custody

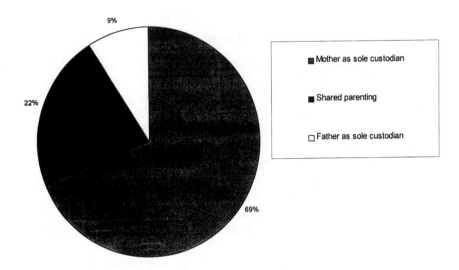

FIGURE 12.1 Postdivorce parenting agreements.
Note: From the U.S. Census Current Population Survey, National Center for Health Statistics, 1997.

arrangement. Because the definitions of shared parenting vary across states and because of difficulties in accurately reporting this arrangement in government documents, actual numbers involved in shared or joint parenting could be somewhat higher or lower.

Joint custody is, to say the least, a challenging enterprise, particularly because its participants have decided to separate. Ending intimate ties between two people can result in residual unresolved conflict, hurt, and anger. Successful co-parents must be able to rise above them if their joint custody is to work. Thus, success with joint custody depends in part upon the capacities and attitudes of divorcing parents; at best they must be equipped with maturity and reasonably developed communication skills. Having a social network that supports their parental role can also be valuable.

Joint custody is also still a debatable policy issue, both at the local and state levels. A firm, unequivocal commitment from state legislatures, local court systems, judges, and divorce attorneys is likely needed if joint custody is to gain wider acceptance. In 1979, California was the first state to pass a joint-custody statute. Since then 19 states have enacted statutes that give preference to joint custody if it can be worked out between the parties. These states include California, Connecticut,

Florida, Iowa, Idaho, Louisiana, Michigan, New Mexico, and Washington. Other states have added legal language that does not go as far as a presumption of joint custody but does encourage consideration of this option. The remaining states have not yet taken a position favorable to joint custody. It is important to add that definitions of joint custody vary among states, including the possibility of restrictions and limitations. The Web site *www.fatherhood.org* lists the most up-to-date status for each state on possible joint custody legislation.

The future of joint custody is also dependent upon the positions and actions of numerous women's groups as their perspectives continue to evolve about what is in the best interest of women. Many of these groups feel that the mother is placed at an undue disadvantage if she has to negotiate directly with the father. Such negotiations, they claim, can leave some women vulnerable to intimidating and controlling behavior of angry fathers.

Generally, it is not necessarily sound policy to depend exclusively on joint custody as a means of involving divorced fathers. Joint custody is not a panacea for all postdivorce families. Its potential weaknesses must be addressed, including some that are identified by women's groups. Furthermore, certain types of people for whom it is contraindicated should not be encouraged to seek this option. In addition, the relevance of joint custody to unmarried parents who separate is still largely an unexplored area.

A wider range of custody options and shared-parenting arrangements must be explored, particularly for parents who are unlikely to be given any custodial responsibility. Changes are occurring gradually in this area. For example, noncustodial parents' rights have expanded in most states to include access to information about their children's school work and medical information (Kelly, 1997). Noncustodial parents in some states can make emergency medical decisions when their children are in their care.

Split custody and alternating custody are two other options that are seldom awarded by judges because the children often have more difficulty in adjusting. Split custody gives one or more children to each of the parents; and alternating custody involves alternating primary custody between each parent for longer periods such as a year or two. Split custody often becomes the informal preference for many families as the children get older; for example, a son may move to his father's home during the teen years while the daughter remains with the mother.

CUSTODY OPTIONS

Many custody options are available, including variations in the joint custody category:

- Sole or primary custody: One parent assumes all residential and legal responsibilities.
- Split custody: One or more children live with and are the responsibility of one parent and the remaining children live with and are the responsibility of the other parent.
- Alternating custody: Each parent has the children for alternating blocks of time, often for a year or two, with the other parent having visiting rights.
- Joint residential (or physical) custody: Both parents assume some residential responsibilities.
- Joint legal custody: Both parents share major decision-making in their children's lives.

JOINT CUSTODY OPTIONS

Joint legal and joint residential custody can be worked out in one of three ways:

- Joint legal and joint residential custody: The parents share both residential and legal responsibilities.
- Joint legal and sole residential custody: One parent assumes the primary residence but shares legal responsibilities with the other parent (this is the most popular shared option).
- Joint residential and sole legal custody: One parent assumes the legal responsibilities but shares major residential responsibilities with the other parent (this is an unusual option).

Two Major Types of Joint or Shared Custody

The concept of joint custody has developed into two distinct options, joint residential and joint legal. In *joint residential custody,* both parents are expected to provide a primary home for their children and assume major child-raising responsibilities. Important decisions about the children's welfare are usually but not always shared. Joint residential custody does not necessarily mean equal residential time-sharing. The children's schedule for living with both parents can vary widely and should depend on the unique circumstances of each family. Examples of schedules for children over 5 years include:

- One parent has the children on Monday and Tuesday, the other parent on Wednesday and Thursday, and they alternate weekends. This schedule offers the parents equal time and gives each parent a weekend off every other week. The child is with each parent for either 2 or 5 consecutive days each week.
- One parent has the children during the school week and the other parent has them on weekends. This schedule works well when the parents live some distance apart, particularly when one of the parents lives quite a distance from the children's school. It also works well if one parent has a job primarily on the weekend.
- An alternate-week schedule in which one parent has the children one week and the other parent has them the next week. This arrangement minimizes the child's movement from one parent's household to the other.
- A popular arrangement for parents who live a considerable distance from each other (over 50 miles) consists of one parent having the children during the school year and the other parent having them during the summers and longer school holidays such as Thanksgiving and spring break.

Age-appropriate issues need to be considered in schedules as well, particularly for children 5 years old and under. One issue to consider is parental bonding. Both parents need sufficient contact with their young children in order for emotional bonding to occur. Another likely issue is the need of very young children to have the stability of one primary residential home along with frequent contact with the other parent. Addressing both of these issues may mean a primary residence with one parent and substantial daytime contact with the other parent. Some experts suggest that very young children should have only short lapses of time without seeing either parent while older children can have longer time lapses between contacts. The Fatherhood Project offers the following guidelines (www.fatherhood.org):

Age of child	Recommended contact with both parents
Under 1 year old	Part of each day
1 to 2 years	Every other day
2 to 5 years	Not more than two days without seeing each parent
5 to 9 years	Alternate weeks, with the "off duty" parent getting a mid-week visitation
Over 9 years	Alternate weeks

The intention of these guidelines is to support emotional bonding between the child and both parents. This is particularly important during the child's first few years of life. Obviously a strong parental partnership is critical to implementing such a schedule successfully because of the frequent contact and cooperation expected between the parents.

Joint legal custody means shared parental responsibility for major decisions involving the children. This shared-custody option has become more common than joint residential custody in most states, with the mother typically being given primary residential custody. In their study, Braver and O'Connell (1998) found that joint legal custody is a popular means of enfranchising fathers because it says that they are still the child's parent.

Joint legal custody does not require that both parents share substantially in child-raising responsibilities or work closely together. A father with joint legal custody, for example, can have much less contact with his children than his former spouse does, perhaps seeing the children every other weekend. With this custody option, a balance can be created so that both parents are involved and have rights without imposing the demands of close contact and cooperation between the parents. Most important, fathers with joint legal custody have been found to be more involved with their children than noncustodial fathers (Pearson & Thoennes, 1990).

One mother expressed her feelings about having joint legal custody. After raising concerns about feeling manipulated by the anger of the other parent, she went on to say:

> Then we realize that it's not such a bad thing that the other parent loves our children as much as we do. And I suppose in the long run, we learn that beyond all the anger and distress, it is the children who benefit from the loving interaction they have with both parents, and we learn to "let go" a wee bit. And for the children, that is the best thing that can happen." (Braver & O'Connell, 1998, p. 186)

With this custody option major decisions to be shared between parents can vary considerably. "Major decisions" depend, in part, on what is important to each family. Many states require that the parents identify in their parenting agreement the major decisions that are to be shared to avoid any misunderstandings at a later time. Examples of major decisions include

- the school a child will attend
- changes in child care arrangements
- the type of religious training the children will receive if any
- whether or not nonemergency surgery is needed
- whether or not to have orthodontal work
- extracurricular activities that require a commitment of time or money by both parents
- developmental matters such as dating, driving, curfew, birth control, etc.
- how to arrange for grandparents to have quality time with the children

Decisions that are shared between the parents do not include minor ones that are made on a day-to-day basis.

Joint legal custody can be a preference for families unable to share residential parenting because of a variety of circumstances. One example is when both parents agree that one parent is exceptional in handling child-raising responsibilities and the other parent is more career-oriented. Another example would be when the conflicts between the parents suggest that sharing residential parenting is inadvisable or possibly when considerable geographic distance between the parents precludes an active physical role by both parents.

Joint legal custody is in some respects a compromise between joint residential custody and sole custody for the mother. This option can elevate the father's rights and responsibilities to a point where he feels that he is enfranchised and valued as a parent. As some fathers have put it, joint legal custody means more than just being a "wallet." His input and direct involvement are recognized along with his financial support.

Studies indicate that joint legal custody fathers are likely to go to greater lengths to assume their economic responsibilities to their children than those without any custodial rights (Seltzer & Meyer, 1996; Shively, 1999). Braver and O'Connell (1998) conclude from their Arizona study that fathers who had joint legal custody were more likely to pay child support and to have significantly more contact with their children than those without any custody responsibilities. They found that even when joint legal custody was awarded despite the mother's preference for sole custody, child support and frequency of contact were significantly higher than for mothers having sole custody.

As with joint residential custody, the joint legal custody option requires cooperation between the parents and assumes that fathers will take on some child-raising responsibilities. This option, like any co-parent arrangement, works best when both parents are mature enough to put their children's interests first and not to use such opportunities to control or manipulate the other parent or get even for past infractions. It is often most challenging for the parent who has been the primary decision-maker in the past to accept this arrangement because she or he is used to making decisions on her or his own (Wilson, 2000). When this option is mandated by a judge against the will of at least one parent, it is less likely to work, in part because of the conflicts and unresolved disagreements between the parents deriving from the legal proceedings.

Perspective: An Example of a Joint Legal Custody Family

Anthony and Jeanne have joint legal custody of their two children. Jeanne is a devout Catholic and Anthony is an agnostic. Because Anthony has less at stake in the religious training of his children, he has agreed to defer decisions about religious training to Jeanne. On the other hand, both parents are very interested in their children's health and medical needs. Their mediated parenting agreement states that Anthony's medical insurance will provide coverage for their children. When Anthony's medical insurance was recently up for renewal, new health-care provider options were offered by his employer. As a result, Anthony and Jeanne got together to decide which HMO they would select for the children. Both parents investigated the advantages and disadvantages of each HMO related to children's medical needs before they got together to pick a HMO together.

We must also consider the potential difficulties that mothers may have with a joint legal or residential custody arrangement. A father's greater involvement with his children may be viewed as a threat to the interests of mothers, and some mothers may feel more secure when they have full control over their children's daily routine. She may also wish to have her former spouse totally out of their lives so they can start over again. Sharing custody means that the father remains in the mother's life as well as the children's. It means that an effort must be made to communicate and work with the father. The father's involvement can be viewed as an added burden or another obligation for the mother. For example, he could hold views about his children's after-school arrangement that are in conflict with the mother's views, or he may lack sympathy for the demands of the mother's job that affect the children.

Another view to consider, however, is that increasing the involvement of fathers may be in the best interests of mothers, assuming that the father takes on greater parental responsibility. Mothers can share their concerns and decisions about their children with the father rather than carrying the burden alone. In addition, a father's time with the children offers mothers more time to get on with their own lives. Joint custody can be a win for mothers and a win for fathers rather than a win-lose equation.

At times parents cannot make joint decisions about their children because shared decision-making can be very difficult when divorced or separated parents have opposing views on an issue. Making joint decisions about the children's welfare requires putting the needs of the children before the parents. Family mediators and other conciliatory professionals may be needed as a neutral party to help resolve the parents' differences. If Anthony and Jeanne (the couple in the Perspective) could not agree on an HMO for their children's health care, they would involve their family mediator as a next step. In their case, they anticipated that this problem could occur and they included a provision in their court-sanctioned parenting agreement that they would use the services of their family mediator whenever they could not make a joint decision on their own.

When Joint Custody is Not Recommended

Both joint legal and residential custody are to be discouraged in some situations. When fathers (or mothers) have serious personal problems that prevent then from becoming positively involved as parents, they should not be encouraged to pursue the joint custody options (Gardner, 1984). At least three such situations need to be mentioned: serious mental illness, a substance abuse problem that is not under control, or abusiveness toward a spouse or children (Braver & O'Connell, 1998).

Many mental illnesses (such as a psychopathic personality disorder, psychotic episodes, or severe mood swings) can unduly interfere with a person's capacity to be mature and reliable enough to care for the needs of his children (Dion, Braver, Wolchik, & Sandler, 1997). Examples are fathers who are pathological liars who cannot be trusted or who regularly disregard time schedules for picking up and returning the children.

Similarly, people with a serious alcohol or drug problem who are not in recovery are not likely to be a responsible parent (Braver & O'Connell, 1998). Supervising children during a drinking or drug episode, for example, could easily place the children in harm's way, and such behavior could easily interfere with a child's developing moral code.

However, if a father is recovering from a substance abuse problem, possibly a different position could be taken. Having renewed contact with his children may benefit therapeutically both a father and his children (Dudley, 1991c). In some cases a father might be more optimistic about returning to a healthy status if he could reunite with his children.

Domestic violence is another factor that weighs heavily against a successful joint custody arrangement. Parents and children who are the victims of such violence must have the protection of the courts when divorce and custody decisions are being made (Goodman, Koss, & Felipe Russo, 1993). A co-parental arrangement with someone who has a history of violence and uses his power to intimidate and threaten other family members is destined to fail. Such an arrangement could not only result in emotional and physical harm to family members but also could continually subvert their needs out of fear of the perpetrator.

While relatively infrequent, abuse is sometimes alleged falsely by one parent to gain an advantage in winning custody. Occasionally false claims are an intentional strategy by attorneys and their clients. To prevent such claims from succeeding, the court must conduct a careful evaluation before making a domestic abuse charge (Stahl, 1996). Unfortunately, the accused is stigmatized even when the charges are disproved (Braver & O'Connell, 1998).

We need to distinguish between an abuser with a history of threats and violence and a parent who has no history of violence but commits an isolated act (perhaps shoving) during one of the most intense times of uncoupling. While the latter behavior must also be viewed as unacceptable, usually it should not be grounds for denying a parent the opportunity to raise his children.

Reflection
If you were a family mediator, how would you go about determining if a charge of domestic abuse alleged by one parent against the other was true or false?

THE PROCESS OF DEVELOPING PARENTING AGREEMENTS

Divorcing fathers and mothers are naturally in conflict with each other as they go through the divorce process. Feelings of anger, hurt, and hostility between divorcing couples is to be expected. Actually, these feelings may often be traced back to many years of unresolved conflicts or unmet needs. In brief, most people who become divorced are bound to be in some conflict. It is clearly a major challenge for parents who are uncoupling to comfortably continue a parental partnership while terminating their intimate relationship.

How a divorce is obtained is likely to impact several important postdivorce family outcomes (Benjamin & Irving, 1995; Hochberg & Kressel, 1996), including the custody decision, financial support, the quality of the postdivorce parental partnership, and the willingness of both parents to implement the parenting agreement. Mediated child-custody settlements more than litigated ones seem to lessen the conflicts between parents, giving greater assurance that shared parenting can occur (Dudley, 1991a; Kitzmann & Emery, 1994). Each parent needs to be heard by the other parent in the divorce or custody process. This process should help both parents gain a fuller understanding of the needs of all family members. Hopefully, the process can also be an opportunity for divorcing parents to come together to make good decisions on behalf of all family members. Effective strategies for resolving conflicts and fostering common understanding are essential to this process if these ideals are to be achieved.

Unmarried parents who split up need parenting agreements that address child custody, child support, and visitation matters. The processes that are selected to determine their agreements are similarly important in terms of their impact on the children and other family members. The literature on mediation almost exclusively focuses on divorcing parents and is referred to as divorce mediation. Yet mediation is available and quite relevant to unmarried and teen parents as well. More research is needed to determine how frequently unmarried and teen parents use mediation, and how effective mediation can be in helping them.

The two most common strategies for obtaining a divorce are (a) proceedings involving two attorneys and (b) mediation. These two strategies have distinctly different philosophies, outcomes, and strategies.

Proceedings Involving Attorneys

Proceedings involving two opposing attorneys are usually adversarial in that each attorney represents one parent in a contest against the other parent. Attorneys are known to vary greatly in their negotiation styles (Fisher & Ury, 1981). They can be soft bargainers who place a high priority on minimizing conflict and reaching an agreement. Or they can be hard bargainers who engage in legal game-playing to win victory over their opponent. A third style is to be a principled bargainer who places the greatest emphasis on achieving a fair agreement. A range of negotiation processes can occur by mixing combinations of these styles. In adversarial proceedings, an attorney represents each parent in what can easily turn out to be a win-lose strategy with the other party. Problems are often resolved when one party is perceived to be gaining and the other party losing. Unfortunately, seizing what is exclusively "mine" is more important in adversarial proceedings than discovering what could exist for "us"-the areas of common ground and mutual benefit.

A major danger of using adversarial attorneys is that the conflicts may broaden and end up in litigated court proceedings. Litigated proceedings are the most adversarial stage of negotiations when the two attorneys put all of their energies into persuading a judge to rule in their favor. Their interest is in manipulating the law to place their client in the most positive light and the other parent in the most negative light (Girder, 1985). At this point little if any opportunity is left for discovering common ground between the parents; instead, a win-lose strategy automatically dominates. While attorneys vary in their negotiation styles in litigated proceedings, quite often they encourage their client to partake in potentially destructive behavior. Girder (1985) points out that attorneys have no other choice but to encourage their clients to do such things as pump their children for information about the other parent, coach them on what they should and should not say in court, and, most destructively, influence how the children feel about the other parent.

What types of families are most likely to need and benefit from litigation is a question not fully answered. However, adversarial proceedings are particularly relevant when two parents have unsuccessfully attempted to resolve their family differences in a voluntary manner. In addition, these proceedings may be preferred for families with special problems, including instances of potential harm to a child or parent, evidence of abuse or threats of violence, or when a family member has a mental illness or a substance abuse problem.

Another question that needs greater consideration is how to reduce the number of cases that end up being litigated when their disputes could have been resolved in a less adversarial way. Unfortunately, adversarial proceedings have been the preferred choice much too often because mediation services were not readily available or a court system was not committed enough to mediation. Alternatives to adversarial proceedings are more prevalent in some states than others largely because of variability in state laws and differing levels of commitment by states to court-sponsored and private mediation and arbitration.

Adversarial proceedings have been found to be particularly problematic for many fathers. Several studies have reported that an adversarial legal system was not usually helpful to fathers (Dudley, 1996; Emery, 1994). Attorneys and the courts, fathers claimed, did not adequately take into account their rights or needs. Their attorneys and the judges presiding in their court hearings did not work with them to increase their level of parenting. Shared and sole paternal custody were often overlooked or discouraged as options. They were not helped to find more effective ways of working with their ex-wives. If anything, many of their adversarial legal battles insured the opposite—that parental partnership in a postdivorce era would be improbable.

It is not evident how often the adversarial legal system exacerbates conflicts or creates them. Existing adversarial legal systems typically are not set up to help parents prepare to be partners in raising children after divorce (Girdner, 1985). Rather, divorcing or uncoupling parents are encouraged to reduce their efforts to communicate with each other, increase their distrust, and diminish any possible grounds of mutual understanding. Litigated proceedings, in particular, are likely to exacerbate the conflicts that parents are experiencing, which can easily result in lessening the father's contact with his children (Koch & Lowery, 1984). Needless to say, when such proceedings are anticipated to lead to such outcomes, they should be avoided if at all possible.

It is important to note that many mothers may have different views than fathers about divorce negotiations and custody arrangements. What would be the preferred legal proceedings for divorcing mothers? Many may not agree with divorcing fathers that it is most advantageous to have the father spend more time with his children, particularly if this is going to create additional difficulties for the mother. Also, mothers may have reservations about using mediation to resolve their disputes. They may feel intimidated when communicating with their ex-husband or uncomfortable negotiating without an attorney. They may also believe that they have the most favorable outcome in the legal system when adversarial proceedings are used. Whatever the reservations of the mother are, they need to be explored and recognized as legitimate concerns.

Alternatively, many women may prefer mediation to adversarial proceedings because they know that they will get more cooperation from their former partners by this method. Some may also prefer mediation to avoid further aggravating their former spouse because they know that aggravating him can easily backfire on them (Wilson, 2000).

The Mediation Process

Family mediation is the other most common approach in obtaining a divorce or deciding custody. Divorce mediation in particular has become increasingly popular in recent years as many court systems have added it to their service provisions, often as a mandatory initial step in negotiations. Mediation is not adversarial. Typically, one mediator meets with both parents without representing either one. If anything, the mediator represents the children's interests, particularly when their needs are overlooked by either parent. Each parent is encouraged to have an attorney represent them, but attorneys are only involved as advisors about the law and almost never become involved in mediation sessions. The mediator helps the parents to clearly define the issues to be resolved, helps in identifying their overlapping interests, and assists in developing an agreement. The agreement is likely to consist of compromises between the parents and takes into account the interests of all family members (Folberg & Taylor, 1984; Kressel, 1985).

Because of its emphasis on cooperation, mediation is designed to achieve a favorable outcome for all family members. The agreement is worked out and developed by the parents. The mediator does not make decisions for them. For these reasons, the agreement is likely to be supported and followed later by both parents. Several studies have reported that a mediated settlement is more likely to provide a favorable postdivorce adjustment, including agreements that are more satisfactory to the parents, have greater compliance, and lead to greater involvement by the father than an adversarial negotiation (Benjamin & Irving, 1995; Dillon & Emery, 1996; Emery, 1995; Kelly, 1994; Pearson & Thoennes, 1990). Mediation services are most helpful if provided early in the separation and divorce process. These services are usually more efficient and cost-effective than adversarial processes (Benjamin & Irving, 1995).

In some instances, including children in the mediation process may be beneficial to positive family outcomes (Gentry, 1997). Numerous reasons have been given for inclusion of children such as keeping some of the focus on the children's needs, keeping the children informed, and providing children with an opportunity to share their views. Other reasons may be given for excluding children from mediation; for example, the children are too young or immature, participation may impose a greater burden on the children, a parent or the children may be against the idea, or the children may need to be protected from parental game-playing (Lansky, Manley, Swift, & Williams, 1995).

MEDIATION IS NOT FOR ALL FAMILIES

Mediation is not recommended for all families. Mediators often pose several general questions to divorcing parents to determine if mediation should be considered (McKay, Rogers, Blades, & Gosse, 1999, pp. 143–145): Do both parents seem ready and willing to get divorced? Are they willing to cooperate in arriving at a fair and equitable parenting agreement? Are they willing to consent to full disclosure of their resources? If one or both parents respond negatively to such questions, mediation is not likely to work.

Mediation should not be encouraged if it places any family members in danger, for example in instances of family violence. Other

family problems such as a parent having a mental illness or a substance abuse problem that is not under control may also preclude
mediation. In these special situations, adversarial lawyers, with special
sensitivity for the vulnerable parties and the impact on the children,
seem more appropriate.

COURT-SPONSORED VERSUS PRIVATE MEDIATION

Mediation services can be either court-sponsored or private. In both
cases, the mediators usually have formal training. Parents who use
court-sponsored mediation are likely to be known to the court as
having difficulty resolving their custody, child support, and property
issues; otherwise, they would probably have resolved them outside the
court (Benjamin & Irving, 1995). Thus, these parents are more involuntary than voluntary because mediation is being imposed on them;
they may even prefer to litigate their differences but are deterred from
doing so by the court system. In contrast, parents using private mediation are likely to be voluntary participants and are less likely to be
embroiled in high-intensity conflicts. Those using private mediation
are also suspected of being from middle or upper income families more
than lower income groups. In this regard, lower income families may
be less likely to use private mediation because of income restraints and
a lack of awareness about these services and their merits. They may
also be less informed about the harmful effects of adversarial proceedings. Overall, privately mediated cases are suspected of having more
success than court-sponsored mediation cases.

Court-ordered mediation is now available in many states. Several
states including California, Maine, and New Mexico have mandated
or court-ordered mediation service as a first step in resolving custody
or visitation disputes. Other states and numerous local court systems
offer mediation service on a discretionary basis. Some states require it
for such things as child custody disputes but not for disputes over
child support and alimony. Unfortunately, in these instances the non-
mediated issues often create conflicts that spill over into mediation.
And public mediation programs can become coercive if parents feel
undue pressure to either settle in mediation or face the consequences
in court (Emery, 1995). Court-sponsored mediation services are usually free or involve minimal fees. The number of sessions available,
however, is often limited.

Private mediation is most often provided by professional practitioners or a family mediation agency. The mediators are most likely to be mental health professional or attorneys, with each bringing different types of expertise beyond specialized mediation training. The former usually bring more background in child and family development and family therapy while the latter have a stronger legal background.

Currently, private mediation is available and can be used for settling all of the issues in a divorce, including settling property, child support, and custody (Kelly, 1997). In this respect, private mediation can be comprehensive while court-sponsored mediation is more likely available for only custody or visitation disputes. Fees for private mediation tend to be relatively high ($70–$100 per hour) but still are usually less than attorney's fees. More information about mediation can be found on several Web sites (e.g., Academy of Family Mediators: www.mediators.org).

Unmarried and teen parents are likely to benefit from both court-sponsored and private mediation. Court-sponsored mediation of child custody decisions usually does not distinguish between whether the couple is married or unmarried (Wilson, 2000). Many of the decisions to be made on behalf of the children are similar regardless of the parents' marital status. However, we suspect that private mediation is less likely to be used by unmarried couples than by divorcing parents.

Reflection

If you were the presiding judge in a family court, which approach would you give preference to in most custody and divorce proceedings: adversarial lawyers or a mediator? What are the advantages and disadvantages of the approach that you favor?

A Continuum of Negotiation Approaches

What would be a preferred legal proceeding for an individual family? While mediation and adversarial proceedings are the most common approaches to consider, a further gradation of choices is often available. A continuum ranges from working out a parenting agreement on your own at the lowest level of contest to litigation at the highest level of contest (Kelly, 1997). Using this continuum, the preferred choice for facilitating positive outcomes for families and fathers should naturally begin at the lowest level of contest agreeable to both parents and move to the next highest level if they are not successful. Exceptions need to be made for families with special problems such as domestic violence or mental illness.

Perspective: A Continuum of Approaches to Negotiations
1. Developing agreements without assistance
2. Assistance from an outside family consultant
3. Professional private mediation
4. Professional court mediation
5. Arbitrator
6. Adversarial negotiations with two attorneys
a. Soft bargainers
b. Principled bargainers
c. Hard bargainers
7. Litigated court proceedings

DEVELOPING AGREEMENTS WITHOUT OUTSIDE ASSISTANCE

This simplest approach is likely to involve a low level of contest. The parents can discuss the needs of their children and their preferences and reservations without any outside assistance. Using an outline of decisions provided by the courts or a mediation agency they proceed to develop their own parenting agreement, including the custody arrangement and the children's residential schedule, major decisions to involve both parents, economic arrangements (child support and alimony), and the property settlement. Ideally, this agreement begins to get worked out as soon after separation as possible, and no costs are incurred beyond preparing a legal document for court approval.

ASSISTANCE FROM AN OUTSIDE FAMILY CONSULTANT

Seeking an outside family consultant may be the next step to consider. Trusted friends or colleagues are invited to help with the communication processes in the areas that are difficult. This trusted resource person could be a clergy person, a family member, counselor, or friend. Otherwise, this approach would be similar to having the agreement worked out with no outside assistance.

PROFESSIONAL PRIVATE MEDIATION

Private mediation would likely be the next step. Mediators have specialized training and would be offering a framework for developing a comprehensive parenting agreement that would eventually become an order of the court. The work with a mediator would emphasize cooperation and finding common ground in making decisions. Mediators would not make decisions for the parents.

PROFESSIONAL MEDIATION SPONSORED BY THE COURT SYSTEM

A court-sponsored mediator could come next if private mediation failed. This mediation service would likely be available only for specific issues like custody and visitation, unless you are fortunate enough to live in a state like Maine, which has mediation services available for all issues pertinent to divorce. This mediation service may also be time-limited. There may be a special incentive to resolve any disputes at this stage because the only alternative may be to resolve the dispute before a judge. With this option, some aspects of a divorce agreement, usually the property settlement and child support, would probably need to be worked out with adversarial attorneys.

ARBITRATION

Arbitration could become the next option if it is available. Arbitration services are not currently available in most states. Arbitration is a nonlitigious approach that does not directly involve attorneys. One person or a panel hears the views of both parents related to a dispute and then makes the decision for them. A special masters program in California is an example (Kelly, 1997). In this case, the special master, usually a mental health professional with extensive training and experience, is empowered by the courts to settle the continuing disputes of a relatively small group of high-conflict, postdivorce families who keep returning to court. Sometimes, this arbitrator attempts first to mediate the dispute, hoping to get the parents to work out their own resolution; if this fails, the arbitrator makes the decision for them. The special master's decision can be challenged in a superior court but seldom is.

ADVERSARIAL NEGOTIATIONS WITH TWO ATTORNEYS

Adversarial negotiations come next and may already be involved if court-sponsored custody mediation is occurring. The attorneys can address all of the issues in a divorce agreement, including custody, economic arrangements, and property settlement. This approach has a built-in win-lose strategy, which sets up competition between the parents. Attorneys have different negotiating styles, which influences how quickly an agreement can be arranged and how much common ground is discovered. Three negotiation styles of attorneys were described earlier in this chapter: soft bargainers, principled bargainers, and hard bargainers. Usually, the attorneys representing both parents must adopt the same negotiation style to reach an agreement that takes into account the needs of both parties. Soft bargainers usually offer the least adversarial negotiations and hard bargainers the most.

LITIGATED COURT PROCEEDINGS

Litigated court proceedings take over if the two competing attorneys fail to work out an out-of-court settlement. These proceedings are the most adversarial of all and are likely to be destructive to relationships between the parents and their children. This step is considered the last resort and typically is very costly. Litigated proceedings are very likely to lead to the withdrawal of one parent, usually the father, from involvement with the children because of the animosity generated (Dudley, 1991a; Emery, 1994). Yet litigated proceedings are warranted if harm is a likely consequence of other negotiations or if conflicting parents cannot resolve their disputes using other approaches.

Educational Programs

Along with mediation, another component of a preferred conflict-resolution approach would be an educational program for parents that systematically prepares them for the divorce (Buehler, Betz, Ryan, Legg, & Trotter, 1992; Devlin, Brown, Beebe, & Parulis, 1992; Warren & Amara, 1984). Such a program would be designed to describe the various options for custody, along with specific information on how parents can determine which option is most suitable to their family. The advantages and limitations of mediation and adversarial proceedings could also be described along with the potentially harmful effects of each approach on the children and parents. It is especially important to introduce this educational intervention as early as possible to encourage maximum cooperation and to prevent or minimize the likelihood of any counterproductive activity. Chapter 11 provides information about postdivorce educational programs.

Diversity Issues, Custody, and Mediation

Cultural and socioeconomic issues need to be considered when exploring joint custody or mediation. The growing interest among men in being more active as fathers may still be primarily a middle- and upper-class phenomenon (Kelly, 1997). However, joint custody and mediation may also be very appropriate options for other types of families such as those from lower socioeconomic backgrounds and minority ethnic groups that emphasize an active father figure. When working with parents who have separated, the important thing to consider is the impact of cultural issues. Questions that could be asked include: Are these options relevant to them? Are they feasible? Are there any potential conflicts between a family's cultural heritage and these options?

Lower income families in particular may have major difficulty with the economic aspects of both joint custody and paying for mediation services. For example, how feasible is it for them to set up two households for joint residential custody (Donnelly & Finkelhor, 1993)? Working out alternative housing arrangements may be a critical issue if they are to succeed with joint custody. Can the home of the extended family be used for overnight arrangements with the father, or would it make more sense for the father to be primarily involved during the daytime hours? Lower income families may also hold traditional views about parental roles and may not expect the father to assume an active nurturing role with his children. If such a role is foreign to a man, he may need ongoing assistance in learning how to meet his responsibilities, like changing diapers, bathing his child, expressing affection, and responding to the child's nutritional needs.

We also need to ask if mediation services are workable for the varied parenting arrangements evident in society. Unmarried parents, for example, have been increasingly utilizing court-mandated mediation. One study suggests that mediation works well for them. Raisner (1997) found that unmarried parents using court-sponsored mediation reached agreement on custody and parenting issues at about the same rate as divorced parents.

A case example of an unmarried family arrangement in the next Perspective illustrates what can happen in the relations between unmarried parents and the impact that it can have on their children.

Mediation services, offered in a timely manner, may have been able to avert many of their conflicts.

Perspective

A young father and mother knew each other while attending the same high school during their teen years. While in their early 20s, they became intimate for a time and gave birth to a child. Both parents and their families decided to work together to raise the child. The child stayed with the paternal grandmother during the day while the mother worked. The father and his family contributed clothing and other tangible items but not a regular child support payment. When the child was 18 months old, the mother lost her job and went on welfare. Unbeknownst to the mother, the welfare office filed a petition for child support against the father. The father and his family, thinking that the mother was being greedy, decided to cut off all informal connections and support. The father later filed a petition for custody, and the relationship between the two parents worsened further, all to the detriment of their child (Raisner, 1997).

The assumptions held by the mediator may need to be adjusted for unmarried parents, gay parents, and others. Unmarried parents, for example, may have issues quite different from divorcing parents. For example, the mediator may need to help in the formation of *new* relationships between parents rather than changing previous ones. It is very possible that unmarried parents may not be in a continuing relationship with each other. Giving birth to a child could be the one thing that connects them to each other. This can happen when a pregnancy results from casual dating or a one-night sexual experience. Also, in some unmarried custody cases, a child may not have had any contact with one of the parents prior to the time that custody issues were raised. For example, a father may not discover that he has a child until long after the birth. In this case, it may be important to gradually ease the father into his child's life. A graduated time schedule could be devised, particularly for a young child, with the assistance of a mediator. The schedule may begin with supervised day contact and gradually develop into unsupervised day contact. Eventually a transition could be made to overnight stays with the father. The father may need other kinds of assistance as well to help in bonding with his child.

Unmarried parents who have had a long term relationship and are now living apart may also need special assistance from the mediator (Wilson, 2000). Among other things, mediators will need to be aware of any prejudices that they or others may have toward their circumstances. Their child may be viewed as "illegitimate" by some, but can be warmly received and accepted by the couple, their extended families, and subculture. Mediation can help work out these concerns as well as foster a stronger tie between the father and his child.

In the case of same-sex couples, other issues may further complicate the mediation assistance that they need. Gay relationships are often not accepted or fully valued by many people and groups in our culture. Nevertheless, they may have as much a need for mediation services as anyone. For example, the nonbiological parent in the relationship may need special assistance in exploring his or her parental role because this parent may have no legal protection. Mediation services may help such a couple clarify the needs and rights of the nonbiological parent and explore ways to strengthen this parent's bonds to the children.

PARENTING AGREEMENTS

An approach to mediation should be creative and build on the strengths of all family members. Wilson (2000) usually begins her child custody negotiations between parents with questions like, "What are each of your hopes and dreams?" She then suggests that they think back to a happier time for them and their children to help create some positive images. Other questions that she asks are, "What do you want for your children?" and "What kind of relationship do each of you want to have with the children?" The children's best interests often get focused attention using this strategy. After creating a positive, child-centered atmosphere the parents can proceed to specific issues that need to be resolved.

Typical Issues to Cover in a Parenting Agreement

Parenting agreements arranged through mediation are usually much more detailed than agreements derived from an adversarial divorce proceeding or other approaches (Kelly, 1993). While agreements with less specificity and more flexibility can be useful in some instances,

Perspective

Patrick and Sandy have four children and are seeking a divorce. They responded to the mediation question, "What are each of your hopes and dreams?" with these comments:

- "I want our children to have a good education and to eventually attend college."
- "I hope that the children start their careers before starting a family like we did."
- "I want to be able to understand our family better, how we can make it work."
- "To have the children know that we both love them and will have done our best for them."
- "That we parents will be able to set and achieve goals."
- "That we will be able to be respectful of ourselves and others."
- "That we will change what we can, and let go of what we can't change."
- "Peace of mind—that we won't fight, we can get along, and that we both will be involved in the children's lives."
- "A strong spiritual foundation."

generally the preference is for greater specificity to prevent unnecessary confusion and conflict. If possible, parents who are experiencing serious conflicts in particular should have a parenting agreement that leaves nothing to be negotiated later.

Issues typically included in parenting agreements could include the following (McKay et al., 1999; Wilson, 2000):

- The regular daily schedule where the children will reside—how often, how long, and at what times. For example, every other Monday through Friday, beginning at 3:30 p.m. on Monday after school and ending at 9:00 a.m. on Friday morning when the children leave for school.
- Specific plan for parent-child contacts for specific holidays and vacations.
- Times, locations, and parental responsibilities for pick-ups or drop-offs when the children regularly go to the other parent's residence.

- Circumstances under which changes can be made in the schedule.
- Communication patterns desired, such as not expressing negative things about the other parent in the children's presence or not having the children be messengers for the parents.
- Major decisions that will be made jointly and how much say the children will have in these decisions.
- House rules that both parents can agree on, such as bedtime at each home.
- A disciplinary approach that both parents agree on if possible; for example is a spanking or time-out the discipline approach to emphasize?
- Recreation, sports, and other after-school activities and any sponsoring organizations for these activities.
- School-related problems and issues, such as doing homework, dealing with low grades, behavior problems.
- School activities for parents—who will attend parent-teacher conferences, who will chaperone field trips, attend soccer games.
- Clothing—what clothes to buy, wear, launder, and whether they are shared between households.
- Medical decisions and care—what physician will be seen, what medication, health insurance.
- Financial issues such as child support payments, who pays what bills, how to handle income tax matters.
- Types of information about the children that are to be shared.
- Any agreements about dating when the children are present.
- Alcohol use when the children are present.
- Children's access to the other parent by phone.

Parenting agreements should anticipate the possibility that one parent could choose to move some distance away in the future, and this can be addressed by proposing a mutually agreed-upon plan for residential custody if this occurs. This plan should also include an agreement that the children will have regular contact with the other parent and specify how the costs of the children's travel between households will be worked out. Such a contingency plan will help facilitate negotiations if a move does occur at a later time, and it may serve as a deterrent for either parent's moving away.

Perspective: Sample Parenting Agreement

1. Jim Seligman and Marcia Seligman are the parents of Alan, Sandra, and Laura Seligman.
2. Jim and Marcia agree to contribute to the children's support in proportion to their incomes (currently 40% for Marcia and 60% for Jim). All outlays for the children will be added up at the end of the month and a payment or adjustment made so that each parent is contributing at the agreed percentage.
3. If the income of either Marcia or Jim falls below 25% of their total income, he or she will still be responsible for contributing 25% of the children's support.
4. The children will live with Jim Friday night through Monday morning and with Marcia Monday night through Friday morning. Schedule changes may be renegotiated at any time.
5. Jim will continue to pay the children's health and dental insurance.
6. Jim and Marcia will jointly make and be responsible for educational, health, and welfare decisions for their children.
7. Both parents will have access to all school, medical, and other records of the children.
8. All child-care arrangements and baby-sitters will be chosen jointly and paid at the same ratio given in paragraph 2 above.
9. Either parent can have the children for a two-week vacation. Longer periods are to be negotiated.
10. The children will be with a particular parent on alternating holidays.
11. Marcia and Jim will live no further than 10 miles from each other for the next four years.
12. If either Marcia or Jim move away from the Chicago area, she or he will give up primary parenting responsibilities.

Signed, Marcia Seligman and Jim Seligman

(McKay, Rogers, Blades, & Gosse, 1999, pp. 239–240)

An arrangement should also be included for how the parents will work out disagreements when they arise. For example, a designated time and place can be set aside for such occurrences, or the parents can agree to try to work out unresolved issues with a particular mediator before either can take court action. Specific principles for negotiating disagreements without outside help are listed in McKay, Rogers, Blades, and Gosse (1999, p. 125).

Questions for Discussion

1. If you were getting a divorce, which approach would you want to use for resolving custody, child support, and other pertinent issues? Why do you favor this approach?

2. If you were the family court administrator reviewing the parenting agreement between Jim and Marcia in the Perspective, would you approve it? What concerns, if any, would you want to raise with them? If Jim and Marcia had intense conflicts with each other, what additional information would you want to include in the agreement?

3. Why do you suppose that joint custody and mediation services have not been utilized by teen and unmarried parents as much as by divorced parents? How could these options be made more available to these groups?

4. What issues do you think that a gay couple (two men) who are splitting up would have in working out a parenting agreement if one of them is both the biological and custodial parent and the other one has developed a close bond with their child? How would you explore the possible concerns of the non-biological parent around custody and visitation?

GLOSSARY

The language that we use in helping two parents work out a parenting agreement after separation or divorce can be extremely important. The following glossary suggests some preferred terms that could be used in place of more traditional ones.

Glossary of Preferred and Problematic Terms

Preferred Term	Traditional Term
Two parents	One parent (and an absent parent)
Primary and secondary parent	Custodial and noncustodial parent
Binuclear family	Single-parent family
Viable parenting roles for both parents	Winning custody
Cooperative	Competitive and conflictual
Parenting agreement	Custodial decisions

Afterword: Visioning a Future for Fathering

The most important thing a man can do in his life is to be a good father. All else pales—money, celebrity, fame, and fortune pass. As the saying goes, "You can't take it with you." But with a child you leave something of yourself behind. If you don't take this opportunity to do your best by your sons and daughters, you fail them and you fail your own humanity. (Senator Bill Bradley)

What can we expect of fatherhood in the 21st century? Will a significantly larger percentage of fathers be actively raising their children in this new century? Will the nurturing-father role discovered in the late 20th century become the norm for all socioeconomic and ethnic groups or will it remain largely a middle-class phenomenon? And what will happen to nonresidential fathering? Will fathers who don't live with their children become more widespread? Will divorced, unmarried, and teen fathers become more involved parents? Or will the biological mothers of their children be left bearing the major responsibility along with greater dependency upon existing and new social institutions? In short, will "nonresidential fathering" become synonymous with "active and valued parenting" or will it be more associated with absence?

ACTING ON BEHALF OF FATHERS

We don't know the answers to these questions any more than anyone else. We do believe, however, that if our society does nothing more than it is currently doing, the continuation of existing trends seem inevitable and the times ahead will become increasingly troubling. What can be done then to promote more involved fathering? We have attempted to answer this pivotal societal question throughout the pages of this book. A retrospective summary of our message is offered at this point.

Our position is that nonresidential fathering is a reality that often cannot be changed. In brief, it's not a question of whether it is good or bad fathering. The important question is, Is it workable? The purpose of the book is to propose ways to make nonresidential fathering workable, particularly when it is beneficial for the children. We highlight and illustrate numerous ways of helping these fathers and their families throughout the book.

Three Groups of Fathers

Initially, we argued that fathering can be at risk for many different groups of fathers. We chose to focus on the risks for divorced, unmarried, and teen nonresidential fathers. They have much in common, including two major challenges: living for the most part separate from their children; and depending upon the cooperation of their children's mother. Each of these groups also has its own unique personal and environmental obstacles to parenting, many of which we have identified. Divorced fathers, for example, often have an unsympathetic and sometimes unfriendly family court system to face when custody, child support, and their children's residential schedule are being worked out. Unmarried fathers have to make special efforts to claim their responsibilities and rights as parents because they can easily be ignored and forgotten except for child-support obligations. And teen fathers are usually unprepared to adequately assume their parental responsibilities without also receiving assistance with their own developmental needs.

Enfranchise Fathers

Overall, we have argued that we must try to help males feel more enfranchised as parents. This may entail awarding them greater legal rights as a parent, including more routinely considering joint custody. Fathers are also enfranchised when they are given greater recognition and encouragement as parents from other family members and friends. If a father is unmarried, he is enfranchised when paternity is established as early as possible. Enfranchisement also means that males should have access to a range of relevant programs that can help them become more effective parents.

We also must become more sensitive to the myriad ways that we disenfranchise fathers. For example, we must work more diligently to overcome early socialization processes that teach boys not to cry or not to hug their moms, or that communicate to males that there is any positive value in being dominant over females. Stereotypes such as the bungling, irresponsible, and insensitive father can be replaced with more positive images in the media and in print material and by prominent role models. In brief, while a father's deficits must be addressed, let's not overlook their strengths.

Seeking Change On Many System Levels

We believe that change on behalf of fathers must occur simultaneously on several system levels, including personal help in individual, family, and group counseling; educational programs; mentoring provided by older men; employment and training initiatives; spiritual interventions; sex education and family preparation in the schools; family-friendly policies and practices in the workplace; positive media coverage; and public policies supporting active fathering and marriage. Also, family court policies and practices are needed that will encourage fathers to become more involved with their children and that will limit the use of punitive measures and adversarial proceedings to instances when voluntary measures cannot work.

Human-services professionals are challenged to utilize practice theories that take into account the benefits of fathers to families. Holistic family assessments and gender-sensitive practice approaches are needed. The strengths perspective is of central importance, and multicultural factors must be taken into account throughout the helping process. Professionals must learn new ways of positively engaging the emotional and spiritual energies of fathers. Professionals should also be equipped with mediation skills and other relevant family system approaches that build cooperative and collaborative relationships between parents. A binuclear family structure should be forged and sustained whenever possible, and fathers' support groups, fathers' rights groups, and teen mentoring and employment programs must be readily available and encouraged. In short, we must work on numerous fronts!

More Father-Based Research

Throughout the book we have noted the general lack of research on fathers. Much of what we know about fathering is based on the reports of mothers or children. There is valuable information to be gained by directly interviewing and observing fathers. Here is a sample of some of the important research questions that need further exploration:

- From the father's perspective, what are the psychosocial factors that contribute to nonresidential fathers becoming absent parents?
- How can nonresidential fathers become better equipped to parent while residing in a separate household?
- How can we help resistant fathers become more motivated to want what society expects of them?
- How effective are the growing number of fatherhood programs that are designed to increase the involvement of nonresidential fathers with their children?
- What strengths do fathers have that contribute to the development of a healthy child?
- How will welfare reform affect nonresidential fathers? What additional policies are needed to make welfare reform truly work for families?
- How can mothers be included more effectively in efforts to involve nonresidential fathers?
- How can fathers actualize their own form of nurturing?
- How does fatherhood change over the developmental life span?

As we move into and through this new century, it is hoped that the renewed research interest in fatherhood will give greater consideration to these and other relevant research questions.

The Challenge of Prevention

We would be remiss if we did not consider the proposition that nonresidential parenting is less than ideal for children (and many parents). Often nonresidential parenting can be averted or prevented in the first place. This is particularly the case when such parenting appears not to be in the best interests of the child.

Two overall prevention strategies seem critical: preventing unwanted births and preventing the breakup of a potentially workable marriage. Frankly, too few effective policies and programs exist today that
are designed to prevent unwanted pregnancies and divorce. Innovative
strategies are needed, for example, to discourage people from getting
married or having children before they are ready. Improved strategies
are also needed for educating people about marriage—how to develop
satisfying marriages and having realistic expectations of a mate. We
can do much more to educate and persuade potential parents to perceive a birth as an awesome decision rather than just one more thing
that can happen to families. New strategies are needed for helping
couples decide whether or not to have children, and parenting skills
need to be taught to all potential parents. Most important of all,
strategies need to be created that encourage parents to put the needs of
a new baby before their own.

We know that marriage is a family structure within which fathering
can thrive; yet society has not instituted enough visible rewards for
parents to stay together to raise their children. Clearly, more attention
needs to be given to promoting healthy marriages by all sectors of
society, particularly when marriage is likely to offer the most positive
benefits for raising child.

Implement Bold New Initiatives

We have described numerous program and policy initiatives that have
been tried across the country on behalf of nonresidential fathers. They
have been identified throughout the book as Innovative Programs. We
believe that these initiatives are truly innovative and deserve to be
models to be emulated by other communities.

Many more program strategies are waiting to be discovered and
tried, and recruiting and sustaining the participation of fathers is a
continued challenge for many programs. How do we get uninvolved
fathers motivated, for example, to more deeply want what they are
expected to do as parents? Is early intervention a significant factor in
reaching them? If so, what additional early prevention programs can
we envision for the school systems and youth and family agencies?

More program initiatives are needed that involve fathers helping
fathers. Perhaps the best ally that a father can have is another active
father, yet countless males overlook or resist the potential source of
support that can come from male bonding and shared problem-solv-

ing. More male counseling groups, informal men's groups, and peer support groups are definitely favorable trends. Programs that help fathers bond with their children are also too rare. Play groups and other educational strategies involving fathers and their children in activities together can have a definite positive impact.

New policy initiatives need to be discovered that target lower income families. Welfare reform, for example, took away an obstacle to a father's participation in his family, but has not yet replaced it with positive incentives for lower income mothers and fathers to successfully parent together. Being successfully employed also has a direct impact on paying child support, but we still have a long way to go in linking employment and training programs to child-support enforcement efforts.

CONCLUSION

Our prescription for promoting nonresidential fathering is an evolving enterprise that continues to unfold. As bold new initiatives are tried, we gain more knowledge about what works and what doesn't. One success can build upon another. But without a doubt, more must be done if we want to expand the role of fathering to all groups in society–all income and ethnic groups, recent immigrants and long-term Americans, the unmarried and married, teen fathers and older dads.

In order to expect more to be done to support fathering, the women's and men's movements must work more closely together in discovering and advocating for common goals. Different factions of the men's movement must discover common ground with each other as well. Religious and spiritual groups must commit anew to their traditional responsibilities of preparing and strengthening families. Government at all levels has a primary obligation to promote policies that strengthen families. And public policy-makers must base their policy initiatives on empirical evidence that suggests these policies can work for families. Both helping professionals and the media can become better messengers of the importance of fathers in families. Above all, men must do all that they can to prepare themselves to be good fathers. Their challenge is to develop an enduring commitment to fathering. They are called to make immense sacrifices for their children and to be bold in their faithfulness to future generations. Everyone has a responsibility if we are to succeed! (The authors have set up a website [www.FatheringAtRisk.com] to encourage continued exchange of information on the topic of fathering.)

Appendix: Fathers' Organizations and Web Sites

American Coalition for Fathers and Children
1718 M Street NW, Suite 187
Washington, DC 20036
800–978–DADS
http://www.acfc.org/

The Center on Fathers, Families, and Public Policy
Family Resource Center
200 South Michigan Avenue
Chicago, IL 60601
312–341–0902

Center for Successful Fathering
13740 Research Boulevard, G-4
Austin, TX 78750
1–800–537–0853
(TX-based group)
http://www.fathering.org

Dad-to-Dad
61 Brightwood Avenue
North Andover, MA 01845
(Stay-home dads)
http://www.slowlane.com/d2d

The Fatherhood Project
Families and Work Institute

Bank Street College of Education
610 West 112th Street
New York, NY 10025
212–465–2044
http://www.fatherhoodproject.org

Mens/Fathers Hotline
807 Brazos, Suite 315
Austin, TX 78701
512–472–3237

Men's Health Network
P.O. Box 770
Washington, DC 20044
202–543–6461

National Center for Fathering
10200 West 75th Street, Suite 267
Shawnee Mission, KS 66204–2223
913–384–4661

National Center on Fathers and Families
University of Pennsylvania
Graduate School of Education
3700 Walnut Street, Box 58
Philadelphia, PA 19104–6216
215–573–5500
http://www.ncoff.gse.upenn.edu

National Center for Fathering
P.O. Box 413888
Kansas City, MO 64141
(MO-based group)
1–800–593–3237
http://www.fathers.com

National Center for Strategic Nonprofit Planning and Community
Leadership
2000 L Street NW, Suite 815
Washington, DC 20036
202–822–6725
www.npcl.org

National Fatherhood Initiative
One Bank Street, Suite 160
Gaithersburg, MD 20878
301–948–0599
(MD-based organization)
http://www.fatherhood.org

Single and Custodial Father's Net-
work
1700 E. Carson Street
Pittsburgh, PA 15203
In PA 412–381–4800
Outside PA Toll-free 877–488–SCFN

At-Home Dad Newsletter
http://www.parentsplace.com/
family/dads/gen/0,3375,10234,
00.html

Center for Children's Justice
http://www.childrensjustice.com/

FatherWork: Generative Fathering Ideas
http://fatherwork.byu.edu/

Father's Rights to Custody
http://www.deltabravo.net/custody

The Department of Health and Human Services: Fatherhood Initiative
http://fatherhood.hhs.gov

Father's World: Web sites on fathering
http://www.fathersworld.com/

Men and Grief
http://www.webhealing.com/

Men's Movement Organizations
http://www.vix.com/men/orgs/
orgs.html

National Fathers Network
http://www.fathersnetwork.org/
mn/index1.html

National Partnership for Women and
Families
http://www.nationalpartnership.
org

Nurturing Fathers Program
http://www.nurturingfathers.com

Promoting Responsible Fathering
http://www.vev.ch/en/

Website for the book,
Fathering At Risk
http://www.FatheringAtRisk.com

References

Abrahamse, A. F., Morrison, P. A., & Waite, L. J. (1988). *Beyond stereotypes: Who becomes a single teenage parent?* Santa Monica, CA: Rand Corporation.

Achatz, M., & MacAllum, C. (1994). *Young unwed fathers: Report from the field.* Philadelphia: Public/Private Ventures.

ACT Coalition of Davidson County, NC. (1999). *All children together: Fathering initiative proposal.* Baptist Children's Home, Davidson County, NC.

Adams, G., & Pittman, K. (1988). *Adolescent and young adult fathers: Problems and solutions.* Washington, DC: Children's Defense Fund.

Ahmed, F., (1990). Unmarried mothers as a high-risk group for adverse pregnancy outcomes. *Journal of Community Health, 15,* 35–44.

Ahrons, C. (1979). The binuclear family: Two households, one family. *Alternative Lifestyles, 2,* 499–515.

Ahrons, C. (1983). Predictors of parental involvement postdivorce: Mothers' and fathers' perceptions. *Journal of Divorce, 6,* 59–66.

Aldous, J. (1987). New views on the family life of the elderly and near-elderly. *Journal of Marriage and Family, 49,* 227–234.

Allen, W., & Connor, M. (1997). An African American perspective on generative fathering. In A. Hawkins & D. Dollahite (Eds.), *Generative fathering: Beyond deficit perspectives* (pp. 52–70). Thousand Oaks, CA: Sage.

Allen, W., & Doherty, W. (1996). The responsibilities of fatherhood as perceived by African American teenage fathers. *Families in Society, 77,* 142–155.

Allen-Meares, P. (1984). Adolescent pregnancy and parenting: The forgotten adolescent father and his parents. *Journal of Social Work and Human Sexuality, 3,* 27–38.

Amato, P. R. (1994). Father-child relations, mother-child relations, and offspring psychological well-being in early adulthood. *Journal of Marriage and the Family, 56*(4), 1031–1043.

Amato, P. R. (1996). Explaining the intergenerational transmission of divorce. *Journal of Marriage and the Family, 55,* 628–640.

Amato, P. R., & Keith, B. (1991). Parental divorce and the well-being of children: A meta-analysis. *Psychological Bulletin, 110,* 26–46.

Anderson, E. (1989). Sex codes and family life among poor inner-city youths. *The Annals of the American Academy of Political and Social Science, 59–78.*

Anderson, E. (1990). *Streetwise: Race, class, and change in an urban community.* Chicago: University of Chicago Press.

Anderson, J., & Stewart, S. (1983). *Mastering resistence: A practical guide to family therapy.* New York: Guilford Press.

300

Andronico, M. (1996). *Men in groups: Insights, interventinos, and psychoeducational work.* Washington, DC: American Psychological Association.

Angel, R., & Angel, J. (1996). Physical comorbidity and medical care use in children with emotional problems. *Public Health Reports 111,* 140–145.

Angel, R., & Worobey, J. (1988). Single motherhood and children's health. *Journal of Health and Social Behavior, 29*(1), 38–52.

Angel, R., & Worobey, J. (1996). Single motherhood and children's health. *Journal of Health and Social Behavior, 29,* 27–38.

Arbuthnot, J., & Gordon, D. (1996). Does mandatory divorce education for parents work? A six-month outcome evaluation. *Family and Conciliation Courts Review, 34*(1), 60–81.

Arbuthnot, J., Kramer, K., & Gordon, D. (1997). Patterns of litigations following divorce education. *Familiy and Conciliation Courts Review, 34,* 60–81.

Arditti, J., & Allen, K. (1993). Understanding distressed fathers' perceptions of legal and relational inequities postdivorce. *Family and Conciliation Courts Review, 31,* 461–476.

Arendell, T. (1992). After divorce: Investigation into father absence. *Gender and Society, 6,* 562–586.

Arendell, T. (1995). *Fathers and divorce.* Thousand Oaks, CA: Sage.

Asante, M. (1989). *Afrocentricity.* Trenton, NJ: African World Press.

Bailey, C. E. (1998). An outcome study of a program for noncustodial fathers: Program impact on child support payments, visitation, and the coparenting relationships. *Dissertation Abstracts International.* UMI Number: 9939311.

Barnett, R. C., Marshall, N. L., & Pleck, J. H. (1992). Adult son-parent relationships and their associations with son's psychological distress. *Journal of Family Issues, 13,* 505–525.

Barret, R., & Robinson, B. (1982). A descriptive study of teenage expectant fathers. *Family Relations, 31,* 349–352.

Barth, R., Claycomb, M., & Loomis, A. (1988, Fall). Services to adolescent fathers. *Health and Social Work, 13*(4), 277–287.

Baumeister, R. F., & Sommer, K. L. (1997). What do men want? Gender differences and two spheres of belongingness: Comment on Cross and Madson. *Psychological Bulletin, 122,* 38–44.

Beaty, L. (1995). Effects of paternal absence on male adolescents' peer relations and self-image. *Adolescence, 30*(120), 873–880.

Beman, D. (1995). Risk factors leading to adolescent substance abuse. *Adolescence, 30*(120), 201–206.

Bengston, V. L., Rosenthal, C., & Burton, L. (1990). Families and aging: Diversity and heterogeneity. In R. H. Binstock & L. K. George (Eds.) *Handbook of aging and the social sciences* (pp. 263–287). San Diego, CA: Academic Press.

Benjamin, M., & Irving, H. H. (1995). Research in family mediation: Review and implications. *Mediation Quarterly, 13,* 53–82.

Bereczkei, T., & Csanaky, A. (1996). Evolutionary pathway of child development: Lifestyles of adolescents and adults from father-absent families. *Human Nature, 7*(3), 257–280.

Berg, C., Atrash, H., Koonin, L., Tucker, M. (1996). Pregnancy-related mortality in the United States, 1987–1990. *Obstetrics and Gynecology, 88,* 161–167.

Bernadett-Shapiro, S., Ehrensaft, D., Shapiro, J. (1996). Father participation in childcare and the development of empathy in sons: An empirical study. *Family Therapy, 23,* 77–93.

Bertoia, C. E., & Drakich, J. (1995). The fathers' rights movement: Contradictions in rhetoric and practice. In W. Marsiglio (Ed.), *Fatherhood: Contemporary theory, research, and social policy* (pp. 230–254). Thousand Oaks, CA: Sage.

Biller, H. (1993). *Father and families: Paternal factors in child development.* Westport, CT: Auburn House.

Billingsley, A. (1968). *Black families in White America.* Englewood Cliffs, NJ: Prentice-Hall.

Billingsley, A. (1992). *Climbing Jacob's ladder: The enduring legacy of African-American families.* New York: Simon & Schuster.

Blaisure, K., & Geasler, M. (2000). The Divorce Education Intervention Model. *Family and Conciliation Courts Review, 38*(4), 501–513.

Blankenhorn, D. (1995). *Fatherless America: Confronting our most urgent social problem.* New York: Basic Books.

Blossfeld, H. P. (Ed.) (1995). *The new role of women.* Boulder, CO: Westview.

Bly, R. (1990). *Iron John: A book about men.* New York: Addison-Wesley.

Borman, L. (1979). New self-help and support systems for the chronically mentally ill. Paper presented at the Pittsburgh Conference on Neighborhood Support Systems, Pittsburgh, PA, June 15, 1979.

Bowman, M., & Ahron, C. (1985). Impact of legal custody status on fathers' parenting postdivorce. *Journal of Marriage and the Family, 47,* 481–488.

Brannen, J., & Collard, J. (1982). *Marriage in trouble.* London: Tavistock.

Braver, S., & O'Connell, D. (1998). *Divorced dads: Shattering the myths.* New York: Tarchner/Putnam.

Braver, S., Salem, P., Pearson, J., & DeLuse, S. (1996). The content of divorce education programs: Results of a survey. *Family and Conciliation Courts Review, 34*(1), 41–59.

Bray, J., & Berger, S. (1993). Nonresidential parent-child relationships following divorce and remarriage. In C. Depner & J. Bray (Eds), *Nonresidential parenting: New vistas in family living* (pp. 156–181). Newbury Park, CA: Sage.

Brock, G., Oertwein, M., & Coufal, J. (1993). Parent education: Theory, research, and practice. *Handbook of family life education, Vol. 1: Foundations of family life education; Vol. 2: The practice of family life education* (pp. 87–114). Thousand Oaks, CA: Sage.

Bronars, S. G., & Grogger, J. (1994). The economic consequences of unwed motherhood: Using twin births as a natural experiment. *American Economic Review, 84,* 1141–1156.

Brown, E. (1997). Comprehensive divorce mediation. In E. Kruk (Ed.), *Mediation and conflict resolution in social work and the human services* (pp. 37–54). Chicago: Nelson-Hall Inc.

Brown, S. (1990). *If the shoe fits: Final report and program implementation guide of the Maine Young Father's Project.* Portland, ME: University of Southern Maine, Human Services Development Institute.

Buehler, C. (1989). Influential factors and equity issues in divorce settlements. *Family Relations, 38,* 76–82.

Buehler, C., Betz, P., Ryan, C. M., Legg, B. H., & Trotter, B. B. (1992). Description and evaluation of the orientation for divorcing parents: Implementation for postdivorce prevention programs. *Family Relations, 41,* 154–162.

Buehler, C., & Ryan, C. (1994). Former-spouse relations and noncustodial father involvement during marital and family transitions: A closer look at remarriage following divorce. In K. Pasley & M. Ihinger-Tallman (Eds.), *Stepparenting: Issues in theory, research, and practice* (pp. 127–150). New York: Greenwood.

Bumpass, L., & Lu, H. (2000). Trends in cohabitation and implications for children's family contexts in the United States. *Population Studies, 54*(1), 29–41.

Bursik, K. (1991). Correlates of women's adjustment during the separation and divorce process. *Journal of Divorce and Remarriage, 14,* 137–162.

Camara, K., & Resnick, G. (1988). Interparental conflict and cooperation: Factors moderating children's post-divorce adjustment. In E. Hetherington & J. Arasteh (Eds.), *Impact of divorce, single parenting, and stepparenting on children* (pp. 169–195). Hillsdale, NJ: Lawrence Erlbaum.

Carlson, N. (1987). Woman therapist: Male client. In M. Scher, M. Stevens, G. Good, & G. Eichenfield (Eds.), *Handbook of counseling and psychotherapy with men* (pp. 39–50) Newbury Park, CA: Sage.

Carr, A. (1998). The inclusion of fathers in family therapy: A research based perspective. *Contemporary Family Therapy: An International Journal, 20*(3), 371–383.

Castro-Martin, T., & Bumpass, L. L. (1989). Recent trends in marital disruption. *Demography, 26*, 37–51.

Cherlin, A., & Furstenburg, F. (1986). *New American grandparent: A place in the family, a life apart.* New York: Basic Books.

Chelser, P. (1972). *Women and madness.* Garden City, NY: Doubleday.

Children's Defense Fund. (1988). *What about the boys? Teenage prevention strategies.* Washington, DC: Adolescent Pregnancy Prevention Clearinghouse.

Chilman, C. (1980). Social and psychological research concerning adolescent childbearing. *Journal of Marriage and Family, 42*, 793–805.

Clawson, M. (1989). *Constructing brotherhood: Class, gender, and fraternalism.* Princeton, NJ: Princeton University Press.

Cleveland, H. (1985). The twilight of hierarchy: Speculations on the global information society. *Public Administration Review, 45*, 194–195.

Clinton, W. (1996, August 1). Text of President Clinton's Announcement on Welfare Legislation. *The New York Times*, p. 24.

Cohen, P. N. (1999). *Racial-ethnic and gender differences in returns to cohabitation and marriage: Evidence from the current population survey.* Population Division Working Paper No. 35, May, 1999. Washington, DC: U.S. Bureau of the Census.

Collins, D., Jordan, C., & Coleman, H. (1999). *An introduction to family social work.* Itasca, IL: F. E. Peacock.

Coney, N., & Mackey, W. (1998). On whose watch? The silent separation of American children and their fathers. *Journal of Sociology and Social Welfare, 25*(3), 143–178.

Cooksey, E., & Fondell, M. (1996). Spending time with his kids: Effects of family structure on fathers'and children's lives. *Journal of Marriage and the Family, 58*, 693–707.

Coontz, S. (1992). *The way we never were: American families and the nostalgia trap.* New York: Basic Books.

Culbertson, P. (1992). *The future of male spirituality: New Adam.* Minneapolis: Fortress Press.

Cutrona, C., Hessling, R., Bacon, P., & Russell, D. (1998). Predictors and correlates of continuing involvement with the baby's father among adolescent mothers. *Journal of Family Psychology, 12*, 369–387.

Dadds, M., Sanders, M., Behrens, B., & James, J. (1987). Marital discord and child behavior problems: A description of family interactions during treatment. *Journal of Clinical Psychology, 16*, 192–203.

D'Andrea, A. (1983). Joint custody as related to paternal involvement and paternal self-esteem. *Conciliation Courts Review, 21*, 81–87.

Danziger, S. K. (1987). *Father involvement in welfare families headed by adolescent mothers.* (Discussion Paper 856–887). Madison: University of Wisconsin, Institute for Research on Poverty.

Danziger, S. K., & Radin, N. (1990). Absent does not equal uninvolved: Predictors of fathering in teen mother families. *Journal of Marriage and the Family, 52*, 636–642.

Del Carmen, R., & Virgo, G. N. (1993). Marital disruption and nonresidential parenting: A multicultural perspective. In C. E. Depner & J. H. Bray (Eds.), *Nonresidential parenting: New vistas in family living* (pp. 13–36). Newbury Park, CA: Sage.

Denham, T., & Smith, C. (1989). The influence of grandparents on grandchildren: A review of the literature and resources. *Family Relations, 38*(2), 345–350.

Depner, C. E., & Bray, J. H. (Eds.). (1993). *Nonresidential parenting: New vistas in family living.* Newbury Park, CA: Sage.

DePoy, E., Hartmann, A., & Haslet, D. (1999). Critical action research: A model of social work knowing. *Social Work 44*(6), 560–569.

Devlin, A., Brown, E., Beebe, J., & Parulls, E. (1992). Parent education for divorced fathers. *Family Relations, 41*, 290–296.

DeWitt, P. M. (1994). The second time around. *American Demographics, 16*, 11–14.

Dillon, P. A., & Emery, R. E. (1996). Divorce mediation and resolution of child custody disputes: Long-term effects. *American Journal of Orthopsychiatry, 66*(1), 131–140.

Dion, M. R., Braver, S. L., Wolchik, S. A., & Sandler, I. N. (1997). Alcohol abuse and psychopathic deviance in noncustodial parents as predictors of child support payment and visitation. *American Journal of Orthopsychiatry 67*:70–79.

Doherty, W. (1997). The best of times and worst of times: Fathering as a contested arena of academic discourse. In A. Hawkins & D. Dollahite (Eds.), *Generative fathering: Beyond deficit perspectives* (pp. 217–227). Thousand Oaks, CA: Sage.

Doherty, W. J., Kouneski, E., & Erickson, M. (1998). Responsible fathering: An overview and conceptual framework. *Journal of Marriage and the Family, 60*, 277–292.

Dollahite, D., Hawkins, A., & Brotherson, S. (1997). Fatherwork: A conceptual ethic of fathering as generative work. In J. Hawkins & D. Dollahite (Eds.). *Generative fathering: Beyond deficit perspectives*, pp. 17–35. Thousand Oaks, CA: Sage.

Dominic, K., & Schlesinger, B. (1980). Weekend fathers: Family shadows. *Journal of Divorce, 3*, 241–247.

Donnelly, D., & Finkelhor, D. (1993). Who has joint custody? Class differences in the determination of custody arrangements. *Family Relations, 42*, 57–60.

Dragonas, T., & Christodoulou, G. (1998) Prenatal care. *Clinical Psychology Review, 18*(2), 127–142.

Dudgeon, T. C. (1999, February). On-the-spot mediation and supervised visitation: A pilot project comes to Courtroom 2003. *Brief*, 20–23.

Dudley, J. (1991a). The consequences of divorce proceedings for divorced fathers. *Journal of Divorce and Remarriage, 16*(3/4), 171–193.

Dudley, J. (1991b). Exploring ways to get divorced fathers to comply willingly with child support agreements. *Journal of Divorce and Remarriage, 15*(2), 121–135.

Dudley, J. (1991c). Increasing our understanding of divorced fathers who have infrequent contact with their children. *Family Relations 40*, 279–285.

Dudley, J. R. (1996). Noncustodial fathers speak about their parental role. *Family and Conciliation Courts Review, 34*, 410–426.

Earls, F., & Siegel, B. (1980). Precocious fathers. *American Journal of Orthopsychiatry, 50*(3), 469–480.

Edin, K. (1995). Single mothers and child support: The possibilities and limits of child support policy. *Children and Youth Services Review, 17*(1/2), 203–230.

Edin, K., & Lein, L. (1997). Work, welfare, and single mothers' economic survival stategies. *American Sociological Review, 62*(2), 253–266.

Egan, G. (1990). *The skilled helper: A systematic approach to effective helping.* Pacific Grove, CA: Brooks/Cole Publishing Company.

Eichler, M. (1997). *Family shifts: Families, policies, and gender equality.* Toronto: Oxford University Press.

Ellis, J. W. (1990). Plans, protections, and professional intervention: Innovations in divorce custody reform and the role of custody reform and the role of legal professionals. *University of Michigan Journal of Law Reform, 24*, 65–188.

Elster, A., & Lamb, M. (1986). *Adolescent fatherhood.* Hillsdale, NJ: Lawrence Erlbaum.

Emery, R. E. (1994). *Renegotiating family relationships: Divorce, child custody, and mediation.* New York: Guilford.

Emery, R. E. (1995). Divorce mediation: Negotiating agreements and renegotiating relationships. *Family Relations,* 44(4), 377–383.

Emery, R. E., Hetherington, E. M., & Dalaila, L. F. (1985). Divorce, children and social policy. In H. Stevenson and A. Siegel (Eds.), *Child development research and social policy.* Chicago: University of Chicago Press.

Erikson, E. H. (1950). *Childhood and society.* New York: Norton.

Evans, T. (1994). Spiritual purity. In *Seven promises of a promise keeper* (pp. 73–81). Colorado Springs, CO: Focus on the Family.

Faludi, S. (1992). *Backlash: The undeclared war against American women.* New York: Crown.

Feldman, L. (1992). *Integrating individual and family therapy.* Philadelphia, PA: Brunner/Mazel, Inc.

Fish, L., New, R., & VanCleve, N. (1992). Shared parenting in dual-income families. *American Journal of Orthopsychiatry, 62,* 83–92.

Fisher, R., & Brown, S. (1988). *Getting together: Building relationships as we negotiate.* New York: Penguin Books.

Fisher, R., & Ury, W. (1981). *Getting to yes.* Boston, MA: Houghton Mifflin.

Fitzgerald, H., Mann, T., & Barratt, M. (1999). Fathers and infants. *Infant Mental Health Journal, 20*(3), 213—221.

Fliegelman, J. (1982). *Prodigals and pilgrims: The American revolution against patriarchal authority, 1750–1800.* Cambridge, England: Cambridge University Press.

Fogel, A. (1997). *Infancy: Infant, family, and society.* St. Paul, MN: West.

Folberg, J. (Ed.) (1984). *Joint custody and shared parenting.* Washington, DC: Bureau of National Affairs, Association of Family and Conciliation Courts.

Folberg, J. (1991). Custody overview. In J. Folberg, (Ed.), *Joint custody and shared parenting* (2nd ed., pp. 3–10). New York: Guilford Press.

Folberg, J., & Taylor, A. (1984). *Mediation:* A comprehensive guide to resolving conflicts without litigation. San Francisco: Jossey-Bass.

Fong, J., & Walsh-Bowers, R. (1998). Voices of the blamed: Mothers' responsiveness to father-daughter incest. *Journal of Family Social Work, 3*(1), 25–41.

Foster, C., & Miller, G. (1980). Adolescent pregnancy: A challenge for counselors. *Personnel and Guidance Journal, 59,* 236–240.

Fox, G. L. (1985). Noncustodial fathers. In S. M. Hanson & F. W. Bozett (Eds.), *Dimensions of fatherhood* (pp. 393–415). Newbury Park, CA: Sage.

Frieman, B., Garon, R., & Mandell, B. (1994). Parenting seminars for divorcing parents. *Social Work, 39,* 607–610.

Frisbie, W. P. (1986). Variations in patterns of marital instability among Hispanics. *Journal of Marriage and the Family, 48,* 99–106.

Furstenberg, F. (1995). Fathering in the inner city: Paternal participation and public policy. In W. Marsiglio (Ed.), *Fatherhood: Contemporary theory, research, and social policy* (pp. 119–147). Thousand Oaks, CA: Sage.

Furstenburg, F. (1988). Good dads-bad dads: Two faces of fatherhood. In A. Cherlin (Ed.), *The changing American family and public policy* (pp. 201–202). Washington, DC: Urban Institute

Furstenberg, F., & Cherlin, A. (1991). *Divided families: What happens to children when parents part.* Cambridge, MA: Harvard University Press.

Gallagher, M. (1998). Father hunger. In C. R. Daniels (Ed.), *Lost fathers.* New York: St. Martin's Press.

Gallup Poll. (1996). Available: www.fathers.com/gallup.html

Gardner, R. A. (1984). Joint custody is not for everyone. In J. Folberg (Ed.), *Joint custody and shared parenting* (pp. 63–71). Washington, DC: Bureau of National Affairs, Association of Family and Conciliation Courts.

Gavazzi, S., Alford, K., & McKenry, P. (1996). Culturally specific programs for foster care youth: The sample case of an African American rites of passage program. *Family Relations, 45,* 166–174.

Gentry, D. B. (1997). Including children in divorce mediation and education: Potential benefits and cautions. *Families in Society, 78*(3), 307–315.

Girder, L. (1985). Adjudication and mediation: A comparison of custody decision-making processes involving third parties. *Journal of Divorce, 9,* 33–47.

Goldberg, H. (1976). *The hazards of being male: Surviving the myth of masculine privilege.* New York: New American Library.

Goldsmith, J. (1980). Relationships between former spouses: Descriptive findings. *Journal of Divorce, 4,* 1–20.

Goldsmith, J. (1982). The postdivorce family. In F. Walsh (Ed.), *Normal family processes* (pp. 243–256). New York: Guilford Press.

Goodman, L. A., Koss, M. P., Felipe Russo, N. (1993). Violence against women: Physical and mental health effects. Part I: Research findings. *Applied and Preventive Psychology 2,* 79–89.

Greif, G. (1997). Group work with noncustodial parents. In G. Grief and P. Ephross (Eds.), *Group work with populations at risk* (pp. 84–93). New York: Oxford University Press.

Griswold, R. L. ((1993). *Fatherhood in America: A history.* New York: Basic Books.

Guidubaldi, J., & Cleminshaw, H. (1985). Divorce, family health, and child adjustment. *Family Relations, 34,* 35–41.

Guitierrez, L. (1988, August). *Culture and consciousness in the Chicano community: An empowerment perspective.* Paper presented at the meeting of the American Psychological Association, Division 9 (Society for the Psychological Study of Social Issues), Atlanta, GA.

Alan Guttmacher Institute. (1994). *Sex and America's teenagers.* New York: The Alan Guttmacher Institute.

Hall, A., & Kelly, K. (1996). Noncustodial fathers in groups: Maintaining the parenting bond. In M. Andronicus (Ed.), *Men in groups: Insights, interventions, and psychoeducational work.* Washington, DC: American Psychological Association.

Hanson, S., Morrison, D., & Ginsburg, A. (1989). The antecedents of teenage fatherhood. *Demography, 26,* 579–596.

Hardy, J., Duggan, A., Masnyk, K., & Pearson, C. (1989). Fathers of children born to young urban mothers. *Family Planning Perspectives, 21,* 159–163, 187.

Hardy, J. B., & Zabin, L. S. (1991). *Adolescent pregnancy in an urban environment. Issues, programs, and evaluation.* Washington, DC: Urban Institute Press.

Harvey, D., Curry, C., & Bray, J. (1991). Individuation and intimacy in intergenerational relationships and health: Patterns across two generations. *Journal of Family Psychology, 5*(2), 204–236.

Hawkins, A., & Dollahite, D. (1997). *Generative fathering: Beyond deficit perspectives.* Thousand Oaks, CA: Sage.

Heiss, J. (1996). Effects of African American family structure on school attitudes and performance. *Social Problems, 43,* 246–264.

Hecker, L. (1991). Where is dad? 21 ways to involve fathers in family therapy. *Journal of Family Psychotherapy, 2,* 31–45.

Hendricks, L. (1988). Outreach with teen fathers: A preliminary report on three ethnic groups. *Adolescence, 23,* 711–720.

Hendricks, L., & Solomon, A. (1987). Reaching Black male adolescent parents through nontraditional techniques. *Child & Youth Services, 9*(1), 111–124.

Heppner, P., & Gonzales, D. (1987). Men counseling men. In M. Scher, M. Stevens, G.

Good, & G. Eichenfield (Eds.), *Handbook of counseling and psychotherapy with men* (pp. 30–38). Newbury Park, CA: Sage.

Hepworth, D., Rooney, R., & Larsen, J. (1997). *Direct social work practice: Theory and skills.* Boston, MA: Brooks/Cole Publishing Company.

Hernandez, D. J. (1993). *America's children: Resources from family, government, and the economy.* New York: Russell Sage Foundation.

Hetherington, E. M. (1989). Coping with family transitions: Winners, losers, and survivors. *Child Development, 60*(1), 1–14.

Hetherington, E. M., Arnett, J., & Hollier, E. A. (1988). Adjustment of parents and children to remarriage. In S. A. Wolchick & P. Karoly (Eds.), *Child of divorce: Empirical perspectives on adjustment* (pp. 67–107). New York: Gardner.

Hetherington, E. M., Cox, M., & Cox, R. (1976). Divorced fathers. *Family Coordinator, 25*(4), 417–428.

Hetherington, E. M., Cox, M., & Cox, R. (1978). The aftermath of divorce. In J. H. Stevens, Jr., & M. Mathews (Eds.), *Mother-child, father-child relations* (pp. 149–176). Washington, DC: National Association for the Education of Young Children.

Hetherington, E. M., Cox, M., & Cox, R. (1979). Family interaction and the social-emotional and cognitive development of children following divorce. In V. Vaughn & T. Brazelton (Eds.), *The family setting priorities* (pp. 89–128). New York: Science and Medicine Publishing Company.

Hetherington, E. M., & Clingempeel, W. G. (1992). Coping with marital transitions. *Monographs of the Society for Research in Child Development, 57*(2–3). Hochberg, A. M & Kressel, K. (1996). Determinants of successful and unsuccessful divorce negotiations. *Journal of Divorce & Remarriage, 25*, 1–21.

Hochberg, A. M., & Kressel, K. (1996). Determinants of successful and unsuccessful divorce negotiations. *Journal of Divorce and Remarriage, 26*, 1–21.

Hodges, W. F. (1990). *Interventions for children of divorce: Custody, access, and psychotherapy.* New York: Wiley and Sons.

Horn, A., Jolliff, D., & Roth, E. (1996). Men mentoring men in groups. In M. Andronicus (Ed.), *Men in groups: Insights, interventions, and psychoeducational work* (pp. 97–112). Washington, DC: American Psychological Association.

Horn, W. (1998). *Father facts* (3rd ed.). Gaithersburg, MD: The National Fatherhood Initiative.

Hosley, C., & Montemayor, R. (1997). Fathers and adolescents. In M. Lamb (Ed), *The role of father in child development.* New York: Wiley & Sons.

Huey, J. (1994). Waking up the new economy. *Fortune, 129*(13), 36–46.

Ihinger-Tallman, M., Pasley, K., & Buehler, C. (1995). Developing a middle-range theory of father involvement postdivorce. In W. Marsiglio (Ed.), *Fatherhood: Contemporary theory, research, and social policy* (pp. 57–77). Thousand Oaks, CA: Sage.

International Telework Association and Council (1999). [On-line]. Available: http://www.telecommute.org/twa/1999_research_results. shtml

Jackson, A. (1999). The effects of nonresident father involvement on single Black mothers and their young children. *Social Work, 44*(2), 156–166.

Jain, A., Belsky, J., & Crane, K. (1996). Beyond fathering behaviors: Types of dads. *Journal of Family Psychology, 10*, 431–441.

Johnson, E. S., Levine, A., & Doolittle, F. C. (1998). *Fathers' fair share: Helping poor men manage child support and fatherhood.* New York: Russell Sage Foundation.

Johnston, J., & Roseby, V. (1997). *In the name of the child: A developmental approach to understanding and helping children of conflicted and violent divorce.* New York: The Free Press.

Johnston, J. R. (1994). High conflict divorce. *The Future of Children, 4*, 165–182.

Johnston, J. R., Kline, M., & Tschann, J. T. (1989). Ongoing postdivorce conflict: Effects on children of joint custody and frequent access. *American Journal of Orthopsychiatry, 59,* 576–592.

Jordan, C., & Franklin, C. (1995). *Clinical assessment for social workers: Quantitative and qualitative methods.* Chicago, IL: Lyceum.

Jordan, P. (1988). The effects of marital separation on men. *Journal of Divorce, 12,* 576–582.

Jordan, P. (1992). Counseling men confronted by marital separation. *Journal of Divorce and Remarriage, 18,* 109–126.

Katz, A. H., & Bender, E. I. (1987). *The strength in us: Self-help groups in the modern world.* Oakland, CA: The Charles Press.

Kauth, B. (1992). *A circle of men: The original manual for men's support groups.* New York: St. Martin's Press.

Kelly, J. (1988). Longer-term adjustment in children of divorce: Converging findings and implications for practice. *Journal of Family Psychology, 2*(2), 119–140.

Kelly, J. (1993). Developing and implementing post-divorce parenting plans: Does the forum make a difference?" In C. Depner & J. Bray (Eds.), *Non-Residential Parenting: New Vistas in Family Living* (pp. 136–155). Newbury Park, CA: Sage.

Kelly, J. (1994). The determination of child custody. *The Future of Children, 4,* 121–142.

Kelly, J. (1997). *The determination of child custody in the USA* [On-line, last modified in July, 1997]. Available: http://wwlia. org/cus1

Kiselica, M., & Sturmer, P. (1993). Is society giving teenage fathers a mixed message? *Youth and Society, 24*(4), 487–501.

Kiselica, M. (1995). *Multicultural counseling with teenage fathers: A practical guide.* Newbury Park, CA: Sage.

Kiselica, M. (1996). Parenting skills training with teenage fathers. In M. Andronico (Ed.), *Men in groups: Insights, interventions, and psychoeducational work.* Washington, DC: American Psychological Association.

Kiselica, M., Rotzien, A., & Doms, J. (1994). Preparing teenage fathers for parenthood: A group psychoeducational approach. *Journal for Specialists in Group Work, 19,* 83–94.

Kiselica, M., Stroud, J., Stroud, J., & Rotzien, A. (1992). Counseling the forgotten client: The teen father. *Journal of Mental Health Counseling, 14,* 338–350.

Kitson, G., & Roach, M. (1989). Independence and social psychological adjustment in widowhood and divorce. *Older bereaved spouses: Research with practical applications* (pp. 167–183). Washington, DC: Hemisphere Publishing Corporation.

Kitzmann, K. M., & Emery, R. E. (1994). Child and family coping one year after mediated and litigated child custody disputes. *Journal of Family Psychology 8,*(2), 150–159.

Kivett, V. R. (1991). Centrality of the grandfather role among older rural Black and White men. *Journals of Gerontology, 46*(5), S250–S258.

Kline, M., Johnston, J., & Tschann, J. (1991). The long shadow of marital conflict: A model of children's post-divorce adjustment. *Journal of Marriage and the Family, 53,* 297–309.

Koch, M. A., & Lowery, C. R. (1984). Visitation and the noncustodial father. *Journal of Divorce, 8,* 47–65.

Koestner, R., Franz, C., & Weinberger, J. (1990). The family origins of empathic concern: A twenty-six year longitudinal study. *Journal of Personality and Social Psychology, 58,* 709–717.

Krampe, E. M., & Fairweather, P. D. (1993). Father presence and family formation: A theoretical reformulation. *Journal of Family Issues 14*(4), 572–591.

Kressel, K. (1985). *The process of divorce: How professionals and couples negotiate settlements.* New York: Basic Books. Kruk, E. (1991). Discontinuity between pre- and post-divorce father-child relationships: New evidence regarding parental disengagement. *Journal of Divorce and Remarriage 16*(3/4), 195–227.

Kruk, E. (1991). The grief reaction of noncustodial fathers subsequent to divorce. *Men's Studies Review, 8*(2), 17–21.

Kruk, E. (1992). Psychological and structural forces contributing to the disengagement of noncustodial fathers after divorce. *Family and Conciliation Courts Review, 30,* 81–101.

Kruk, E. (1994). The disengaged noncustodial father: Implications for social work practice with the divorced family. *Social Work, 39*(1), 15–25.

Kurdek, L. (1986). Custodial mothers' perceptions of visitation and payment of child support by noncustodial fathers in families with low and high levels of preseparation interparent conflict. *Journal of Applied Developmental Psychology, 7,* 307–323.

Lamb, M. E. (1986). The changing roles of fathers. In M. Lamb (Ed.), *The father's role: Applied perspectives.* New York: John Wiley.

Lamb, M. E. (1987). The emergent American father. In M. E. Lamb (Ed.), *The father's role: Cross-cultural perspectives* (pp. 3–26). Hillsdale, NJ: Lawrence Erlbaum.

Lamb, M., Sternberg, K., & Thompson, R. (1997). The effects of divorce and custody arrangements on children's behavior, development, and adjustment. *Family and Conciliation Courts Review, 35,* 393–404.

Landry, D., & Forrest, J. (1995). How old are U.S. fathers? *Family Planning Perspectives, 27,* 159–161.

Lansky, D. T., Manley, E. E., Swift, L. H., & Williams, M. (1995). The role of children in divorce mediation. In Academy of Family Mediators, *Workshop Proceedings Book: 1995 Annual Conference* (pp. 31–33). Golden Valley, MN: Academy of Family Mediators.

LaRossa, R. (1988). Fatherhood and social change. *Family Relations, 36,* 451–458.

Lerman, R. (1986). Who are the young absent fathers? *Youth and Society, 18,* 3–27.

Lerman, R. (1993). A national profile of young unwed fathers. In R. Lerman & T. Ooms (Eds.), *Young unwed fathers: changing roles and emerging policies* (pp. 27–51). Philadelphia, PA: Temple University Press.

Lerman, R. I., & Ooms, T. J. (1992). *Young unwed fathers: Changing roles and emerging policies.* Philadelphia: Temple University Press.

Levant, R. (1992). Toward the reconstruction of masculinity. *Journal of Family Psychology, 5,* 309–315.

Levine, J., & Pitt, E. (1995). *New expectations: Community strategies for responsible fatherhood.* Families and Work Institute.

Levine, J., & Pittinsky, T. (1997). *Working fathers: New strategies for balancing work and family.* AddisonWesley Longman.

Levinson, D., Darrow, C., Klein, E., Levinson, M., & McKee, B. (1978). *The seasons of a man's life.* New York: Knopf.

Lewis, R. A. (1990). The adult child and older parents. In T. H. Brubaker (Ed.), *Family relations in later life* (pp. 68–85). Newbury Park, CA: Sage.

Libassi, M., & Maluccio, A. (1986). Competence-centered social work: Prevention in action. *Journal of Primary Prevention, 6*(3), 168–180.

Lorenz, F., Simons, R., Chao, W. (1997). Family structure and mothers' depression. In R. Simons (Ed.), *Understanding differences bewteen divorced and intact families: Stress, interaction, and child outcome* (pp. 65–77). Thousand Oaks, CA: Sage.

Luepnitz, D. (1986). A comparison of maternal, paternal, and joint custody: Understanding the varieties of post-divorce family life. *Journal of Divorce, 9*(3), 1–12.

Lund, M. (1987). The noncustodial father: Common challenges in parenting after di-

310 References

vorce. In C. Lewis & M. O'Brien (Eds.), *Reassessing fatherhood: New observations on fathers and the modern family* (pp. 212–224). Newbury Park, CA: Sage.
Maccoby, E. E., & Mnooken, R. H. (1992). *Dividing the child: Social and legal dilemmas of custody.* Cambridge, MA: Harvard University Press.
Manlove, J. (1998). The influence of high school dropout and school disengagement on the risk of school-age pregnancy. *Journal of Research on Adolescence, 8,* 187–220.
Mann, B., Borduin, C., Henggeler, S., & Blaske, D. (1990). An investigation of systemic conceptualizations of parent-child coalitions and symptom change. *Journal of Consulting and Clinical Psychology, 58,* 336–344.
Manning, W. D., & Landale, N. S. (1996). Racial and ethnic differences in the role of cohabitation in premarital childbearing. *Journal of Marriage and the Family, 58,* 63–77.
Marlow, C. (1998). *Research methods for generalist social work* (2nd ed.). Pacific Grove, CA: Brooks/Cole.
Marsiglio, W. (1986). Teenage fatherhood. In A. Elster & M. Lamb (Eds.), *Adolescent fatherhood.* Hillsdale, NJ: Lawrence Erlbaum.
Marsiglio, W. (1988). Adolescent fathers in the United States: Their initial living arrangements, marital experience, and educational outcomes. *Family Planning Perspective, 19,* 240–251.
Marsiglio, W. (1995). Young nonresident biological fathers. *Marriage and Family Review, 20*(3/4), 325–348.
McGovern, M. (1990). Sensitivity and reciprocity in the play of adolescent mother and young fathers with their infants. *Family Relations, 39,* 427–431.
McKay, M., Rogers, P., Blades, J., & Gosse, R. (1999). *The divorce book: A practical and compassionate guide.* Oakland, CA: New Harbinger.
McKenry, P., McKelvey, M., Leigh, D., & Wark, L. (1996). Nonresidential father involvement: A comparison of divorced, separated, never married, and remarried fathers. *Journal of Divorce and Remarriage, 25*(3/4), 1–13.
McKenry, P. C., & Price, S. J. (1990). Divorce: Are men at risk? In D. Moore & F. Leafgren (Eds.), *Problem solving strategies and interventions for men in conflict* (pp 95–112). Alexandria, VA: American Association for Counseling and Development.
McLanahan, S. (1997). Parent absence or poverty: Which matters more? In G. Duncan & J. Brooks-Gunn (Eds.), *The consequences of growing up poor* (pp. 35–48). New York: Russell Sage Foundation.
McLanahan, S. (1998). Growing up without a father. In C. R. Daniels (Ed.), *Lost fathers* (pp. 85–108). New York: St. Martin's Press.
McLanahan, S., & Sandefur, G. (1994). *Growing up with a single parent: What hurts, what helps.* Cambridge, MA: Harvard University Press.
Meloy, S. (2000). Comments made by Stan Meloy, Director of the ACT Coalition, in a set of interviews in June–July, 2000.
Messner, M. (1997). *Politics of masculinity: Men in movements.* Thousand Oaks, CA: Sage.
Michael, R., & Tuma, N. (1985). Entry into marriage and parenthood by young men and women: The influence of family background. *Demography, 22,* 515–544.
Miley, K., O'Melia, M., & DuBois, B. (1998). *Generalist social work practice: An empowering approach.* Needham Heigths, MA: Allyn & Bacon.
Miller, B., McCoy, J., Olson, T., & Wallace, C. (1986). Parental discipline and control attempts in relation to adolescent sexual attitudes and behavior. *Journal of Marriage and Family, 48,* 503–512.
Mills, T. (1999). When grandchildren grow up: Role transition and family solidarity among baby boomer grandchildren and grandparents. *Journal of Aging Studies, 13*(2), 219–239.
Mincy, R., & Sorenson, E. (1998). Deadbeats and turnips in child support reform. *Journal of Policy Analysis and Management, 17,* 44–51.

Mintz, S. (1998). From patriarchy to androgyny and other myths: Placing men's family roles in historical perspective. In A. Booth & A. C. Crouter (Eds.), *Men in families: When do they get involved? What difference does it make?* Mahwah, NJ: Lawrence Erlbaum Associates.

Mintz, S., & Kellogg, S. (1988). *Domestic revolutions: A social history of American family life.* New York: Free Press.

Mirande, A. (1991). Ethnicity and fatherhood. In F. Bozet & S. Hanson (Eds.), *Fatherhood and families in cultural context* (pp. 53–82). New York: Springer.

Momeni, J. A. (1984). *Demography of racial and ethnic minorities in the United States.* Westport, CT: Greenwood Press.

Moore, K., Snyder, N., & Hall, C. (1992). *Facts at a glance.* Washington, DC: Child Trends.

Myers, M. (1989). Angry abandoned husbands: Assessment and treatment. *Marriage and Family Review, 9,* 31–42.

National Center for Education Statistics. (1997). *Fathers' involvement in their children's schools.* Government Printing Office, Washington DC.

National Center for Fathering. (2000, January 10). *Building stairs* [On-line]. Available: http://www.fathers.com/articles/articles.asp?ic=1&cat=1

National Center for Health Statistics. (1982). Advance report of final nativity statistics, 1980. *Monthly vital statistics report, 31*(8), Suppl., November 30, 1982. Hyattsville, MD: U.S. Public Health Service.

National Center for Health Statistics. (1993). Advance report of final nativity statistics, 1991. *Monthly Vital Statistics Report, 42*(3), Suppl., September 9, 1993. Hyattsville, MD: U.S. Public Health Service.

National Center for Health Statistics (1995). *Vital statistics of the United States, 1992* (Vol. 1 Natality). Washington, DC: U.S. Public Health Service.

National Center for Health Statistics (1999). *National vital statistics reports (Births and deaths: Preliminary data for 1998)* (Vol. 47). Washington, DC: Public Health Service.

National Research Council. (1989). Washington, DC: National Academy Press.

Nelson, R. (1989). Parental hostility, conflict, and communication in joint and sole custody families. *Journal of Divorce, 13,* 145–157.

Newberry, A., Alexander, J., & Turner, C. (1991). Gender as a process variable in family therapy. *Journal of Family Psychology, 5,* 158–175.

Nilles, J. (1991). Telecommuting and urban sprawl: mitigator or inciter? *Transportation, 19,* 411–432.

Nord, C. W., & Zill, N. (1996). *Noncustodial parents' participation in their children's lives: Evidence from the survey of income and program participation, Vol. 1.* [On-line]. Summary of SIPP analysis. Available: http://aspe.os.dhhs.gov/fathers/SIPP/NONCUSP1.htm

Norman, J., & Wheeler, B. (1996). Gender-sensitive social work practice: A model for education. *Journal of Social Work Education, 32*(2), 203–213.

Norton, G. (1977). *Parenting.* Englewood Cliffs, NJ: Prentice-Hall.

Nydegger, C., & Mitteness, L. (1991). Fathers and their adults sons and daughters. *Marriage and Family Review, 16,* 249–256.

O'Brien, M. (1988). Men and fathers in therapy. *Journal of Family Therapy, 10,* 109–123.

O'Connell, M. (1993). *Where's papa?: Father's role in child care.* Washington, DC: Population Reference Bureau, Inc.

Oliver, W. (1989). Black males and social problems: Prevention through Afrolicentric socialization. *Journal of Black Studies, 20,* 15–39.

Osherson, S. (1992). *Wrestling with love: How men struggle with intimacy.* New York: Fawcett Columbine.

Pable, M. (1996). *The quest for the male soul: In search of something more.* Notre Dame, IN: Ave Maria Press.

Parke, R., & Brott, A. (1999). *Throwaway dads.* New York: Houghton & Mifflin.

Parke, R., Power, T., & Fisher, T. (1980). The adolescent father's impact on the mother and child. *Journal of Social Issues, 36,* 88–106.

Pasley, K., & Minton, C. (1997). Generative fathering after divorce and remarriage: Beyond the "disappearing father." In A. J. Hawkins & D. C. Dollahite (Eds.), *Generative fathering: Beyond deficit perspectives,* (pp. 118–133). Thousand Oaks, CA: Sage.

Patterson, C. J. (1995). Lesbian mothers, gay fathers, and their children. In A. R. D'Augelli & C. F. Paterson (Eds.), *Lesbian, gay, and bi-sexual identities over the lifespan* (pp. 262–290). New York: Oxford University Press.

Patterson, C. J., & Chan, R. W. (1997). Gay fathers. In M. E. Lamb (Ed.), *The role of the father in child development* (3rd ed., pp. 245–260). New York: Wiley.

Pearson, J., & Thoennes, N. (1990). Custody after divorce: Demographic and attitudinal patterns. *American Journal of Orthopsychiatry, 60,* 233–249.

Peterson, G., Mehl, L., & Leiderman, H. (1979). The role of some birth-related variables in father attachment. *American Journal of Orthopsychiatry, 49*(2), 330–338.

Peterson, V., & Steinman, S. B. (1994). Helping children succeed after divorce: A court-mandated educational program for divorcing parents. *Family and Conciliation Courts Review, 32,* 55–61.

Phares, V. (1996). Conducting nonsexist research, prevention, and treatment with fathers and mothers: A call for a change. *Psychology of Women Quarterly, 20,* 55–77.

Pine, B., & Warsh, R. (1996). Protecting children and supporting families: An essay review. *Children and Youth Services Review, 18,* 469–472.

Pirog-Good, M. (1988). Teenage paternity, child support, and crime. *Social Science Quarterly, 69,* 527–546.

Pirog-Good, M. (1993). In-kind contributions as child support: The Teen Alternative Parenting Program. In R. Lerman & T. Ooms (Eds.), *Young unwed fathers: Changing roles and emerging policies* (pp. 251–266). Philadephia: Temple University Press.

Pirog-Good, M. (1995). The family background and attitudes of teen fathers. *Youth and Society, 26,* 351–376.

Pleck, E. (1987). *Domestic tyranny: The making of social policy against family violence from colonial times to the present.* New York: Oxford University Press.

Pleck, E., & Pleck, J. (1997). Fatherhood ideals in the United States: Historical dimensions. In M. E. Lamb (Ed.), *The role of the father in child development.* New York: Wiley.

Pleck, J. H. (1991) Family supportive employer policies: Are they relevant to men? *Center for Research on Women.* Wellesley, MA.

Popenoe, D. (1996). *Life without father: Compelling new evidence that fatherhood and marriage are indispensable for the good of children and society.* New York: Free Press.

Power, T., McGrath, M., Hughes, S., & Manire, S. (1994). Compliance and self-assertion: Young children's responses to mothers versus fathers. *Developmental Psychology, 30,* 980–989.

Price, S., & McKenry, P. (1988). *Divorce.* Newbury Park, CA: Sage.

Public Health Reports (1998). New study identifies infants at greatest health risk. *Public Health Reports, 113,* 371.

Rabinowitz, F. E., & Cochran, S. V. (1994). *Man alive: A primer of men's issues.* Pacific Grove, CA: Brooks/Cole.

Radin, N., & Russell, G. (1983). Increased father participation and child development outcomes. In M. Lamb & A. Sagi (Ed.), *Fatherhood and social policy* (pp. 191–218). Hillsdale, NJ: Lawrence Erlbaum.

Raffoul, P. R., & McNeese, C. (1996). *Future issues for social work practice.* Boston, MA: Allyn & Bacon.

Raisner, J. K. (1997). Family mediation and never-married parents. *Family and Conciliation Courts Review, 35*(1), 90–101.

Rasheed, J. (1999). *Social work practice with African American men.* Thousand Oaks, CA: Sage.

Rappaport, J. (1987). Terms of empowerment/exemplars of prevention: Toward a theory of community psychology. *American Journal of Community Psychology, 15,* 121–145.

Redmond, M. (1985). Attitudes of adolescent males toward adolescent pregnancy and fatherhood. *Family Relations, 34,* 337–342.

Rees, S. (1991). *Achieving power: Practice and policy in social welfare.* Sydney, Australia: Allen & Unwin.

Reissman, C. (1990). *Divorce talk: Women and men make sense of personal relationships.* New Brunswick, NJ: Rutgers University Press.

Reissman, F. (1987). Forward. In T. Powell (Ed.), *Self-help organizations and professional practice* (pp. ix–x). Silver Spring, MD: National Association of Social Workers.

Resnick, M. D., Wattenberg, E., & Brewer, R. (1994). The fate of the non-marital child: A challenge to the health system. *Journal of Community Health, 19,* 285–301.

Rhein, L., Ginsburg, K., Schwartz, D., Pinto-Martin, J., Zhao, H., Morgan, A., & Slap, G. (1997). Teen father participation in child rearing: Family perspectives. *Journal of Adolescent Health, 21*(4), 244–252.

Rhoden, J., & Robinson, B. (1997). Teen dads: A generative fathering perspective versus the deficit myth. In A. J. Hawkins & D. C. Dollahite (Eds.), *Generative fathering: Beyond deficit perspectives* (pp. 105–117). Thousand Oaks, CA: Sage.

Ricci, I. (1980). *Mom's house, dad's house.* New York: Macmillan.

Richters, J., & Martinez, P. (1993). Violent communities, family choices, and children's chances: An algorithm for improving the odds. *Development and Psychopathology, 5,* 609–627.

Robbins, C., Kaplan, H., Martin, S. (1985). Antecedents of pregnancy among unmarried adolescents. *Journal of Marriage and Family, 47,* 567–583.

Roberto, K. (1990). Grandparent and grandchild relationships. In T. Brubaker (Ed.), *Family relations and later life.* Newbury Park, CA: Sage.

Robertson, J., & Fitzgerald, L. (1990). The (mis)treatment of men: Effects of client gender role and life-style on diagnosis and attribution of pathology. *Journal of Counseling Psychology, 37,* 3–9.

Robinson, B. (1988a). *Teenage fathers.* Lexington, MA: Lexington Books.

Robinson, B. (1988b). Teenage pregnancy from the father's perspective. *American Journal of Orthopsychiatry, 58,* 46–51.

Robinson, B., & Barrett, R. (1985). Teenage fathers. *Psychology Today, 19,* 66–70.

Robinson, H. L. (1985). Joint custody: Constitutional imperatives. *Cincinnati Law Review, 54,* 27–65.

Rosenthal, K., & Keshet, H. (1981). *Fathers without partners: A study of fathers and the family after marital separation.* Totowa, NJ: Rowman and Littlefield.

Rotter, J. B. (1966). Generalized expectancies for internal versus external locus of reinforcement. *Psychological Monographs, 80,* 8–15.

Roy, K. (1999). Low income single fathers in an African American community and the requirements of welfare reform. Paper presented at American Sociological Association Annual Meeting, Chicago, IL.

Rubin, L. (1983). *Intimate strangers.* New York: Harper & Row.

Sachs, B. (1986). Mastering the resistance of working-class fathers to family therapy. *Family Therapy, 13*(2), 121–132.

Saleebey, D. (Ed.). (1997). *The strengths perspective in social work practice* (2nd ed.). White Plains, NY: Longman.

Saleeby, D. (1992). Biology's challenge to social work: Embodying the person-in-environment perspective. *Social Work, 37*(2), 112–118.

Sanchez-Ayendez, M. (1988). The Puerto Rican American family. In C. H. Mindel, R. W. Habenstein, & R. W. Wright (Eds.), *Ethnic families in America: Patterns and variations* (pp. 173–195). New York: Elsevier.

Sander, J., & Rosen, J. (1987). Teenage fathers: Working with the neglected partner in adolescent childbearing. *Family Planning Perspectives, 39*, 107–110.

Savage, E. (1895). Desertion by parents. *Proceedings of the National Conference of Charities and Corrections, 22*, 213–215.

Scharlach, A., & Grosswald, B. (1997). The Family and Medical Leave Act of 1993. *Social Service Review, 71*(3), 335–359.

Scher, M. (1979). On counseling men. *Personnel and Guidance Journal, 58*, 252–254.

Sedlak, A., & Broadhurst, D. (1996). *The Third National Incidence Study of Child Abuse and Neglect: Final Report.* Washington, DC: U.S. Department of Health and Human Services, National Center on Child Abuse and Neglect.

Seligman, M. (1996). A creditable beginning. *American Psychologist, 51*(10), 1086–1088.

Seltzer, J. A. (1991). Relationship between fathers and children who live apart: The father's role after separation. *Journal of Marriage and the Family, 53*, 79–101.

Seltzer, J. A., & Meyer, D. (1996). Child support and children's well-being. *Focus at 34*, Fall, 1996.

Shiono, P., & Behrman, R. (1995). Low birth weight: Analysis and recommendations. In *The future of low birth weight, 5*, 4–18. Los Altos, CA: Center for the Future of Children. David and Lucile Packard Foundation.

Shively, C. (1999). Examining the link between access to children and payment of support. *Divorce Litigation, 11*(5), 85–112.

Silverstein, L. (1996) Fathering is a feminist issue. *Psychology of Women Quarterly, 20*, 3–37.

Silverstein, L., & Auerbach, C. (1999). Deconstructing the essential father. *American Psychologist, 54*, 6, 397–407.

Silverstein, L., Auerbach, C., & Grieco, L. (1999). Do Promise Keepers dream of feminist sheep? *Sex Roles, 40*, 665–688.

Smith, J., Brooks-Gunn, J., & Klebanov, P. (1997). Consequences of living in poverty for young children's cognitive and verbal ability and early school achievement. In G. Duncan & J. Brooks-Gunn (Eds.), *Consequences of growing up poor.* New York: Russell Sage Foundation.

Smollar, J., & Youniss, J. (1985). Parent-adolescent relations in adolescents whose parents are divorced. *Journal of Early Adolescence, 5*(1), 129–144.

Snarey, J. (1993). *How fathers care for the next generation: A four decade study.* Cambridge, MA: Harvard University Press.

Soliday, E., McCluskey-Fawcett, K., & O'Brien-Mof, M. (1999). Postpartum affect and depressive symptoms in mothers and fathers. *American Journal of Orthopsychiatry, 69*(1), 30–38.

Sonenstein, F. (1986). Risking paternity: Sex and contraception among adolescent males. In A. B. Elster & M. E. Lamb (Eds.), *Adolescent fatherhood* (pp. 31–54). Hillsdale, NJ: Lawrence Erlbaum.

Sonenstein, F., Holcomb, P., & Seefeldt, K. (1990). Paternity practices at the local level: A preliminary view from a national survey. Paper presented at the Association for Public Policy and Management's Twelfth Annual Research Conference, San Francisco, CA.

Sorenson, E. (1999). *Obligating dads: Helping low-income noncustodial fathers do more for their children.* Washington, DC: The Urban Institute.

Stahl, P. (1996). Second opinions: An ethical and professional process for reviewing child custody evaluations. *Family and Conciliation Courts Review, 34*(3), 386–395.

Steinman, S., Zemmelman, S., & Knoblach, T. (1985). A study of parents who sought joint custody following divorce: Who reaches agreement and sustains joint custody and who returns to court. *Journal of the American Academy of Child Psychiatry, 24*(5), 554–562.

Stoltenberg, J. (1995). Whose God is it anyway? Male virgins, blood covenants, and family values. *On the Issues, 25*–29, 51–52.

Stone, G. (in press). Father postdivorce adjustment: An exploratory model. *Journal of Genetic Psychology.*

Stone, G., & McKenry, P. (1998). Nonresidential father involvement: A test of a mid-range theory. *Journal of Genetic Psychology, 159,* 313–336.

Stone, G., McKenry, P., & Clark, K. (1999). Father participation in a divorce education program: A qualitative evaluation. *Journal of Divorce and Remarriage, 30,* 99–113.

Suzuki, B. (1985). Asian-American families. In J. Henslin (Ed.), *Marriage and family in a changing society* (pp. 104–119). New York: Macmillan

Taylor, R. J. (1988). Aging and supportive relationships among Black Americans. In J. S. Jackson (Ed.), *The Black American elderly: Research of physical and psychosocial health* (pp. 259–281). New York: Springer.

Teachman, J. D. (1991). Contributions to children by divorced fathers. *Social Problems, 38,* 358–371.

Thomas, J. (1994). Older men as fathers and grandfathers. In E. Thompson, Jr. (Ed.), *Older men's lives.* Thousand Oaks, CA: Sage.

Thoreson, R., & Budd, F. (1987). Self-help groups and other group procedures for treating alcohol problems. In W. Cox (Ed.), *Treatment and prevention of alcohol problems: A resource manual* (pp. 157–181). San Diego, CA: Academic Press.

Tiedje, L., & Darling-Fisher, C. (1993). Factors that influence fathers' participation in child care. *Health Care for Women International, 14,* 99–107.

Toomey, B., & Christie, D. (1990). Social stressors in childhood: Poverty, discrimination, and catastrophic events. In L. E. Arnold (Ed.), *Childhood stress* (pp. 423–456). New York: Wiley.

Toseland, R., & Rivas, R. (1998). *An introduction to group work practice.* Boston, MA: Allyn and Bacon.

Tracy, E., & Whittaker, J. (1990). The social support network map: Assessing social support in clinical practice. *Families in Society, 71,* 461–470.

Trad, P. (1991). *Interventions with infants and parents: The theory and practice of previewing.* New York: Wiley-Interscience.

Tschann, J. M., Johnston, J. R., & Wallerstein, J. S. (1989). Resources, stressors, and attachment as predictors of adult adjustment after divorce: A longitudinal study. *Journal of Marriage and the Family, 51,* 1033–1046.

Umberson, D. (1987). Family status and health behaviors: Social control as a dimension of social integration. *Journal of Health and Social Behavior, 28,* 306–319.

Umberson, D., & Williams, C. L. (1993). Divorced fathers: Parental role strain and psychological distress. *Journal of Family Issues, 14,* 378–400.

U.S. Bureau of the Census. (1981). Marriage status and living arrangements: March 1980. *U.S. Bureau of the Census, Current Population Reports* (Series P-20, No. 365). Washington, DC: Government Printing Office.

U.S. Bureau of the Census. (1990). Remarriage among women in the United States: 1985. *Studies in Household and Family Formation* (Series P-23, No. 169). Washington, DC: Government Printing Office.

U.S. Bureau of the Census. (1991). Marriage status and living arrangements: March 1990. *U.S. Bureau of the Census, Current Population Reports* (Series P-20, No. 450). Washington, DC: Government Printing Office.

U.S. Bureau of the Census. (1992). Marriage, divorce, and remarriage in the 1990's. *U.S. Bureau of the Census, Current Population Reports* (Series P-23, No. 180). Washington, DC: Government Printing Office.

U.S. Bureau of the Census. (1995). Household and family characteristics: March 1994. *U.S. Bureau of the Census, Current Population Reports* (Series P-20, No, 483). Washington, DC: Government Printing Office.

U.S. Bureau of the Census. (1997). Current population survey. *National Center for Health Statistics*. Washington, DC: Government Printing Office.

U.S. Bureau of the Census. (1998). Marriage status and living arrangements: March 1998 (Update). *U.S. Bureau of the Census, Current Population Reports* (Series P-20, No. 514). Washington, DC: Government Printing Office.

U.S. Department of Labor. (1965). *The Negro family: The case for national action.* Washington, DC: Government Printing Office.

U.S. General Accounting Office. (1998). *Teen mothers: Selected socio-demographic characteristics and risk factors, 98, 141.* Washington, DC: U.S. General Accounting Office.

U.S. House of Representatives, Committee on Ways and Means. (1993). *Overview of entitlement programs.* Washington, DC: U.S. Government Printing Office.

Vaden-Kiernan, N., Ialongo, N., Pearson, J., & Kellam, S. (1995). Household family structure and children's aggressive behavior: A longitudinal study of urban elementary school children. *Journal of Abnormal Child Psychology, 23*(5), 553–568.

Vaz, R., Smolen, P., & Miller, C. (1983). Adolescent pregnancy: Involvement of the male partner. *Journal of Adolescent Health Care, 4*(4), 246–250.

Veach, T. (1997). Cognitive therapy techniques in treating incestuous fathers: Examining cognitive distortions and levels of denial. *Journal of Family Psychotherapy, 8*(4), 1–20.

Vosler, N., & Robertson, J. (1998). Nonmarital co-parenting: Knowledge building for practice. *Families in Society, 79*(2), 149–59.

Waldrop, D., Weber, J., Herald, S., Pruett, J., Cooper, K.,& Juozapavicius, K. (1999). Wisdom and life experience: How grandfathers mentor their grandchildren. *Journal of Aging and Identity, 4*(1), 33–46.

Wall, J., & Levy, A. (1994). Treatment of noncustodial fathers: Gender issues and clinical dilemmas. *Child and Adolescent Social Work Journal, 11,* 295–313.

Wallerstein, J. S., & Blakeslee, S. (1989). *Second chances: Men, women, and children a decade after divorce.* New York: Ticknor & Fields.

Wallerstein, J. S., & Kelly, J. B. (1980). *Surviving the breakup: How children and parents cope with divorce.* New York: Basic Books.

Warfield-Coppock, N. (1990). *Africentric theory and applications, Volume I: Advances in adolescent rites of passage.* Washington, DC: Baobab Associates.

Warren, N. J., & Amara, I. A. (1984). Educational groups for single parents: The parenting after divorce programs. *Journal of Divorce, 8,* 79–96.

Wattenberg, E. (1987). Establishing paternity for nonmarital children: Do policy and practice discourage adjudication? *Public Welfare, 45,* 8–13.

Wattenberg, E. (1991). Unmarried fathers: Perplexing questions. *Children Today, 19,* 25–31.

Weinstein, E., & Rosen, E. (1994). Decreasing sex bias through education for parenthood or prevention of adolescent pregnancy: A developmental model with integrative strategies. *Adolescence, 29,* 723–732.

Weitzman, L. (1985). *The divorce revolution: The unexpected social and economic consequences for women and children in America.* New York: The Free Press.

Westney, O., Cole, O., & Munford, T. (1986). Adolescent unwed prospective fathers: Readiness for fatherhood and behaviors toward the mother and the expected infant. *Adolescence, 21*(84), 901–911.

Williams, E., Radin, N., & Coggins, K. (1996). Paternal involvement in childrearing and the school performance of Ojibwa children: An exploratory study. *Merrill-Palmer Quarterly, 42*(4), 578–595.

Williams, R. (1979). *Mental health education: The untapped resource.* Unpublished paper, University of Wisconsin Extension.

Wilson, B. (2000). Interview with Ms. Becky Wilson, divorce mediator with the Mecklenburg County Child Custody Mediation Program, Charlotte, NC.

Wood, J., & Lewis, G. (1990). The coparental relationship of divorced spouses: Its effect on children's school adjustment. *Journal of Divorce and Remarriage, 14*(1), 81–95.

Wu, L. (1996, June). Effects of family instability, income, and income instability on the risk of a premarital birth. *American Sociological Review, 61.*

Wyndham, A. (1998). Children and domestic violence: The need for supervised contact services when contact with the violent father is ordered/desired. *Australian Social Work, 51*(3), 41–48.

Yogman, M., & Brazelton, T. B. (1986). *In support of families.* Cambridge, MA: Harvard University Press.

Yogman, M., Kindlon, D., & Earls, F. (1995). Father involvement and cognitive/behavioral outcomes of preterm infants. *Journal of the American Academy of Child and Adolescent Psychiatry, 34*(1), 58–66.

Zastrow, C. (1993). *Social work with groups* (3rd ed.). Chicago: Nelson-Hall Publishers.

Zemmelman, S. E., Steinman, S. B., & Knoblach, T. M. (1987). A model project on joint custody for families undergoing divorce. *Social Work, 32*(1), 32–37.

Zimbardo, P. (1985). *Psychology and life.* Glenview, IL: Foresman Scott.

Zuckerman, B., Walker, D., Frank, D., & Chase, C. (1986). Adolescent pregnancy and parenthood. *Advances in Development and Behavioral Pediatrics, 7,* 273–311.

Index

Page numbers followed by f indicate figure. Page numbers followed by t indicate table.